NOURISHING THE SOUL

Nourishing the Soul

Discovering the Sacred in Everyday Life

Edited by
Anne Simpkinson, Charles Simpkinson,
and Rose Solari

A COMMON BOUNDARY READER

HarperSanFrancisco
An Imprint of HarperCollins*Publishers*

FIRST EDITION

Library of Congress Cataloging-in-Publication Data
Nourishing the soul : discovering the sacred in everyday life / edited by Anne Simpkinson,
Charles Simpkinson, and Rose Solari. — 1st ed.
p. cm.
"A Common Boundary reader."
Proceedings of a conference sponsored by the editors of Common Boundary magazine and held in 1993.
ISBN 0–06–251205–6 (pbk.)
1. Spiritual life—Congresses. 2. Soul—Congresses. 3. Psychology, Religious—Congresses. I. Simpkinson,
Anne Adamcewitz. II. Simpkinson, Charles H. III. Solari, Rose. IV. Common boundary.
BL624.N68 1995   95-5087
291.4—dc20   CIP

95 96 97 98 99 ❖ RRD(H) 10 9 8 7 6 5 4 3 2 1

Contents

3 Soul and Community

Acknowledgments

Because this book is based, for the most part, on presentations made at the 1993 Common Boundary conference, "Nourishing the Soul," it seems only right to begin by acknowledging Mary Jane Casavant, Common Boundary's educational program manager, and Kristen Leigh Smith, assistant educational program manager, for handling with great skill, humor, and dedication the innumerable details that go into organizing such an event. We are also grateful to the entire Common Boundary staff for pitching in and taking on conference tasks too numerous to list.

We thank the contributors for the time and effort they put into their essays.

Tami Simon and Devon Christensen of Sounds True did, as always, a highly professional and technically superb job of recording the various sessions.

Mary Jane O'Cumiskey, Common Boundary's executive assistant, and Gail Klotz of the Home Office painstakingly transcribed session tapes, transforming them from the spoken to the written word. Our deputy editor, Bill O'Sullivan, brought a fresh editorial eye to the completed essays.

We also thank Caroline Pincus and Rachel Lehmann-Haupt of HarperSanFrancisco for their perceptive comments and feedback on the manuscripts. Working with them has been a pleasure.

We are also grateful to Shambhala Publications for permission to use Shaun McNiff's piece, which appeared in a slightly different form in his book *Earth Angels;* and to The New Press for use of Jim Wallis's essay that we adapted from his book *The Soul of Politics.*

Special thanks goes to Edith Sullwold, who is alternately adviser, mentor, and soul friend.

NOURISHING THE SOUL

Introduction

Until recently, the twentieth century might have been viewed as the century in which Western culture lost its soul. Sacrificing attention to the inner life for pursuit of the outer life, we have become obsessed with money, convenience, and the illusion of immortality. But while the evidence of a shrinking sense of the spiritual is all around us—most apparent in the lack of respect for the value of human life demonstrated by the rise in violent crime, the diminished concern for the poor and homeless, and the glamorization of war—there remains a conscientious group of thinkers who have always kept their eyes on the less measurable, though nonetheless real, aspects of our existence.

In recent years, there has been a resurgence of attention to the inner life—those aspects of human experience that underlie and animate our everyday pursuits. Suddenly, media that once shied away from spiritual subject matter are filled with evidence of a renewed interest in understanding, defining, and feeding the soul. Magazines as disparate as *Psychology Today* and *Newsweek* have carried major stories on America's interest in spiritual matters. In film, *The Fisher King* and *Little Buddha* feature characters who discover animating soul stories through, respectively, Arthurian legend and Buddhist philosophy; in rock music, bands such as U2, Arrested Development, and The Waterboys are unabashed about their religious influences. On television, programs such as *Northern Exposure* explore indigenous, alternative, and Jewish religious traditions, while on the best-seller lists, books such as Thomas Moore's *Care of the Soul* and Clarissa Pinkola Estés's *Women Who Run with the Wolves* hold their own against lighter fare. Clearly, a quiet revolution is going on.

This book is a product of that revolution. In it, some of the wisest voices of our time offer information and advice on how to feed and attend to our souls. Though they come to the subject from a variety of perspectives—there are, in these pages, essays that reflect Jungian psychology, biochemistry, shamanism, Buddhism, business ethics, and deep ecology—the writers included here all share two goals: the respectful exploration of inner experience, and the bridge building that makes that experience come to life in the world. In recognizing that we can no longer afford to concentrate only on the quantifiable, empirically measured aspects of existence or to develop our interior lives at the expense of the world around us, the writers here share a concern for soul as the ground where human experience can be unified and deeply understood.

As E. M. Forster asserts in his novel *Howards End,* our job is to connect the inner and the outer life. "The businessman," writes Forster, "who assumes that this life is everything, and the mystic who asserts that it is nothing, fail, on this side and on that, to hit the truth." He goes on to say that no compromise between these two approaches will work, either: "Truth, being alive, was not halfway between anything. It was only to be found by continuous excursions into either realm."

The writers of these essays bring to us the results of their continuous excursions. Sometimes philosophically complex, sometimes simple, their ideas, theories, and solutions strike at the center of who we are and what we want for ourselves and our planet. In order to more fully understand the essays in this collection, it is helpful to look at the results of excursions made throughout the centuries, to examine the philosophical, spiritual, and psychological experiences and traditions that help to shape contemporary definitions of the word *soul.*

For Plato and Aristotle, defining the soul was a crucial human endeavor. Their concern was chiefly that of separation: Always preoccupied with what makes a human being human (or, more accurately, with what makes a man a man), classical explorations of soul were concerned with defining categories that would separate us from plants, animals, and rocks. Though they did not deny that other creatures had souls as well, these philosophers made hierarchical distinctions between, for example, the soul of an animal and the soul of a man. In the twelfth century, Thomas Aquinas built on Aristotle's work, adding to it the idea that the soul is not only what distinguishes us from other forms of life but what connects us to the divine; in other words, the soul has a vertical movement, always drawing the person up and out of the self and toward a union with God.

Buddhism, on the other hand, opposes the traditional Christian view of soul as espoused by Aquinas and, indeed, the very concept of soul itself. Buddhism rejects the definition of soul as something that separates us from the world and from others and as something that is not only discrete but unchanging. Throughout the language of the Buddha, there are repeated references to the concept of no-soul or no-self (in Pali, *anatta;* in Sanskrit, *anatman*). Two of the central teachings of Buddhism are that there is nothing inside any of us that is not part of the flowing stream of change that is life, and that there is no separation between one thing and another. While soul, particularly in the definitions above, is a static concept, for Buddhists, life is a process. There is nothing static or separate; all is part of the same river.

Obviously, Aquinas's definition and the Buddhist position are difficult to reconcile in any conventional logical system. But the two seem to blend in the important contribution to the literature of soul that came in the form, not of explicitly theological writing, but of poetry. As the eighteenth century passed into the nineteenth, those poets whom we now call the British Romantics—particularly Wordsworth and Keats— were grounding the soul in the stream of the world. If for Aquinas soul finds itself fulfilled in relationship to God, for these poets the soul is charged and changed through human experience, through its relationship with other people and with nature.

For William Wordsworth in particular, the location of the sacred was not above and unchanging but immediate and present in the fields and paths of his beloved Lake District of England. Though he did believe that the soul had heavenly origins, nature was for him the mirror of that origin, and in poem after poem he pays tribute to that mirror. For example, in "Ode: Intimations of Immortality from Recollections of Early Childhood," he states his belief that the soul "Hath had elsewhere its setting,/And cometh from afar"; however, he goes on to say that the Youth—the universal boy who is the protagonist of the poem—is "Nature's priest" and that nature provides comfort for the human soul until it can be returned to its divine origins. In "Lines"—better known as the Tintern Abbey poem—the poet, upon returning to the countryside, says that in this landscape it is possible to be "laid asleep/In body, and become a living soul."

John Keats, for whom the Tintern Abbey poem was a touchstone, expanded on Wordsworth's explorations of soul to include the possibility of change as well as a positive view of suffering. Like Wordsworth, Keats found a kind of sacred solace in the cycles of nature and in the landscape. For Keats, however, the pains of human experience were not simply to be endured but to be learned from; they, as much as any sensory or aesthetic pleasure, nourished and transformed the soul.

In a letter to his brother, Keats put forth his theory of the world as "the vale of soul-making." Saying that he found his system to be preferable to the Christian views of sin and salvation because it is a "system of Spirit-creation," Keats describes the world as a school in which the soul is educated; we are embodied, therefore, in order to create a soul, just as a child goes to school to learn how to read. "Do you not see," Keats goes on, "how necessary a world of pains and troubles is to school an intelligence and make it a soul?" In opposition to the Christian view, which asserts that the soul suffers because it is separated from God, Keats's position is that the soul is actually created from suffering and that it is the pain and difficulty of being alive that makes us ensouled creatures.

If the British Romantics pulled the concept of soul out of the sky and planted it on the ground, the American Transcendentalists built their own church around it. Ralph Waldo Emerson, a clergyman who had fallen away from his church, found in his quest for self-reliance a new vision of the soul. Influenced by Wordsworth's good friend Samuel

Taylor Coleridge, Emerson, too, found solace and sacredness in nature. But rather than seeing the beauty of nature as a mirror of the realm above, Emerson found God in nature. In 1836, he wrote the influential essay "Nature," in which he shattered the hierarchical notions of the divine on which he had been raised and set off toward something entirely new: "In the woods, we return to reason and faith. . . . Standing on the bare ground,—my head bathed by the blithe air and uplifted into infinite space,—all mean egotism vanishes. I become a transparent eyeball; I am nothing; I see all; the currents of the Universal Being circulate through me; I am part or parcel of God."

Emerson was perhaps never closer to Buddhism than he was in the moment of his conception of the transparent eyeball—and indeed, American Transcendentalism and Buddhism may share much common ground in their perception of the unity of all things.

Perhaps the greatest expression of that vision in this country came, not in Emerson's own writing, but in the poetry of Walt Whitman, who sang of his nonhierarchical spiritual vision, which widened to encompass every man and woman.

Not only was there no division between matter and the divine for Whitman—in the epigraph to *Leaves of Grass,* he stated that his soul and body were one—but he believed he could speak for his country and his time. As a human being, he saw himself as absolutely linked to all other human beings and, in fact, to every living thing. In "Song of Myself," Whitman boldly states, "and what I assume you shall assume,/for every atom belonging to me as good belongs to you." For Whitman, the soul was not only inseparable from the body but from the souls of others.

In their preoccupation with the elements of the human mind and soul, the nineteenth-century thinkers seem to anticipate the new science of psychoanalysis that would emerge at the beginning of the twentieth century. Two poets in particular seem to reach forward in their thinking to the fathers of modern psychoanalytic theory: Keats, who once described the mind as a "mansion of many apartments," might have found much to admire in Sigmund Freud's categorization of id, ego, and superego, while Whitman's ever-expanding view of the human soul is strikingly similar to Carl Jung's concept of the collective unconscious. But though Freud tended to dismiss the spiritual or religious yearnings of his patients as symptoms of an unhealthy psyche, both Jung and the psychologist and philosopher William James took a more receptive view of matters of religion and soul.

Perhaps because he combined the philosopher's quest for locating and pursuing the highest aspirations of humankind with the psychologist's desire to know the mind, James's exploration of the subject of religion is sensitive and sympathetic. Even when noting the pathological extremes certain religious people have gone to—such as the amount of time and energy some Catholic saints spent on devising various forms of self-torture—he nonetheless maintains respect for those aspects of life that we cannot see but still feel as real. James's *The Varieties of Religious Experience* may be the first psychospiritual text. The author, with little apology and great insight, examines a number of first-person accounts that range from the mystical to the practical, from the optimistic worldview James sees as inherent to the "religion of healthy-mindedness" to the pessimism and panic-stricken fear of "the sick soul," for whom religious conviction is perhaps the only thing that keeps the individual from utter despair.

If James united the study of psychology and theology with the broad and disinterested intellect of a philosopher, then Carl Jung united those same two schools with the heart of a poet. Having watched his father, a minister, suffer a crisis of faith late in life, Jung knew the importance of spiritual matters to the very survival of the human psyche and, in his autobiography, described his life's task as the "cure of souls." Deeply concerned with the problems of this world—in the 1950s, after two world wars, he wrote that the central myths of Christianity had failed to enable us to deal with the problem of evil—he chose not to find solutions in any one school or tradition of thought but combined and blended a variety of traditions with his own original thoughts into a set of theories that remain dynamic and generative. He recognized, throughout his life, the importance of the Christ figure as a god who suffered; he took the image of the mandala—which for him symbolized the "wholeness of the self"—from Eastern philosophy; he reached back to pagan mythology for the patterns of his archetypes; he drew on indigenous cultures in noting that many psychological problems have their origin in soul loss. Like a healthy ecosystem, Jung's approach to spirituality reflects diversity and multiplicity, a respect for all the various ways in which human beings have come to explore, define, and school the soul.

Given the impact that Jung has had on the study of soul, it is not surprising that many of the contributors to this volume work in that tradition. Jungian analysts Clarissa Pinkola Estés, Robert A. Johnson, and Marion Woodman offer essays that combine the common ground of that psychoanalytic approach with their own varied experiences and stories. Thomas Moore and Robert Sardello each expand on the archetypal school that is an offshoot of Jungian thought, but in opposite directions: with Sardello, we move forward in time through a new approach to dream work; with Moore, we look back to the wisdom of medieval philosophers.

Angeles Arrien and Sandra Ingerman take us even further back in time, showing how indigenous cultures and their approaches to soul sickness and soul loss have much to offer us today. Stephen Happel and James R. Price take a scholarly, historical approach, giving an overview of definitions of soul ranging from classical to contemporary times.

In virtually all spiritual traditions, there is some recognition of the importance of solitude and contemplation. Here, two Buddhist teachers, Jack Kornfield and Tsultrim Allione, share aspects of their meditative practice and the development of mindfulness. Kornfield combines his training as a Buddhist monk with a background in clinical psychology to show how meditation can awaken us to the sacredness of all life, while Allione, a former Tibetan Buddhist nun, offers a specific practice designed to help us face our demons. Merrill Ware Carrington looks to the recovery of an old contemplative Christian tradition—that of the seasonal honoring of Ember Days—as an opportunity for soul replenishment. Elaine Prevallet, a sister in the Catholic community of Loretto, offers a meditation on the significance of recognizing and tending one's home. In counterpoint to the emphasis, in much literature, on the metaphor of spiritual growth as a journey, these two writers remind us that much can be learned from staying in one place.

Contemplation is only one half of the equation, however; we are also embodied creatures, with a responsibility to the world we inhabit and to other beings. Several contributors take on the details of such responsibility, including Rosemary Radford Ruether, a feminist theologian who notes the sources of our abuse of the planet and offers clear, specific guidelines for healing our relationship with the earth as well as for female empowerment. In essays by Tom Chappell and Jim Wallis, we see how our outer responsibilities include a social consciousness: Chappell offers the story of the growth of his own business, Tom's of Maine, as an example of how respect for the earth and for other people can inform every aspect of business decision-making, while Wallis, founder of *Sojourners* magazine, tells us with great urgency about the necessity of bringing soul back into politics.

Several contributors have staked their territory on the same plot of ground as Walt Whitman: a central belief that soul and body are one. Among those who take such an approach are Joan Borysenko, who combines her training as a psychologist with a respect for the more mysterious aspects of bodily life, and Annemarie Colbin, who finds the sacred in the making of a meal. Because our bodies age, we are presented with certain soul issues reflective of our various stages of growth; David Oldfield and Rabbi Zalman Schachter-Shalomi address these issues in essays that focus on, respectively, the particular soul problems of adolescents and the spiritual aspects of eldering.

And finally, no discussion of soul would be complete without the poets and artists whose job it is to give soul its voice in the world. Poet David Whyte discusses the need to recognize and give voice to the paradoxes of the soulful life; Ysaye M. Barnwell, singer, composer, and member of the female a cappella group Sweet Honey in the Rock, describes the power of a voice raised in community with others. Writer and teacher Deena Metzger explores the ancient tradition of storytelling as a source of soul food, while Shaun McNiff, an innovator in the field of creative arts therapy, finds the healing power of expressing soul wounds in visual art. Therapist Nor Hall offers a sequence of reflections on the therapeutic process that can be read more as a poetic series than as an essay.

Some of these authors are primarily concerned, like Aquinas and Aristotle, with locating the individual soul; some, like Emerson, describe a sense of oneness with all other living beings. Some, like Keats, focus on pain as the soul teacher, while others resemble Wordsworth in their emphasis on nature as the resting place of the divine. But whatever their individual differences in perspective, all are united in the urgency with which they approach their work. All acknowledge that survival—not only of individual people, communities, and countries, but of the earth itself—depends on our ability to clarify and feed our inner life so that we can carry a knowledge of the sacredness of all things into our work in the world.

In Nobel Prize–winner Derek Walcott's stage version of Homer's *The Odyssey,* one character notes of Odysseus that he is engaged in asking "the only question the soul ever asks: Where is home?" Odysseus, with his twenty-year struggle to return to Ithaka, may seem a less happy model for our soul journeys than we would like; however, as we near the end of the twentieth century, his tale is in many ways an instructive one. Wounded in spirit by the Trojan War, Odysseus must fight off temptation after temptation, which appear to him in a variety of terrifying and benign disguises, in order to get back to his wife and son. In this century, we have witnessed more bloodshed and have been offered more avenues of distraction than any generation before; we are only beginning to be aware of the costs of losing ourselves in those distractions, of the toll they take on human life and on our environment. The essays in this book offer ways to rethink our presence here, to survive our trials, and to live as ensouled creatures in healthy relationship with ourselves, with other beings, and with the earth.

Rose Solari

❦ 1 ❦

Mapping the Territory of Soul

Chapter 1

The Art and Pleasure of Caring for the Soul

Thomas Moore

Although not the only proponent of bringing sacredness into everyday life, Thomas Moore has, perhaps, become the best known. Since the publication of his books Care of the Soul *in 1992 and* Soul Mates *in 1994, he has brought the soul into the public dialogue in a way that religious institutions have not been able to.*

His background in religious life, the arts, academia, and psychotherapy has shaped his perspective. He does not separate psychology and religion, for example, and he places soul matters squarely in the realm of the imagination.

In this essay, he explains how the arts, contemplation, pleasure, and community all connect us to and feed our souls.

W hile it is impossible to define precisely what soul is, we can work intuitively toward an understanding of soul by examining how we use the word in everyday conversation. When we say, for example, that someone has soul, or that a piece of music has soul, often we are referring to depth and passion and, most importantly, to a sense of authenticity. The old theological definition, of course, is that soul is what survives us after death. A more intimate way to think about soul would be to say that soul is that mysterious dimension of our own personalities and lives that we will never know fully but that plays an influential role in everything we do.

The more I think and write about soul, the more I believe that it has to do, very simply, with allowing our experience to be. To work with soul is to uncover what is mysteriously problematical and deeply pleasurable about being human.

This fundamentally simple approach is actually quite radical in that it eliminates many of our contemporary concepts of the self and how to work on the self. I believe, in fact, that if we truly, actively work to make our lives more soulful, there will be little room left for psychotherapy.

Psychotherapy sometimes encourages us to look at the mysteries in our lives as problems and to look to our personal past to uncover the source of those problems. According to this approach, whenever you are uncomfortable or unhappy with something in your life, you ask, What did my parents do that was wrong? or What kind of trauma have I had? This "problem" approach to the soul has misled us. The Catholic philosopher Gabriel Marcel said, "There is a difference between a problem and a mystery," and that idea is central to the issue of soul. While psychotherapy encourages us to see our lives as problems to be solved, a soulful approach to life looks at confusion or paradox as a mystery to be respected and explored rather than grasped and digested by our intellect.

Respect for mystery implies a spiritual, rather than a purely intellectual, approach. Concentrating on solving the problems of our lives leads us away from spirituality and moves us into a secular, mechanical way of thinking. We make plans based on how far we think we should have progressed in a certain field by a given age—how much money we should be making, how many degrees we should have. Part of our inheritance as a culture is that we use mechanical metaphors for the deepest, most profound aspects of human life.

In the eighteenth century, the philosopher La Mettrie said that the human being is a clock: Look into the depths of our hearts, and what do we see? Gears. This kind of image is absolutely inappropriate for anything to do with human life—it is as cold as it can possibly be—yet the influences of that kind of thinking are everywhere. Once, during an interview, when I mentioned all the traveling I had been doing, the interviewer said, "Your battery must be wearing down." I said, "I have no batteries." The metaphor doesn't work; that is not what the human soul is.

One of the reasons I find Renaissance philosophy a useful place to turn for an understanding of soul is that it is free of such mechanical metaphors. The Renaissance philosophers used natural metaphors for the soul and felt a strong connection between human beings and the cycles of nature and the planets. Renaissance philosophy also puts the human being very high—next to divinity—in the nature of things.

This approach implies a set of values and beliefs that is radically different from what our culture surrounds us with today. For contemporary people, care of the soul requires a fundamental reorientation. In this age, when we worship technology and efficiency above all else, we need to find a different language to describe ourselves, to find words that are not mechanical, that don't reduce us to pathologies. We also need to find language that is not judgmental. Caring for the soul does not judge what is good and bad in ourselves and our experiences. The soul is neither good nor bad; the soul *is*.

This does not imply that we should simply sit back and wallow in our particular dilemmas. Care is an *active* thing; it requires our full participation. But that participation is not about striving for complete understanding. Oscar Wilde, one of the great spokespeople for soul, said that "only the shallow know themselves." In order to truly care for the soul, we have to give up our logical approach.

In fact, caring for the soul requires that we be able to give up many of our old concepts and ideas. Renaissance philosophers called this the *via negativa*, or negative way: you define your soul by discovering what it is not. One thing we need to give up is our concept of what we ought to be and the vocabulary we have created to reflect it: words such as *normal* and *abnormal, functional* and *dysfunctional, balanced* and *unbalanced.* The soul, particularly when it is in distress or in need, does not present itself in balanced ways, but in extremes.

It is important to recognize those extremes and honor them. Rather than intentionally forcing ourselves in one direction or another, we must recognize and protect the mysterious stuff of our individual identity. Say, for example, that you are feeling sad or melancholy. The ancients would have said that you were in Saturn. You might complain about the presence of Saturn in your life, but it does no good to try to eradicate it or outwit it. Why not appreciate it, cultivate it, and let its mystery take form in your heart?

Marsilio Ficino, a great fifteenth-century philosopher, examined his astrological chart and found Saturn at the center. He looked into his own emotional life and saw melancholy at the center. He was able to accept this, to say, "Well, this is my life. I am going to be sad a lot; I am going to feel heavy. This is my universe."

Of course, I am not suggesting that we each have to look at our lives in astrological terms. But the realization that we no longer have to understand ourselves or make ourselves healthy can be a big relief. It also leaves us with more resources of time and energy, because we are no longer preoccupied with the great task of improving ourselves. Instead of improvement, we can look for pleasure; instead of understanding, we can look for awe. This is where the arts come in. Art of all kinds—painting, poetry, dance, music—is necessary and exquisite food for the soul.

The arts nourish soul in several ways. Perhaps the most obvious has to do with our sense of time. Ficino said that the soul exists partly in time and partly in eternity, and both those sides need attention. Usually we give plenty of attention to those aspects of ourselves that exist in time—taking care of our families, making a living, trying to accomplish certain things by certain deadlines. But the soul needs to maintain some relationship with eternal issues as well as temporal ones. To do that, we need, first of all, to be stopped. One of the primary purposes of the arts is to arrest us. A piece of music, a painting, a beautiful piece of architecture, can lift us off the treadmill of our functional daily lives and show us a piece of eternity where the soul can emerge.

Once we are stopped, we have the opportunity for contemplation. It seems to me that one of the definitions of art is that which leads us into contemplation and intensifies the presence of the world. This is particularly true of certain kinds of paintings. In landscapes and still lifes, for example, the painter is able to show us the world when function and practicality fall into the background. We may notice aspects of shape and form that we never saw before; colors may become more vibrant or more subtle. What does that experience say except that in our day-to-day lives we miss out on a great deal of the richness of detail, the particulars that surround us? Such paintings can guide us, instruct us, and give us images for perceiving and valuing and thinking about our lives. That, in turn, is care of the soul.

If art helps to feed the soul by arresting us in our everyday activities, it can also provide the soul with pleasure. Obviously, not all art provides a completely pleasurable experience; some, in fact, is deliberately intended to disturb or shock. Even in those cases, however, it seems to me that many of us feel pleasure in the intellectual stimulation such art can provide. In the history of Western intellectual life, discussion of soul has always, at its heart, involved an epicurean philosophy, or an approach to life that has to do with pleasure and how we can live our desires.

This can be a difficult idea for our culture to understand. Again, we tend to distrust our desires, especially if they are for things our society does not encourage us to want. There are a few things that we feel absolutely comfortable wanting—money, a nice car, various other status symbols. Perhaps because we don't trust ourselves, we don't know just what we desire beyond those few culturally endorsed objects. For years, I have attempted at various conferences to give a workshop on pleasure, and no wants to come. People ask instead, "Do you have anything on pain?" It seems to me that there is plenty of pain and discussion of pain already going on. In the meantime, we have forgotten the importance of pleasure, of fulfilling our desires.

You see, the soul wants things. It wants to be nourished by texture and color, sound and spice. There is a puritanical drive in America to deny ourselves while we're busy getting everyone's pathologies resolved. We feel a lot of guilt, and we want to make everyone else feel guilty. We repress our desires for pleasure and dwell on our wounds. Yet, when we begin to allow ourselves pleasure, our pain finds its context. It becomes, not the focus of our lives, but just one aspect of living a life. Toward the end of his life, when he was very ill and in tremendous pain, Epicurus himself said that even throughout his suffering, he was comforted by the small pleasures he found around him.

Those small pleasures can be anywhere. Think, for example, of our attitudes toward food. Sometimes food is just fuel—something to keep us going though our work day. The soul, however, craves food—not calories and chemistries, but spices, the right amount of stewing, the appropriate evocation of ethnic fantasy. The soul feeds on the Italian in the food, not the calories within the spaghetti; it feeds on the Indian or the Chinese or the American.

In that way, food, like art, feeds the erotic element in our lives. The relationship between art and eros has obvious and ancient precedents, and yet in the last several years, that relationship has caused quite a scandal in this country. People desire good food and beautiful things to look at, and they desire as well the sensual, sacred pleasures they can bring to one another. This is all very simple and natural. But look at the attitude, for example, that has been reflected in the issue of government funding for art in the last several years. When eros is manifested in the arts, the immediate response from many people is to reject it, to kill it, to say, "No more money."

I had a personal encounter with this kind of rejection a few years ago. I was shopping for a Christmas gift for my teenage nephew and having a very difficult time. When he was a kid and wanted toys, it was very easy to buy him gifts, but when he got to be about sixteen, it became much more difficult for me to know what to get him. I finally selected an art history book, written for people his age, with beautiful re-productions inside and a painting of a nude on the cover. When he opened it, there was an immediate furor. A relative thought I was trying to corrupt my nephew by exposing him to art.

That tells us something very sad about ourselves and about our culture: We don't trust desire. We don't trust the erotic element that appears as we become more pleasure-oriented, less logical and mechanical.

On a certain level, that distrust makes sense. For many people, and particularly for our government, the thought of all of us living more soulful lives could be very threatening. If we are truly living lives that nourish the soul, we will want jobs that serve the soul as well. We won't be able to simply live the life we are all familiar with and just make a few little adjustments; we will have to make a huge shift in values, in behavior, in how we make choices. If we start living our lives as soulful individuals, we will have a revolution in the workplace, because so many of us will have to refuse to put up with the conditions we now work under—bosses who abuse us, for example, or unhealthy working environments. The implications go beyond the personal to a larger social level, in that we will also have to refuse to do work that damages others, that contributes to environmental destruction, that in one way or another injures the soul of the world.

There is clearly a political level to this: if we care for our souls, we cannot let things go on as they are. I often hear of frustrations over this issue from psychologists, therapists, and social workers I speak to. They want to work with their clients on a soul level, but meanwhile, they are employed by institutions that require short-term therapy solutions in order to keep their profits up. You can't care for the soul in six sessions; you can't address the mysteries of an individual while you're labeling pathologies and looking at the clock.

I came across an interesting example of this in my own therapy practice. I was working with a man who had just gotten out of a detox ward; he had had the most abusive childhood imaginable and had lived a life of crime and addiction. He didn't trust the idea of therapy at all; we had something in common because, at that point, I didn't either.

At the time we began working together, he was reading a lot—literature, philosophy—and the material he was reading had become very important and interesting to him. When he came in, it was clear that what he wanted to talk about most was the reading he was doing, and so that was what we talked about. After a few sessions, he said, "Aren't we supposed to be talking about my childhood? You know, I had a pretty rough childhood."

I said, "Well, sure, if you want to. We can talk about whatever you want to talk about."

He said, "Well, to be honest, I'm not really terribly interested in that stuff. I just thought you would be."

So we continued to talk about what *was* interesting to him. It was clear to me that these conversations—about the new and pleasurable world he was discovering though books—were nourishing to him in ways that discussions of his individual past would not be.

The issue of being pulled into a larger world is very important. Caring for the soul cannot be just an individual personality project. The archetypal psychologist James Hillman says that our efforts to work on ourselves have become a narcissistic enterprise. We must imagine our lives more broadly than that. When we are participating in our communities, when we feel and act responsively to the world around us—notice I am using the word *responsively,* not *responsibly*—we recognize that the universe, too, is a part of ourselves. There is no big boundary between you and me, between us and them. In other words, when we are working together to create a world in which each of us is granted respect, the opportunity to do useful and satisfying work, and the right to our own desires, we are caring for our souls.

A primary reason for the existence of art is to help us create a more desirable and beautiful culture to live in. There are some great artists, of course, whom we can learn from—just as we can learn from the great theologians, philosophers, and scholars—but truly, we are all artists. Stravinsky, the great Russian composer, said that for him, writing music was very much like making shoes—both he and the shoemaker labored each day to make the pieces fit together, to find new and beautiful designs. Each of us can bring some element of creativity to our work, to our relationships, and to our daily lives. We can create opportunities to listen to our own imaginations; we can recognize the soul's desires and attend to them. Caring for the soul means making all of life sacred, and then appreciating that sacredness everywhere.

Chapter 2

Minding the Body, Mending the Mind and Soul

JOAN BORYSENKO

For many of us, science and mysticism seem antithetical, locked in an ongoing argument between the validity of personal experience and the solidity of empirical data. But Joan Borysenko, medical scientist and psychologist, moves back and forth between those worlds with ease. A hallmark of Borysenko's work is the ability to blend hard scientific data with a respect for the mystery inherent in all life. This approach has won her the respect of lay audiences as well as scientists and doctors throughout the world.

She and her husband, Myrin Borysenko, a psychoneuroimmunology researcher, are cofounders of Mind/Body Health Sciences, an educational organization that teaches health and mental-health professionals, scientists, and businesspeople about the body-soul connection. Borysenko is also cofounder and former director of the Mind/Body Clinic at Harvard Medical School's New England Deaconess Hospital, as well as the author of several books, including The Power of the Mind to Heal; Minding the Body, Mending the Mind; Guilt Is the Teacher, Love Is the Lesson; *and* Fire in the Soul: A New Psychology of Spiritual Optimism.

B ringing soul into physical healing requires that we be able to distinguish between healing and curing. Though the two are sometimes related—when we develop the capacity to heal, that is, to listen to both our head and our heart and to be present to life, then our physical functioning often improves—they are not the same thing. In most conventional medicine, the focus is on curing rather than healing: we look to medical procedures and pharmaceuticals to remove the most obvious aspects of the problem. But the relationship between mind and body, and between body and soul, is much more complex than such an approach implies.

When I refer to the connection between body and soul, the term I most frequently use is *mind*. I do not see these terms, *soul* and *mind*, as equivalent, but linked. Healing has to do with repairing our bond with self, with the deepest levels of who we are, and that, I think, is where the soul lives. Our mind reflects how clear or muddy our bond with the soul is, and so when I refer to the connection between mind and body, it is always with our bond with soul as the subtext.

There are certain aspects of the mind-body connection that are clearly recognizable on a cellular level. For example, every cell in your body has receptors for the neuropeptides released by anger; when you are angry, your entire chemistry changes due to that particular emotion. That our emotions are the mediator between the images in our minds and the cells of our bodies is not just metaphorically true but actually true. All of our systems are talking to one another all the time, and the images in our minds therefore have a great deal to do with what is happening in our bodies.

The connection between mind and body was illustrated for me by an incident I witnessed when I was very young. My Uncle Dick, who often visited my family, was notoriously finicky about food; he particularly detested cheese. Once when he was at our house for dinner, my mother gave him a piece of cheesecake for dessert without telling him what was in it. He ate it and enjoyed it. About an hour later, my mother decided to tell him that he had actually eaten cheese. As soon as she said the words, he threw up his entire dinner on the living room rug. It was very clear to me that his throwing up had nothing to do with the physiological effect of cheese, but everything to do with an image in his mind.

I had plenty of opportunities to think about that because, from the time I was a child, I have suffered from severe migraine headaches. I realized quite early that the more upset I became or the more I cried, the worse the pain would become. In order to feel better, I had to do what was counterintuitive—I had to learn to relax when every fiber of my being wanted to stiffen up.

Most people do not go to their physicians for purely physical concerns. Statistically, roughly 85 percent of the reasons people visit their doctors are mind-body related. Our current medical system is unequipped to handle this for a number of reasons, one of which is that our physicians are overworked. The average physician can listen to a patient's story for only eighteen seconds before trying to move toward a diagnosis. That isn't nearly enough time for real healing.

I came across this phenomenon myself when I was in training at Harvard Medical School in the late 1960s. At that time, there was very little in the way of treatment for people with stress-related illnesses, and most physicians had very little time for them. I found that out because I was one of those people.

Part of my stress had to do with the gap between what my parents wanted for me and what I wanted for myself. I was raised as the archetypal Jewish American princess—groomed from birth to grow up and marry a doctor. When I rebelled at an early age, saying I would rather be a doctor than marry one, I became a big disappointment to both my parents, particularly my mother. The difference between what your parents envision for you and what you want for yourself is often linked to self-esteem; the farther apart those visions are, the lower your self-esteem is likely to be. Because I was constantly aware of how different my path was from the one my parents had chosen for me, my self-esteem was quite low.

This problem was compounded by my entry into graduate studies at Harvard Medical School. Although medical education varies from place to place, it is very often education via humiliation. The students are not rewarded for what they know but insulted and verbally abused for what they don't know. A more competitive, toxic environment could not possibly be found in which to teach people anything about healing. The stress of the curriculum, coupled with my own view of the world, created some very serious physical problems.

Within my first year of graduate school, my migraines became so severe that they often lasted for two or three days, and I would become dehydrated from the constant vomiting. I also had irritable bowel syndrome, which is like having a migraine in your belly. I developed high blood pressure, as well as a cardiac arrhythmia that was so severe I was afraid of fibrillating and dying. It also became clear that something was very wrong with my immune system—I had chronic bronchitis that kept turning into either pleurisy or pneumonia. For most of the time, I was on antibiotics; occasionally, my problems became so acute that I had to be hospitalized.

It is interesting to me, in retrospect, that not one of my physicians—who were really all quite caring people, although overworked—looked to emotional or soul-related problems for the answer to these severe physical ailments. Though I was grateful for the medicine I received—I would have died without antibiotics—my actual healing came not through medication but through a synchronous experience.

A fellow student of mine, a long-time practitioner of transcendental meditation, took me aside and said, "You have all the symptoms of hyper-arousal of your sympathetic nervous system. You are forming images in your mind of everything you fear in life, and your physiology is carrying out your fearful images because your body cannot tell the difference between what you're imagining and what is happening."

I said, "So what should I do?"

He said, "Learn to meditate. Meditation will help you clear fearful images from your mind and teach you instead to be present to what is."

He was right. I learned how to meditate, and within a period of about six months, all of my illnesses disappeared.

The Austrian psychiatrist and author Victor Frankl, who was incarcerated in four Nazi death camps, writes movingly of the connection between the physical body and the workings of the mind and soul.

In *Man's Search for Meaning,* Frankl says that when his fellow prisoners felt there was no meaning to their suffering, they would usually pick up the first epidemic that passed through the camp and die very quickly, before the ovens had a chance to consume them. But people who in some way had a vision of what their suffering might mean found some way to transform it. These people could endure the most terrible privations—cold, hunger, germs of all sorts—and yet their bodies managed to stay healthy.

It is, however, important to remember that none of what we have discovered about the mind-body connection implies that we should blame ourselves for getting sick or feel guilty about our diseases. We will never know all the reasons why human beings become ill. There is heredity, the environment, behavior, and there is also mystery. When I ran the Mind/Body Clinic at Harvard, I went in one day with a cold, and from the reactions of my patients you would have thought they had just caught the pope walking out of a brothel. I know far too many people—both laypeople and health professionals—who believe that if you really are enlightened, you won't get sick. In a sense, they have become mind-body fundamentalists, and that is a very self-punishing, destructive path.

We can avoid buying into that kind of thinking if we recognize the basic human impulses beneath it. In her book *Adam, Eve, and the Serpent,* the theologian Elaine Pagels says that human beings prefer guilt to helplessness. Guilt at least implies cause-and-effect and suggests a rational explanation for the way things are; when we cannot find a rational explanation, we feel much less secure. Therefore, because being stricken by illness or disease makes us feel helpless, we might try to avoid that feeling by choosing to believe that we are completely responsible for our physical health. I have actually heard people say something like, "If I'm really, really, really good—if I think right, eat right, and meditate right—I'll never get sick." Then, of course, if these people get sick anyway, they still believe it is their fault—there was something, somewhere, that they were doing wrong. This belief is much more comforting, somehow, than accepting the random mysteries of the universe.

We need to remind ourselves of those mysteries. Even people who are psychologically well balanced, who have active spiritual lives, and who eat all the right food, can die when they are very young, and from what everyone else dies from. They die from heart disease, and they die from cancer. I often remind people that the Buddha died of food poisoning. Our approach to mind-body concerns should not be one of guilt— this is not an opportunity to punish ourselves—but rather one of optimism and a sense of the widening possibilities as we continue to research the connection between body and mind.

Most mind-body medical research, and most of my own interest in the area, has focused on stress, because, regardless of where or how we might live, no human being is immune to it. Generally, we experience stress in our lives when an event requires us to adapt or change. The change could be anything from getting a new job to moving to having a loved one die. Though the details obviously vary greatly from case to case, there seem to be two basic ways in which people cope with stress.

One is regressive coping. A regressive coper wants to maintain the status quo and will resist recognizing the inevitability of change. Such a person will usually blame himself or herself—or someone else—if circumstances require adaptation or change. The main goal here is to keep things as they were before the stressful situation developed. This form of coping is associated with both psychological problems and physical illness.

The second approach is transformational coping. A transformational coper is someone who not only adapts to a stressful situation but finds something positive within it that enriches the individual's life. We might say that transformational coping is making lemonade out of lemons. We might also say that it has to do with the way we tell the story of our lives.

Often, people who have had a great deal of difficulty in their lives— those who were abused by their parents, for example, or suffered other kinds of traumas—tell a life story of helplessness and victimization. There are other people, however, with equivalently difficult life experiences who manage to construct, out of similar events, a story with a very different meaning. They might tell their life story as a story of overcoming, of triumphing over adversity and deprivation. Or they might tell a story of suffering transformed—of using their own difficult experiences to help others who have suffered similarly. People who can transform the events of their lives into coherent stories that preserve integrity, compassion, and hope are transformational copers, and such coping is often associated with good health.

Dr. Hans Selye, who is known as the father of stress studies, had an experience in his own life that illustrates very well how transformational coping can work. In his seventies, after a tremendously successful career, he developed a very virulent form of cancer. His doctor told him that he had three months to live.

Rather than falling into despair, he decided to use those three months to write a quick autobiography. He had kept journals from the time he began medical school and decided to go through those journals chronologically as preparation for writing his life story. The first thing he read was an account of how a piece of research had been stolen from him and his colleagues when he was a medical student, and his feelings of anger and betrayal over the event.

Reading the account, Dr. Selye realized that despite the decades that had passed, he was still as furious at the people who had stolen his research as he had been at the time; he had never resolved the anger that he felt. He thought about it and came to the conclusion that it really was time to let go of that anger. He decided that this was not a story he needed to include in his autobiography.

He continued reviewing his old journals, asking himself which events he needed to include in his autobiography and which ones he could leave out. After about a year of reviewing this material, he realized that he hadn't died yet. He went back to the doctor, and it turned out the cancer had gone into remission. He lived for several more very productive years, and he attributed that to having had the opportunity to reexamine and let go of the things that were creating hostile images in his own mind.

Again, it is important not to fall into simplistic thinking—"I'm going to be completely optimistic all the time, then I'll never get sick." If you approach any kind of mind-body study with the goal of never getting sick, you will probably be disappointed. If, however, you explore this material in order to live a life that is more joyful, celebratory, and creative, you can achieve your goal. In fact, the two factors that are most consistently associated with good health are high self-esteem and strong social connections, and these are, it seems to me, two essential elements of a joyful and fulfilling life.

Many of us struggle with the self-esteem part of this equation. I said before that our self-esteem is often connected to the difference between our parents' ambitions for us and our own ambitions. It is also true that the way we are raised can influence us to create a worldview that will confirm whatever ideas about ourselves we have taken in. There is a considerable amount of research in this area and one study in particular that I find very revealing.

This study was based on information drawn from one hundred Roman Catholics. It showed that, within the group considered, each person's self-esteem was connected to how he or she thought of God. Those who believed in a loving and merciful God had much higher self-esteem than those who saw God as being judgmental and punitive, and this, in turn, was related to the way they were raised. Those who were brought up in a very authoritarian and punitive environment developed low self-esteem, which they in turn projected onto the world: they created a punitive God in the image of their parents.

Albert Einstein said that the most important question human beings have to answer is, Is the universe a friendly place or not? This study seems to indicate that the answer to that question hinges on how we have come to see ourselves in that universe. If we believe that we will be punished and belittled for every transgression, then the universe is indeed a hostile place; but if we can believe, whether through therapy, self-study, or the luck of our own upbringing, that we are valuable and significant people, then the universe can in fact be a friendly place, a place that accommodates us just as we are.

This returns us to where we began: the bond with self that is the center of soul in healing. It makes sense that such a bond would be affected by childhood, but we do not have to limit ourselves to that. Erich Fromm writes that good parents view their children with a passion for the possible. In order to truly explore the mind-body connection—in order to develop a healing model that takes soul into account—I think we need to view ourselves and one another with that passion. When I meet a therapist or a physician who I intuitively know is a real healer, and not just technically competent, I know that this is someone capable of sending thoughts of unlimited possibility to his or her patients, and that quality is often far more important than access to advanced technology or so-called medical miracles.

The communication of unlimited potential is healing to even the most damaged or neglected soul. We need to remember that whether that healing leads to a specific physical cure or not, to work with soul is to work with the only part of ourselves that really lasts. It just happens to be a beautiful coincidence that the things that heal our souls can sometimes heal our bodies, too.

Chapter 3

Who Is Teacher?

Clarissa Pinkola Estés

Clarissa Pinkola Estés is an award-winning poet, a senior Jungian analyst, and a cantadora, *or keeper of the old stories, in the Latina tradition. She is former executive director of the C. G. Jung Center for Education and Research in Denver, Colorado, and has been in private practice for the last twenty years.*

Estés is the author of Women Who Run with the Wolves, *a bestselling collection of twenty fairy tales and accompanying psychological commentary about the instinctive nature of women. The book—which has been translated into seventeen languages and has had a profound effect on women all over the world—is the first in a projected five-volume series covering a total of one hundred fairy tales and myths. Estés is also the author of the Jungian Storyteller Series, a collection of audiotapes, and is now branching into new media: in 1995, Theater of the Imagination, a thirteen-part series of Estés's stories, poems, and commentaries, will be broadcast on National Public Radio.*

My thoughts regarding life as teacher are derived from my own contemplations as a *Católico* over five decades. They are only mine, and as such, I do not generalize that they ought to be taken up, as my *abuelita*, grandmother, used to say, "by every last jay in the forest." They do, however, follow familial traditions in my Mexican *meztisa* heritage as well as through my inherited Magyar customs. The resultant weave is religious in the truest sense of the word—from the Latin, *religàre*, meaning the intention and effort to bind all parts together in order to make a whole.

Being called to an intense daily relationship with soul is undeniably a glorious thing. It is also a very difficult thing. Euphemists might say it is "challenging." Realists might say it is ofttimes "painful." Poets might say the process is, at various times, "fiery." Certainly there are as many descriptions of this milieu as there are portals to it, numinous, intellectual, and otherwise. Yet, it seems to me that if relationship with soul is not both difficult and glorious, that it is fairly certain that we have made a wrong turn somewhere along the way, and that it would be good to consider backing up and taking a good long look, for the very nature of soul work is to be flensed to the bone and to receive new life all at the same time.

This is why when I meet a person who is in some clear way called to live a consecrated life in the mundane world, I feel I would like to offer both congratulations and condolences. The inner and outer worlds rarely match up evenly. Living en-souled is rigorous because it demands maintaining a meaningful relationship to the outer world and a closeness to the inner world, all at the same time—regardless of the paradoxes and ambiguities this creates. *Religàre*, bringing these two worlds together, is not a facile task. It requires unforeseen sacrifices and much endurance. So, it is understandable that most of us would feel greatly assisted if we could be blessed with even a small amount of consistent guidance.

You may have heard the saying, "When the student is ready, the teacher appears." Some people are fortunate, it is true. They have had soulful friendships with their elders since birth, or with other kindred spirits, or with a community of souls over a long period of time. Many, however, have been ever so ready for years and yet they are still waiting in the winds at the crossroads, waiting for someone to trot up and in some recognizable way announce themselves as teacher.

Great teachers do not always or often show up exactly on time, or when needed most, or in some cases, ever. And when they do appear, they sometimes say things that may seem rather mumbledy instead of instantly miraculous.

For these reasons, it is a good thing that life itself is a fine, fine teacher. When you are at the lonely crossroads, life can always be depended upon to come riding up. Life is the teacher that shows up when the student is ready. Life is the quintessential escort and preceptor. Life is often the only teacher we are given that is perfect in every way.

Here, then, are some glimpses of "life as teacher," as I understand them from firsthand experience and observation. And just in case a personified teacher appears in your life not too far down the road, here are also some thoughts and caveats derived from twenty-five years of practice as a psychoanalyst and healer.

Remembering is teacher.
Beginning with the most simple and pure facet of all, there is a fact that has been handed down generation after generation through the ages, and particularly through the auspices of religious and spiritual ideas, and that is, that a great Something is the luminous center of all things, and that this great Something is also at the same time far greater than the "all" itself.

This energic center has many names worldwide; The Ineffable, The Imminent, The Omniscient, and The One are but a few. In my tradition, it is explained as the nonpersonified *El todo Dio,* that is, the All God—with a myriad of *las almas* (souls) attached to it. My grandmother, Querida, explained it to me this way: imagine a huge sunflower with infinite numbers of seeds attached to it, and all of them flaming at the center of the universe—each and all constituting the illuminating force behind what we humans call soul.

What has impressed me most about this center of psyche, as I understand it, is how vast and infinite is its continent—by whatever name one calls it; how visible its seasons, how remarkable its precipitations, and especially how evocative it is. It calls to us through night dreams and the events of daily life—all these causing a life-giving memory: that we are the original inhabitants of that God-land forever, that our home is not on *x* street in the town of *x*, but there.

For many persons, the investigation of the nature and meaning of life's difficult passages leads them unrelentingly and directly to this locus, this archway through which lies the original land of the soul itself. Disillusionment about a person or an idea, the suffering of a great loss, an ongoing torture or injustice—these are the most well-defined passages that lead, push, and even force us to remember home.

Through our concern with the soul and the soul's concern with us, we re-learn, re-survey what matters to us most. Instead of being scattered by the wind, we in some way learn to ride it—even if unsteadily at first.

Recalling soul as original shelter and original succor can, in significant ways, mediate grief, assist in filling a paucity of spirit, balance floods of emotion, and ease sustained bewilderment, the latter being one of the greatest sorrows a human can feel.

Experiences carrying the most tension are in some significant way, and often in every way, leading us back and back again to this original memory of true home. It is in this sense that life events are an inestimable teacher, and that this particular memory of the Source remains teacher throughout all of life.

First-order experience is teacher.

When I was seven years old, I was inducted via a great ceremony into *La Sociedad de La Virgen*, a devotional order rising from the *campesino* class in sixteenth-century Mexico, this being a preservation of the admixtures of the healing and religious ways of the Xztecas commingled with the spiritual practices and formal worship patterns of the post-Conquest friars from Old Spain.

This ceremony constituted consecration into one of the oldest time-honored Catholic traditions—lifetime devotion to, and mystical dialogue with, *Nuestra Señora*, Our Lady. This is how She formally became my teacher. Skin against skin. Face to face. Not as in the study of Her, nor as a rhapsodizing about Her, not a précis with footnotes, but first-person and on common ground. My ongoing relationship with Her has always been frightening, awe inspiring, and love drenched, and is meant to be precisely so.

If I were to make a blessing over those who work hard to pursue soulful acts and issues that matter most by their lights, it would be that all that they are and all that they are yet to become derive from first-order experience, that is, up close and immediate—not told to, not read about, nor merely imagined—but lived, day after day after day, face to face.

When one takes first-order experience as one's lifetime teacher, one is sometimes desperately challenged, definitely changed, greatly charged with responsibility, and marked for life in certain ways—ways that cannot be received or learned down to the bones in any other way. Taking an occasional class about spirit and healing won't do it. Fantasizing won't produce first-order experience. Pretending will not make it so. There is so much that cannot be put forth about these matters in such a brief essay. However, this cannot be left out: seeking direct relationship with the numinous is not everyone's desire nor destiny, but when it is, it is a fierce and exacting teacher.

Cultura cura: Culture is teacher.
A heritage or society can carry a *cultura cura* tradition, that is, a belief that through consistent healing and repair, the culture can cure its own populace. The rituals, rites, and binding ties of the culture become full teacher in the soul life of every member. A culture that produces and preserves meaningful, fierce, and joyous rituals and ideals fosters the periodic expansion and mending of every individual's life. My grandmother used to call the rituals of our culture, *los maestritos,* "the little teachers." The culture that cures its own is, in essence, a true humanitarian culture. "Life as teacher" in *cultura cura* is one that instructs and renews through rituals that demonstrate these four basics: love, reception, refuge, and blessing.

The wind of change is teacher.
In the Latino worker community I was born into, besides backs and hands given to labor, we brought with us what I think of as our immense

talent for teaching endurance. We brought too, I think, an innate poetry, certainly our ecstatic rituals and other lifelong traditions—all these acknowledging that death comes so soon for all of us, and that life is a gift made of equal parts of pure gold and pure ashes.

Because we toiled in times of great personal, political, and socioeconomic turmoil—much of which continues in one way or another to this very day—we felt that to hold onto our very souls we had to face a basic truth about the world, and that is: *Los vientos soplan cambios fuertes,* The fierce winds of change blow eternally.

There is much to say about this matter, but in this short time let me only say this—and it will not seem cryptic to those who are on their way already: I am certain that when we are severely tested, we can be sure that we have met the teacher. The teacher always arrives on the wind of change, and often is the wind itself.

Being thwarted is teacher.

When I was little, I aspired to be a child mendicant. I wanted to pack a bindle bag with apples and go off and find Her (and also Her Son, and a host of *santos* [saints] as well), and to be all day in a kind of thrall and not come back to the house until long after dark, and once there, to tell stories in poems of all I had seen and heard.

On quite a few occasions, I had been able to escape to do this very thing. In the process, I drove my family half mad, for there were boxcar hitchhikers and thieves in the woods, and besides there was always work to be done, at least some insisted it was so, even when it was work for no end.

The "big ones" kept more and more an eye on me then, and many times I was thwarted in slipping away to my places in the woods. Subsequently, ever so much of my young life was spent being metaphorically chained to a post within the sight of grown-ups who were both faithful and funny, but who did not always understand the requirements of a child ecstatic. Whereas before, my wanderings had almost driven them over the edge, sometimes being not free to rove almost drove me to the cliffs myself.

Surprisingly, it was through being thwarted thusly that I learnt that

Nuestra Señora was as well understood through the work of the wooden scrub brush, in the steam of the washer-wringer, in the mists of the canning kitchen in summer, and in all worldly workaday locales. This is, in part, how I came to understand that being thwarted is also teacher, for it forces one to see that if called in the proper way, spirit visits every integral act and thought.

I do not believe that one need go anywhere in particular to "see, find, or experience" the numinous—even though I come from a heritage that is completely dedicated to the taking of long pilgrimages to faraway shrines that house the finger bones, ashes, nightshirt, or some such relic of a revered one. Once there, we pilgrims move toward the church steps for at least a quarter of a mile on our knees, preferably in the cold (more reprieve for the souls of the dead in the waiting room of Purgatory) and having fasted from all nourishment, save the Host, for seven days previous.

I believe in pilgrimage and have completed many in my lifetime, mostly to very humble shrines. However, I am certain the power of the numinous does not only choose certain sites to inhabit. I believe it chooses certain minds and many souls as well. Wherever that One is, there is what is needed. Going out and about can be teacher, but so especially can staying.

The personified teacher.
Here I will give some thoughts and caveats about the flesh-and-blood teacher. Say one appears in your life. In a student-teacher relationship that has integrity, there is a primary tenet: the student has regard for the teacher, and the teacher has equal regard for the student.

I have had several lifelong teachers; some are my close blood, several are not, and a few have been seemingly complete strangers. I've a dear friend and colleague, Vasavada, who in the 1950s, traveled from his home in India to study with C. G. Jung in Zurich. Vasavada is a Hindu and a Jungian analyst.

We once attended a conference of Jungian analysts where a great argument broke out—I think it was later described in the minutes as a "lively discussion," which is polite-speak for "blood was drawn."

First this analyst, then that one, argued about how, why, and when a kind of spiritual grace is given by the analyst to the analysand during the analytic work. Back and forth went the debate. Vasavada became quite agitated. He raised his hand to be recognized, but the chairman did not see him, for Vasavada is quite diminutive in stature. Finally exasperated, Vasavada used my shoulder to hoist himself up so he was half-standing on the seat of his chair. In his beautiful lilting East Indian accent he spoke to the assembly, "Oh no, no, no, you have it all wrong, my respected colleagues. It is not the analyst only who brings grace to the analysand, but rather it is more so that the analysand brings grace to us. This is how it is and it should never be forgotten."

There was silence in the room, and people, seeming to remember themselves, began murmuring, many in accord with the truth he spoke. This simple idea, that the teacher may give grace to the student and the student may give grace to the teacher, is the acknowledgment of the reciprocal relationship that is the fundament of a helpful teacher-student or friend-friend relationship. Not in a million years can one hold to one without the other.

Being clay-footed is teacher.
We have a saying in our family: *Los santos tienen los pies de barro,* Even the saints have feet of clay. To have feet of clay means that the heroic and the very human are combined together in one person. Neither one negates the other: humanness does not negate heroism, and especially heroism does not negate humanness.

We have another saying, "Out of sight, oh what perfection!" This means a teacher can remain "perfect" only if the student never lays eyes upon him or her. However, if one were to see any teacher up close every day, one would find that they have tics, some strong preference, some pitiful habit or other, or that they say mostly nonmystical things, such as, "I am hungry, let's eat"; "Where are my shoes?"; "Go away cat, don't bother me now."

Those *pies de barro,* feet of clay, are often known to the teacher; they are the challenge or cross that the teacher is bearing, hopefully thoughtfully. Those *pies de barro* belong to every teacher—no one is without them. Those *pies de barro* are very important: they are meant to be teacher to the teacher. Also they are teacher to the student, that is, the notice of them means, "Wake up! There can be immense goodness without perfection in your teacher, but even more importantly, *in you.*"

Integrity is teacher.

Since I began to practice therapeutically nearly twenty-five years ago, I've seen many fads, events, and evolutions pass through the sometimes obscure culture of psychology. Recently, as I've traveled the country, I've heard many, too many, firsthand accounts of various teachers' tragic intrusions into students' psychic, sexual, financial, and spiritual lives. Most who seek the spiritual are whole in soul and exceedingly sweet in their hearts when they begin. But those who have come under the influence of a teacher who exploits them become like vases that have been broken and, even if glued back together, are never again as they once were.

Because of those who have suffered thusly, I would like to shift the focus of my comments to some of the pitfalls regarding "teacher." From this frame of reference, I'd like to put forth some guidelines regarding the student-teacher relationship, particularly in service of the student.

While it is only proper to show, in many different ways, respect for one's teacher, beware the teacher who needs or wants to be worshiped, who needs you as business manager, baby-sitter, housekeeper, road builder, remodeler, sergeant at arms, or sexual partner—and who claims that any of these will lead to "higher awareness."

Be wary of the teacher who insists on obedience at deleterious costs. Be heedful of the teacher who solicits personal gifts, who encourages behaviors that countermand your own senses, who leads you into anything that is against your moral principles because "it is for your own highest good," "for your own best development," "in order to take you to the next highest level," or because "we are outside it all," or "inside it all," or "above it all." It is not the spiritual teacher's job to force or seduce people into performing any act in service of anyone's "highest good," including the teacher's.

A teacher is supposed to have good ability to differentiate, so that they can teach acute differentiation to those who study with them. The teacher's only and most compassionate work is to suggest, to tell, to teach, and to demonstrate by striving to live their own lives in the best way they have found. The teacher is supposed to show the way through, not act as though they themselves are the way through.

Genealogy is teacher.
I would say this to the young or barely informed person contemplating a teacher, and especially those who are in a temporarily weakened state from, say, a heartache, an existential conflict, or who have experienced a loss of meaning in life: teachers develop from heritages and therefore have genealogy. If you come across a new, suddenly proclaimed person who holds himself or herself out as a teacher or healer, it is good to ask, who are their relatives? Who are their living spiritual forebears? Their testers? From what genealogy are they? Which spiritual practices have they been rooted in for life?

Do they have peers who love them and regard them, and who are awake? With whom do they congregate and consult with on various matters—not because they must, but because they see the ongoing wisdom in such? What is their exact training, with whom and for how long? How is this verifiable? Do they have a good sense of their own foibles? What do they see as their limitations?

To what human authorities are they answerable in addition to spirit and God? Do they have close friendships with other teachers? And particularly, what is their ethical training and how much time was given to it? This list is relevant to anyone who holds themselves out as carrying healing spirit of any kind.

Some years ago I was appointed by the governor of our state to the psychology grievance board. Since that time I've seen many instances of substandard practice by "teachers" with all manner of ethical confusions. Perhaps they have bought a flimflammery "training" of one sort or another, or have undertaken an unsupervised self-education, or have fallen under the spell of a mentor who is snagged in a terminal hubris of their own. Perhaps they have been taught and supervised by someone who pays little or no attention to what their acolytes are up to, or who has never themselves bothered to or found the proper place to be trained in how to train others.

"Wanting to help others" does not prove that one understands the requirements and responsibilities of guiding others. Sincerity is not the issue. Sometimes the self-appointed hope to bypass the required time-tested learnings, but this will not do. The work is the work. There are no shortcuts.

At grievance hearings we see many utterly sincere and very contrite "teachers" who have, sadly, made massive and destructive intrusions into the lives of those who were in trusted ongoing therapeutic and/or spiritual relationships with them. Many were both unconsciously and consciously trying to fulfill personal needs, fulfill personal financial goals, or achieve other ends. As many were grossly undertrained and said they "really didn't know any better." This is tragic for all involved, student and teacher alike. The teacher's accountability is essential, and, even after the fact, so are insights and help for both.

Hard, consistent work is teacher.

One of my close friends, a fine and respected Buddhist teacher, tells me of receiving letters from people who write: "I read your book and took some classes, and I have set up a Buddhist center, and I'm the main teacher." This causes every person who is an experienced teacher, who has been tested and stretched in talent, and who stands with full permission on the shoulders of those who have gone before them, an essential and great alarm.

Unfortunately, there are those whom one might call unsanctioned or self-anointed teachers who hold themselves out as teacher without having done the hard and long work to achieve such. They are recognized by the fact that they invariably mimic the words, styles, and beliefs of those who have done the hard work or the original research, or who are born into the life that produces such. But the self-anointed do so without essentially crediting those they are mimicking, and especially without having lived the kind of life that would produce such thoughts and insights to begin with.

Some even mimic those who have mimicked others, also without having done the fundamental work. The copyist takes without the benefit of guidance, transmission, permission, and testing, and therefore has questionable ethics and superficial development of the ideas. I have, on more than one occasion, cringed to hear people espousing thoughts and ideas that are not only not theirs, but which they have appropriated without the benefit of ever having thought them through. The teachings of such a person versus that of a tested teacher constitute the difference between Kool-aid and mother's milk.

A solid training in healing, helping, and guiding gives a teacher the most important knowing—aside from how to proceed and what to do—and that is, what not to do. *Knowing what not to do* is far more important in many cases than knowing what to do.

Knowing what to do and what not to do requires trained judgment, acute observation skills, and experience. Making the motions without understanding the perils brings to mind the Walt Disney film version of *The Sorcerer's Apprentice*. In the film, the sorcerer's apprentice is lazy and desires sway and comfort. The sorcerer has bade the apprentice to clean the castle while he is away. The apprentice tries a shortcut to gain what he wants—he uses a magical chant that causes the broom and bucket of water to multiply into many brooms and many buckets of water that simultaneously throw the water onto the floor and madly sweep it at the same time.

But the phenomenon he has set in motion careens out of control; the buckets flood the castle instead, and the apprentice is threatened with death by drowning. On top of all this, he fears that his teacher's return will expose his deceit. For though he figured out how to start it all, he does not know how to stop it all. He has only the raw desire for power and ease. And so the entire landscape is flooded and the apprentice's conceit is revealed as not glamorous, but destructive.

A well-trained teacher sees the student's foibles and intervenes to correct them. There are no shortcuts.

Common sense is teacher.

We use a term in our family, *la sabaduría loca,* which translated means, "crazy wisdom." Although I have heard the term "crazy wisdom" used to explain something that is serendipitous, I have also heard reckless and injurious behavior on the part of a teacher being defended (usually by the teacher) as "crazy wisdom." I cannot agree with the latter.

I would like to offer what I believe to be a more integral understanding of *la sabaduría loca.* It is not a "crazy wisdom" used as a way of explaining away irresponsible behavior or exploitation, but rather is understood as a kind of desirable cleverness that one uses in order to protect one's young.

For instance, we point to the killdeer, which is a plover, as being an example of *la sabaduría loca* because it distracts enemies away from its nest by pretending to have a broken wing. It drags and limps across the ground, and when the predator has finally been lured away from the nest, the killdeer, which is of course completely able, flies away.

In the tradition that I understand, "crazy wisdom" is meant to be used to shelter, not to cause students to feel as though they are crazy. In this way, *la sabaduría loca* is really composed of powerful common sense. If teachers profess to use "crazy wisdom" as a technique, then hopefully they will have also investigated the subtle corruptions that creep into the psyches of all who hold power, they will have examined these in themselves, and decontaminate themselves of such on a regular basis.

Custom fit is teacher.

Psychic maturation is an individual and customized endeavor. It cannot be done by rote, cannot be done *en masse* by the thousandfold, and is more easily done in silence and solitude no matter how brief, though most of us labor at it in a daily cacophony.

Psychic maturation is best guided by those who have some— preferably a considerable amount. I like very much the model of Alcoholics Anonymous, and that of other groups, wherein people gather together in private in order to discuss and learn from one another. This,

to my mind, causes a pooling of various maturities and first-order experiences, both negative and positive, of all the group members. The customized fit is worth seeking.

In the end, we each have our own way of proceeding, whether by one
method or another, or by many combined. In my early years of learning
the many devotions to *La Señora* that are a part of my lifelong practice,
the request I made most often was, "Please, tell me if I am holding the
soul map right-side up or upside-down . . . again." In these later years, I
find myself more simply murmuring daily and sometimes hourly,
"Enséñame a me, por favor," or "Show me, please show me."

Whether the teacher is life itself, or whether the teacher is an actual
person, group of persons, or a combination of all of the above, in matters of repair of the psyche, and in its strengthening and maturation
through a soulful life, there are direct analogies to modern science. I
wrote about these in a poem called "Sacred Science."

> . . . If you go long enough,
> stand the cold enough
> stay under and far enough down
> . . . pure carbon crystallizes
> into regular octahedrons
> at those adequate depths
> under proper tension,
> and sufficient time buried
> in darkness.
> In the earth, this phenomenon produces
> diamonds.
> Amongst humans, this phenomenon creates
> a whole person.
> Who is teacher?
> This.

Chapter 4

Learning to Serve the Soul

ROBERT A. JOHNSON

Although the Jungian analyst Robert A. Johnson gives lectures and workshops internationally, he is best known as an author. His ten books explore topics as diverse as romantic love, dreams and active imagination, joy, and shadow aspects of the psyche.

But his most popular subjects and the majority of his work focus on aspects of masculine and feminine psychology. Indeed, his first two books, He *and* She, *a retelling and interpretation of the story of the Holy Grail and the myth of Amor and Psyche, respectively, have each sold more than a hundred thousand copies and have stayed in print since their publication more than twenty years ago.*

The essay that follows, which is based on his book The Fisher King and the Handless Maiden *(1993), discusses the wounded feeling function, which Johnson calls "the most common and painful wound which occurs in our Western world." Without a healthy feeling function, he says, we are incapable of valuing ourselves, family members, friends, or others, including plants, animals, and the natural world.*

Though Johnson offers the Fisher King's story as an illustration of how the masculine feeling function is healed, he points out that it is equally applicable to the masculine side (animus) of women.

The word *feeling* is one of the weakest words in the English language. It is derived from the verb *to feel*, which means to perceive or explore by touch; therefore, it is associated with our tactile sense. But feeling, in its truest meaning, has to do with the capacity to give worth. It is the art of valuing, of treasuring someone or something.

Feeling is different from affect or emotion, which is the energy evoked by the activation of any faculty. You can become emotional, for example, about an idea or physical object. Our capacity for feeling is still so rudimentary that most people confuse feeling and emotion. Perhaps this explains why the noblest quality of feeling is dismissed simply as emotion.

It is difficult to talk about such things because the English language has an inadequate vocabulary in this regard. Sanskrit-based languages have ninety-six words for love, Persian has eighty, Greek has three; we have one. The paucity of terms indicates an inferiority of that faculty in the culture. If there were ninety-six words for love in our vocabulary, I could say exactly what my warmth, feeling, attachment, or devotion is to a particular person. I could tell someone precisely to what degree I value him or her.

People in this culture whose feeling function is high are often thwarted from finding legitimate means of expressing feeling; because of this, they sometimes act explosively or impulsively. In fact, the reason so many people are expressing their feelings violently today is that our culture gives us few legitimate pathways for expressions of feeling.

This experience is the condition of the feeling function, and it is our male heritage. There is scarcely an English-speaking person who is not wounded in this manner. I was horrified to watch young people in India learn English and take on the Fisher King wound by way of the language. When you think in English, you feel in English; you take on the poverty of the feeling function. Because the thinking function is predominant in American culture it automatically follows that feeling is deprived of energy and dignity. The paucity of feeling terms in the English language is striking when one compares it to Spanish, Italian, or Greek. It is discouraging to listen to a bilingual person speak first in English—

with its subdued feeling quality—and then break out into the high energy and feeling-toned cadences of Spanish.

Feeling is one of the four basic faculties that Jung described as making up a human personality. The others are thinking, sensation, and intuition. These faculties tend to pair off, and the pairs fight each other to some degree. For example, if you're a feeling type, your thinking function may be weak because these two tend to be polar opposites.

In all individuals, one faculty is predominant. We are either a feeling or thinking type, a sensate or an intuitive. The personality type appears very early in a child's upbringing. One child, drawn by his or her inborn thinking function, will naturally go off in a corner with books; another, inspired by an inborn sensation function, will build a tree house; still another, driven by the insatiable intuitive faculty of searching out the meaning behind things, won't stop asking questions; and the fourth moons and dreams and leads one to wonder if he will ever get his feet on the earth.

If things go well, the child develops this superior function—the faculty that naturally functions best, that is God's gift, that's effortless. With some training, a second function is developed. It's as if we get another dimension to our being. In the latter part of our adolescence we develop yet a third function, but this one comes hard; we have to work at it. Very few people go beyond this stage. The fourth function is the opposite of the first; it is our inferior function, and everybody has one. It's the Achilles heel of our psychology. It's where we get hurt, where we bungle, where we have two left feet. Our greatest treasures are won by the superior function, but always at the cost of the inferior function.

Knowing your typology—as well as that of your family members, your boss, and so forth—can be a gold mine. If you are one type and have to deal with someone who is another, you can learn to speak the other person's language and avoid many conflicts.

I had a demonstration of this facility in some precious interviews I had with Carl Jung. Not only did he speak English to me rather than his native German, but he spoke my typology as well. I'm an introverted feeling type, a group to which only one percent of the American populace belongs. Not only did Dr. Jung speak English for me, but he chose his vocabulary and talked to me in a manner that was coherent to my type. He used vivid feeling examples to make his points, and talked in the quiet, subdued way that is most accessible to someone with my introverted nature. At first I didn't know he was doing it deliberately. I thought, here's someone who thinks, speaks, and functions just like me; I feel at home.

Only when I saw him in other circumstances did I realize that he spoke quite a different language when left to his own devices. Initially, I felt wounded, left out; I was angry until it dawned on me what he had done. I swore a holy vow that if I grew up and got wise I would try to talk the typological language of the person standing in front of me as far as I possibly could. Doing so creates a bond and prevents much misunderstanding.

Just as individuals have their own superior and inferior functions, so do cultures. Japan, for instance, is a land of sensation. Everything is meticulously clean; everything works. The Swiss are also a sensate people, and they spend their lives making watches and keeping the streets clean. Mexico, on the other hand, is a feeling land.

Our own culture worships thinking. No matter what typology we may have been born into, Americans must speak a language and live in a culture oriented to thinking. Sensation is the next strongest function. Thus, Americans are very good at organization, planning, and management; we are particularly good at mechanics. Our telephones work, we excel at developing computers, and so forth. Those are excellent faculties, and I appreciate them. But by definition, if a culture has developed a superior function, it also has an inferior function, enervated by the high discipline required by its superior function. This is where the trouble comes in.

The wounded feeling function is ubiquitous in America. Italians aren't nearly as wounded as we, nor are Greeks or Mexicans. In our culture, the wound is so deep that most of us spend an inordinate amount of time and energy trying to protect and cover it up. We bear up bravely under it and won't show our hurt. But on the street, if you watch the expressions on people's faces, you know the hurt feelings are there.

Furthermore, we are quite embarrassed by feelings. Good manners insist that we not show our feelings in a personal way. We are not supposed to get close to another person or to inquire into the intimacies of another's life. We are only just learning, as a legacy of the hippies, how to hug each other. A number of years ago, the Anglican Church instituted the "passing of the peace" during Mass. I'll never forget the anguish experienced by Anglican souls when they had to turn around and publicly embrace one another.

The twelfth century struggled with many of the same issues that we grapple with today. In fact, someone once said that the winds of the twelfth century became the whirlwinds of the twentieth century. Science, individuality, a new sense of freedom, and romanticism were all emerging and being defined then. But while great intellectual and scientific advances were made, they exacted a heavy price: the wounding of the feeling function in the modern male psyche.

The formation of the modern Western mind, with its emphasis on the ego and on thinking, can be clearly seen in the twelfth-century myths surrounding the Holy Grail and the quest of the medieval knight. One myth that deals with the wounded feeling function is that of the Fisher King. Although this myth speaks directly to men, it describes a psychology that is also applicable to the masculine side of women.

When we first meet the Fisher King, he is a sixteen-year-old prince. One morning he goes out on his horse, carrying a banner with the word *amour* on it; he's going out to look for love. He's whole, full of life, happy, and bright. He represents the unwounded man. A short way into his journey, the young prince encounters a pagan knight. In the days of chivalry, if a knight encountered a compatriot, he would lower his visor, take out his biggest lance, get his horse going at full speed, and rush full tilt at his opponent. This is what the young prince does.

The prince and the knight meet in a terrible crash. When the dust settles, the pagan knight is dead. The future Fisher King is castrated, and a bit of the pagan knight's lance is embedded in his thigh. This encounter is the personal history of every modern Western male as he takes his place in the competitive world. We may no longer wear armor, but the customs of our male-dominated business meetings, for example, encourage competition and win-lose situations. Such a milieu produces heroic stances but is deadly to any feeling function. The pagan knight—instinct—is killed; the generative capacity is seriously impaired. Instinct is no longer available to use or to depend upon.

In another version of the story—more complex but perhaps richer—the young Fisher King walks into an encampment where a fire is burning and a salmon is roasting over a spit. No one is around. Because the Fisher King is hungry, young, and impetuous, and because the salmon smells so good, he takes a bite of it. It's so hot that he drops the piece of fish and puts his fingers in his mouth to assuage the burn. But he gets a bit of the salmon into his system and suffers the Fisher King wound. The symbolism here tells us that a touch of Christ consciousness—for the fish is an early symbol for Christ—taken too early wounds the genital capacity of the male. A modern equivalent would be the recent theory that learning to read too early deprives children of some of their feeling capacity. This is the Fisher King wound in its contemporary form.

Another version has the young Fisher King attempt to steal the salmon. Someone shoots him with an arrow that goes through his testicles, far enough so it can't be pulled out but not far enough to kill him. In all of these stories, the Fisher King is badly wounded—too ill to live, yet unable to die.

When a man bears the Fisher King wound, he gets frightened of his potency or of his ability to create. He starts asking if he's any good: Is he as good as his neighbor? Why didn't he get a better raise? Why didn't he get a better position in the corporation? His sense of worth, which is a touchy thing in a man, is wounded. If you inadvertently touch a man's Fisher King wound, he'll flare up in a most inordinate manner. Assuage his wound a little, pat him on the back, validate him, please him, and he aches a little less. He'll be grateful to you forever. This is what modern English-speaking and, in general, Western men carry around with them. Men show off all the Tarzan display in a desperate attempt to keep that gnawing Fisher King wound under control. But the ploy doesn't work very well.

The prince eventually becomes king of his realm, but most of the time he can only lie on a litter groaning in pain. As a result, nothing prospers in the kingdom. If the king is in trouble, the whole kingdom is in trouble.

The Fisher King lives in the Grail Castle, which keeps as a relic the chalice from which Christ drank at the Last Supper. Every night there's a procession: a fair damsel comes with the paten that bore the bread of the Last Supper, another fair damsel comes with the lance that pierced the side of Christ, and yet another comes carrying the Grail itself. The procession reflects the fact that, for a man, salvation almost always is brought to him by a feminine carrier, a "psychopomp." She is the guide. Dante's Beatrice is the best illustration, in Western literature, of a woman as guide for the soul of man. Beatrice is *la femme inspiratrix,* who guides Dante through hell and purgatory into heaven.

At one point, all present drink from the Grail. When they do, whatever wish they carry with them is immediately fulfilled. Everyone, that is, except for the Fisher King. This is the worst suffering: to be in the presence of pure beauty, in the presence of happiness, in the presence of the most valuable thing in the world, and to be unable to touch it or be touched by it. One realizes then that it is the capacity for enjoyment or happiness that is lacking, rather than objective things to be happy about. One has only to cross the border into Mexico to see people with seemingly little to be happy about who nonetheless have the capacity for experiencing pleasure.

What we call a midlife crisis is usually the discovery of the Fisher King wound. This is because though you can kid yourself for most of your life—as soon as I get married or divorced, get a new house or another job, I'll feel better—there comes a time when you are in the presence of everything you could ever wish for and you cannot enjoy it. This is pure cruelty; this is the Fisher King's dilemma. Everyone drinks from the Grail except the poor man in the litter.

I remember an incident like this. I was in my twenties and on my way home to spend Christmas with my parents. Driving through San Francisco, I saw Handel's *Messiah* advertised for that Sunday evening at Grace Cathedral. Because nowhere in the world is *Messiah* done better, I postponed my plans in order to attend. But twenty minutes into the performance, I couldn't stand it. I had to leave. I could not stand the presence of that much beauty in contrast to the misery, loneliness, and suffering inside myself. The beauty only made me feel worse. That's the Fisher King wound.

For the Fisher King, fishing is the only respite for his suffering, so he spends most of his day fishing in the moat in his little rowboat. If you're doing inner work—if you paint, write poetry, make music, garden, or pursue something artistic in nature—you are "fishing" in the unconscious, and that activity will make you feel a little bit better. It won't get you very far, but it will take some of the edge off your suffering.

Meanwhile, the residents of the Grail Castle take comfort in the legend that one day an innocent fool will come and ask a question that will release the Fisher King from his wound. The name Parsifal, in German, means "innocent fool." In this myth, the character Parsifal is destined to bring healing to the wounded Fisher King.

Parsifal has no father. His father and all of his older brothers were killed in heroic knight-errantry battles before his birth. His mother, Heart's Sorrow, shields Parsifal from this knowledge. She tells him nothing about knights because she doesn't want to lose her last son. She clothes him in a single garment of homespun, which symbolizes his simple, rustic background. Eventually, however, Parsifal finds out about his lineage and follows his destiny. He blunders about and, more by luck than ability, finds himself in King Arthur's Court, where he is knighted for slaying the tyrant Red Knight.

One day late in the afternoon, Parsifal is by himself in the forest. It's getting dark, and he needs a place to stay. He sees a man in a boat fishing—the Fisher King. Parsifal hails him and asks, "Where can I stay tonight?"

The man in the boat says, "There's no habitation within thirty miles." Parsifal is upset, but the Fisher King says, "If you go down the road a little way, turn left, and go over the drawbridge, you can stay at my house tonight."

If you're stuck in your thinking function, you will only hear a contradiction. But the king has just uttered the formula for healing the hurts in us. The story says that there is no habitation for thirty miles; that is, in the three-dimensional world, there's nothing that's going to help you. However, if you go down the road just a bit and turn left—which means go into the unconscious, the imaginative world—and cross the drawbridge, you will find yourself in the Grail Castle. If you're traveling in a disciplined, straightforward way, you're in the three-dimensional world. If you can shift gears, you can enter the imaginative realm. We are so wedded to the "rightness" of life that we have made the "leftness" of life inferior. The story's promise is that if you take a left, you can find the Grail Castle—the world of dreams—any night of your life. The prescription for the healing of loneliness or woundedness is in the castle, in the world of imagination.

Parsifal reaches the Grail Castle and comes upon the procession. He is awestruck and speechless by what he sees. But a terrible thing happens. Although he is bursting with curiosity, he remembers advice that his mother gave him. She said, "Don't ask so many questions." So he doesn't ask the question. The procession comes and goes; the Fisher King is not healed. Parsifal spends the night in the castle and wakes up in the morning, and the Grail Castle has vanished.

I have yet to find recorded information for this, but I'm convinced that the reason Parsifal didn't ask the question that would have freed the Fisher King was the one-piece, homespun garment that his mother had given him. The homespun is a man's mother complex. It makes him impotent or sufficiently weak so that he doesn't ask the critical question when he should. Parsifal must at some point get his one-piece homespun off. Most of what a man does between the ages of twenty and forty is to rid himself of his homespun. This undertaking is analogous to separating from the mother, turning from a boy into a man. It's a difficult process. A woman doesn't go through anything comparable because a woman is born with her womanness. A man has to win his manness.

For the next thirty years Parsifal goes about as a knight. He fights dragons, conquers many enemies, rescues fair maidens, succors the poor. He does many good things. (Today these challenges have different names—mortgages, educational debts, etc.) After thirty years, he's tired. Knighthood wears thin at about forty. Two times in our lives the veil between consciousness and the unconscious grows thin—once in adolescence and again in midlife. Parsifal was innocent at sixteen, and his innocence was his original entree into the Grail Castle; at forty-six, he's worn out. At either stage you can get into the kingdom of heaven quite easily. Parsifal is traveling one day when pilgrims stop him. They say, "What are you doing with your armor on on the day of the death of our Lord? Don't you know it's Good Friday?"

"No," he replies.

The pilgrims convince him to take his armor off and confess to a hermit who lives nearby. The old man gives Parsifal a bad time, reminding him of all the stupid things he's done, all the mistakes he's made, and all the chances he's missed. Wise old hermits know about these things because they are etched in the face of every human being.

But the hermit suddenly becomes kinder and encouraging. He says, "Go down the road, turn left, and go over the drawbridge."

Parsifal goes down the road, turns left, crosses the drawbridge, and once again finds himself at the Grail Castle. The procession is going on as it has gone on every night. This time Parsifal asks the question: "Whom does the Grail serve?" That is, "What is the meaning of life?"

If you ask that question today, almost everyone will say, "It serves me." What is life for? It's to get ahead, build equity in the house, get a better job, get better insurance coverage so the family will be taken care of. All these things are ways of saying, "The Grail serves me." That's the modern heresy we live in.

But the answer that comes from the Grail Castle is that the Grail serves the Grail King, a thin disguise for God. In Jungian language, one would say that the meaning of life is to serve the Self or the soul, not the ego.

I take enormous pleasure from the fact that Parsifal needs only to ask the question; he doesn't have to answer it. That's a relief and a generosity beyond imagination. It means that we don't have to answer the questions of life; we just have to formulate them.

Because Parsifal has asked the right question, the wounded Fisher King rises up healed—in Wagner's opera, the Fisher King sings the most wonderful aria, which is full of strength, vitality, and healing—and the whole kingdom comes alive. Parsifal is a great hero, of course. The Fisher King dies three days later.

This may seem to be a strange ending, but I believe it means that the wounded part of us can be left behind once it has fulfilled the development of the psyche. Once it has served its purpose, it is no longer needed.

Another way to look at it is to say that there are certain questions in this world that cannot be answered. There are questions that a person agonizes over at forty years of age. But if you remind him of the questions at fifty, he may say, "They just went away." Most of the seemingly insoluble questions that one tortures oneself with can only be dropped. But you have the right to drop them only when you have done the work of formulating the question. The old proverb is correct: A question well-formulated is mostly answered.

Thus, if a man can find Parsifal within himself, if he can find the Grail Castle and finally ask the question "Whom does the Grail serve?" he will be able to heal himself. He will remember that he is not here necessarily to find happiness. He is here to serve the Grail King, to serve God, to serve something larger than himself. Paradoxically, in doing so, he will be flooded with happiness. He will have healed his feeling function and become capable of appropriately valuing and cherishing life—his life, the life of all creatures in the world, and, most important, the Source of all life.

This old tale, which seems so innocent in its mythological content, is in fact a very wise treatise addressing the most painful wound we face today: the inadequacy of feeling and relatedness in our modern world. Beneath the archaic language of Grail Castles, fair damsels, and homespun garments, we can find a coherent statement about where we are at the close of this century. We can find, too, some very wise advice about treating contemporary manifestations of the Fisher King wound.

Chapter 5

Geography of the Soul: An Intellectual Map

STEPHEN HAPPEL AND JAMES R. PRICE III

Stephen Happel chairs the Department of Religion and Religious Education at The Catholic University of America. He has coauthored two books; written articles on worship and the arts, the transformative power of religious language and culture, and religion and literature; and is currently working on a book entitled The Kiss of Judas: Christianity's Betrayal of Culture.

James R. Price III directs the Shriver Peaceworker Program at the University of Maryland, Baltimore County. The two-year graduate program for returned Peace Corps volunteers combines theory, practice, and ethics and aims to transform conditions in the cities through community service projects. He is currently writing on the subjects of values, community service, and higher education.

In their essay, Price and Happell look at concepts of the soul, from the medieval perspective represented by Thomas Aquinas through the Enlightenment's rejection of soul to a contemporary viewpoint that uses psychological language to map the soul's landscape.

In an illustration from the fifteenth-century Rohan *Book of Hours*, a dead knight lies diagonally at the left corner, his body stripped naked among skulls. In the upper right-hand corner of the painting, an immense, crowned, elderly God calls to him. In between the two, a battle rages: a scarlet demon and a sword-wielding archangel fight over the possession of a tiny, wraithlike doll. That doll, torn between reward and damnation, is a medieval image of the soul.

This image has dominated the Western understanding of the soul for hundreds of years. On the one hand, the eternal significance of the human person is at stake, the level traditionally named "soul." On the other, the soul is conjured as simply a smaller version of our most palpable self, the body. Even when we imagine it in a more subtle way—such as an inner light—the soul is still often defined as a thing, a concrete object among other concrete objects. Many religions, in fact, view the soul as a divine thing that inhabits the body but will one day escape it.

Why is this image a problem? In our culture, driven by logical, empirical modes of thought, this image no longer intelligibly conveys the meaning of what the soul is. To contemporary understanding, the image appears either primitive or absurd. As a result, many people find themselves estranged from ideas of what the soul is, rejecting even the possibility of its existence.

To recover an interpretation of soul that is both adequate to the realities affirmed by tradition and available to our contemporary sensibilities, we will provide an intellectual map that charts the soul, including how our definitions of the word have developed over time, and what thinkers and historical periods have contributed to our grasp of it. A fruitful place to begin is with the classical understanding of the soul, set forth in the thirteenth century by the philosopher and theologian Thomas Aquinas.

A Classical Understanding of the Soul

Aquinas agreed with Aristotle's assertion: "To attain any knowledge about the soul is one of the most difficult things in the world." Aquinas wanted to discern what distinguishes living from nonliving elements in the world, so he formulated a series of questions: If things are not simply material, what are they? How does human life differ from other forms of reality? How can human life be distinguished from divine life?

Aquinas used a notion of the soul to create an intellectual map by which matter, motion, the body, mind, and God can be distinguished yet related. In the *Summa Theologiae*, he defined the soul as "the first principle of life" in those things that know and move. "Ancient philosophers," Aquinas says, "presumed that the principle of these actions was something corporeal." They assumed that only bodies were real things and that what was not corporeal was nothing. In order to believe in the existence of the soul at all, they had to believe that it had a bodily form—as in the illustration from the *Book of Hours*. But, said Aquinas, "it is clear that to be a principle of life, or to be a living thing, does not belong to a body as such; since, if that were the case, every material body would be a living thing."

Aquinas understood the soul as a principle of unifying activity, ordering itself and other entities. On this basis, he was able to identify the "souls" of various organisms. For example, Aquinas understood plants to have a vegetative or nutritive soul—an inner principle of activity that feeds and grows and is fed by its environment. Without that principle of unifying activity, plants would not be plants but mere aggregates of accumulated mass, like rocks. Animals sense things, desire objects, and move; they possess a sensitive soul. The animal soul is distinguished from that of plants because unlike flowers and trees, animals can move of their own accord. In human beings, the soul integrates the activities of nutrition, sense, desire, and motion with the power of intelligence and choice. Aquinas calls this unifying principle the rational soul.

The soul is the principle of human freedom, our way of moving through the world as human beings. To be human, of course, means to have these powers as potential. But not everyone exercises this potential in the same way. As a result, Aquinas focuses on the capabilities of the human soul for understanding, evaluating, and deciding, since these activities relate most directly to his ultimate concern—the relationship of human beings to God. For him, the soul is both very much of this world and yet transcendent. Though he does not identify the soul with the material world, his definition nonetheless insists that the soul is present as a dimension of the world we know. Simultaneously, however, the soul's operations and habits allow us to connect with a divine reality that completely transcends the world of material realities.

According to Aquinas, soul cannot be separated from the body. Although one can distinguish between matter and soul, they cannot be divided. Thus, according to this definition, the human body is actually ensouled matter.

Aquinas also believed that certain operations of the soul—such as knowing, desiring, and loving—can become habits. Individuals tend to ask certain questions, desire characteristic things, and choose particular ways of life. Just as repeating certain physical exercises makes our bodies conform to specific patterns, taking action in repeated patterns makes us recognizable as individuals.

For Aristotle and Aquinas, the proper exercise for the soul is virtue; this is what makes human beings genuinely happy. Though not all human beings develop good habits or virtuous characters, the soul is the principle that leads us to the good. In this sense, the soul is always trying to surpass itself in achieving virtue—telling the truth, appreciating the beautiful, and accomplishing justice. Just as there is a good that is needed by the body to survive, so inquiring, understanding, and loving have a built-in direction toward desiring what is genuinely good for ourselves and others. Therefore, the powers of the soul are self-transcending—they are constantly drawing us out of ourselves and toward, for example, intelligent thought and love of others. We are always on our way toward what is outside the self, toward what is other than we are.

It is important to recognize that, for Aquinas, soul is an *explanatory* term. Explanation is different from description. When we describe something like the soul, we often try to say how it is related to us, to answer the question, What does it mean to me to have a soul? But if we try to explain something, we take some distance from the object being studied. We try to create an objective definition that is true, not just for me or for you, but for all humans. Therefore *soul,* when used as an explanatory term, is an attempt to relate dimensions of human activity that exist whether I feel them or not.

This explanation of soul is vastly different from the medieval image offered in the *Book of Hours*. There, the soul is a tiny, frail body, whereas God is an elderly male ruler with powerful warriors in the form of angels. According to Aquinas, however, the soul is not at all frail. When exercising its capacities for knowing, desiring, and loving, it becomes evidence for human links with a divine reality that knows all, desires all to be saved, and loves unceasingly. Ultimately, for Aquinas, it is God's own life that becomes the prime analogue or model for all created forms of life, and the final happiness of the human soul is to be drawn into a divine reality that is absolutely other than we are.

THE RISE OF SCIENCE AND THE FALL OF SOUL

Though this explanation of the soul is satisfying in many ways, Aquinas's work gradually disappeared from philosophy and from popular images of the soul. Three major factors contributed to this development. First, the language that Aquinas used, as well as the classical framework he borrowed from Aristotle, became suspect with the rise of early modern science in the seventeenth century. Aquinas used the language of metaphysics—the branch of philosophy concerned with the ultimate composition of reality. This terminology and the ideas it represented could not be verified through experimentation. For the modern scientist, theory needed to be based upon empirical observation and repeatable experiments; metaphysics did not fit into those categories. The understanding of what an explanation is had shifted from conceptual logic to empirical analyses, with which neither Aristotle nor Aquinas were primarily concerned.

The second problem was that classical metaphysics did not seem to take into consideration factors of personal or communal history; rather, it treated human nature as being the same in all places at all times. As people became more and more interested in the influence of culture on human thought and action, classical metaphysics began to seem hopelessly outdated. It did not adequately encompass historical developments or the power of personal stories.

Third, early modern science and the Enlightenment movements of the eighteenth century rejected popular images of the soul as well as metaphysical theories explaining it. Aquinas clearly did not believe that the soul was a little waiflike body torn between demons and angels—in fact, his theory was meant to criticize such images—but later thinkers placed metaphysics and popular religious images into the same category. Scientists, who saw themselves as the reformers of the mind, believed that anything that cannot be known through the senses should disappear altogether from the realm of inquiry. Therefore, not only metaphysical explanations for soul but the images of soul that continued to be painted in churches had to be rejected. Moreover, since the churches used these images of soul to "educate" their members, the use of "soul language" became, during the Enlightenment, a political issue. Rejecting the soul as an entity was envisaged as a rebellion, a war for one's freedom from the oppression of priests and churches.

In his essay "What Is Enlightenment?" the German philosopher Immanuel Kant (1724–1804) wrote that enlightenment is our "release from . . . self-incurred tutelage" and our inability to make use of our own understanding without direction from someone else. According to Kant, unless we can find the soul within our own empirical evidence, to continue to believe in it is simply a cowardly decision to let others think for us. "If I have a book which understands for me," he wrote, "a pastor who has a conscience for me, a physician who decides my diet, and so forth, I need not think if I can only pay—others will readily undertake the irksome work for me." Kant believed that our primary task as human beings is to achieve competence based on our own independent authority. "Soul" in this view is a religious import, an alien that should be deported for lack of proper identity papers.

Not only did the Enlightenment reject the language of soul, but it refused to replace it with anything else. Rather, it viewed human beings as material entities, whose explanation can be found through the reasonable exercise of science. This was the beginning of the control of human behavior through medicine, educational institutions, public welfare systems, insane asylums, and prisons, which were considered rational ways to order human action and knowledge without the need for any transcendent principle existing either within or beyond human beings.

THE SOUL: AN INTELLECTUAL MAP
FOR THE PRESENT

The question now is how contemporary people, raised with the aftereffects of the Enlightenment critique of philosophy and religion, can recover a notion of soul. Is it possible to find a language that uses neither metaphysics nor naive images to convey a sense of soul? In order to be adequate for modern minds, such a language would need to respond to the Enlightenment critique while giving rise to an entirely new approach. Perhaps we can look to an image from painting as a place to start.

In the early seventeenth century, the Italian painter Caravaggio captured stories just at the moments of their transition. For example, in a painting called *Sacrifice of Isaac,* we see Abraham at the center of the canvas, quizzically looking to the viewer's left at a nude figure who reaches into the scene, grasping Abraham's right hand. The light rakes across the painting from the upper left to the lower right, where the head and body of Isaac are gripped and tormented by his father's powerful left hand. The boy is in agony, his mouth opened in a silent scream. Abraham is indecisive, his right arm captured still moving toward the boy's neck, despite angelic intervention. To the viewer's right, just above the squeezed skull of the child is a ram, whose soft brown eyes look toward the angel and the viewer with acceptance.

Much occurs in this painting, but the important thing to notice for our purposes is that the painting does not give away the end of the story. Even if the viewer happens to know the tale, what Caravaggio shows us is a moment of choice for Abraham: Should he or should he not sacrifice his son? Is this new messenger any more to be believed than the last one? How is he to know? By making a decision, Abraham will become someone—perhaps a father who kills his child for his God; perhaps a coward who uses any excuse to avoid what he does not want to do; perhaps a believer who trusts that God knows what is meant to be. A moment of human self-agency is captured, an activity that is at once present in the world but not of it.

Insofar as we think, feel, desire, or plan, we experience the movement of soul. This interior life that we sense in Caravaggio's painting—

and in life itself—is the action of the soul. It is the agency that propels our stories: without the energy of questions, understanding, and decisions, we would be static, like rocks, or simply assimilative and responsive, like plants.

To be able to know and understand the soul, we must attend not just to objects "outside" us but to the data of our own conscious life. (This kind of attentiveness began much earlier than the contemporary postscientific age; it is rooted in the work of mystics who were keen to understand their interior connection with God.) A contemporary map of the soul, therefore, seeks to explain the dynamics of human consciousness. The language for such a map can be found in psychology, a science of inner experience that attends to the interior motions and patterns of the heart and mind.

Simply by paying attention, we can become aware of the movement of consciousness within us. We can notice that as human beings, our consciousness engages in all sorts of operations: *questioning* what something is, *analyzing* its contents, *desiring* to possess it for ourselves, *reimagining* it creatively, *deciding* what to do with it, and so forth. In contemporary terms, Aquinas was referring to these operations when he spoke of the rational soul.

We can also become aware that we perform these operations in a number of distinct but interrelated patterns. As human beings we have the capacity to operate in many patterns of consciousness, such as theoretic, pragmatic, aesthetic, interpersonal, and narrative. Spontaneously, effortlessly, and usually without noticing it, we shift back and forth among these various patterns. For example, to be interpersonally focused involves expressing our consciousness to another person at many levels. To be somatically focused is to express our consciousness in a bodily way, the way athletes and dancers do. Consciousness is always available to us to focus on whatever area we wish.

Dancers do not say "my body is dancing" but "I am dancing." For them the body is the medium through which consciousness is expressed. This is a subjective process: just as the dancer is the subject of the sentence "I am dancing," so each of us is a subject who speaks, thinks, yearns, and decides. The many differentiations of consciousness are the media through which we discover who we are and through which we communicate with one another. Each of these media is distinct—dancing is not thinking; art is not mathematics—but they connect in the consciousness of the doer. Not everyone accomplishes all differentiations equally well—some have better skills as thinkers than painters or as mathematicians than athletes—but each can understand the other analogously because each is expressing consciousness, is expressing the soul through a medium.

Imagine yourself engaged with a mountain in three different roles: geologist, developer, and artist. As a geologist, you notice tree lines, rock stratifications, signs of volcanic upheaval. You seek to understand the mountain in relation to itself, to explain what it is made of and how it came to be. The patterning of your consciousness is abstract, analytical, theoretic.

As a developer, you engage with the mountain differently. You wonder about the cost of bringing in power lines, about where a ski lodge should be built, about the problems an environmental impact study may pose. You seek to understand the mountain so it will be useful to you and to others. You are calculating, pragmatic.

Now imagine yourself engaged with the mountain as a painter or poet. How is the aesthetic patterning of your consciousness different from the other two? How is it related? Can the three patterns inform and enrich one another? To answer these questions is to be aware of the dynamics of one's own consciousness.

To take responsibility for these differentiations is to appropriate one's own consciousness, one's own soul. To be able to integrate the various overlapping dimensions of consciousness in an ongoing trajectory is to struggle to be virtuous. Ensouled persons are on a quest to have the true, the good, and the beautiful coincide. They are in a process in which consciousness transcends itself.

Mystics of all traditions maintain that, through meditation and other techniques, it is possible to silence all the patterns and operations of consciousness, to bring all the sensing, questioning, imagining, analyzing, and evaluating to a halt. What emerges from this cessation of activity, this emptiness, is a new kind of fullness, an awareness of what

Meister Eckhart calls the Ground of Consciousness, and what other mystics have referred to variously as True Self, Great Mind, and God.

These, then, are the basic features of a contemporary map of the soul: what we mean by *soul* is human consciousness, which is characterized by various operations that function in various patterns, all of which have their source in a Ground of Consciousness.

The Soul and Its Stories

What we call the awakening of the interior life is the resurrection of the soul. Such awakenings occur in all the forms of differentiation about which we have spoken—somatic, aesthetic, interpersonal, intellectual. But perhaps most characteristic of the contemporary resurrection of the soul is the current trend toward the recovery of storytelling, especially involving stories that prompt us into self-awareness and decision.

One of the classic stories in the Western tradition is the parable of the prodigal son, which Jesus tells in the Gospel of Luke 15:11–32. A father has two children—one who stays at home working on the family farm and another who squanders his entire portion of inheritance on loose living. Finally, after having to take work as a feeder of pigs in order to earn his daily bread, the latter son returns, and his father offers him a lavish welcome. In a typical allegory, that would be the end of the story: good triumphs, and faithfulness vanquishes irresponsibility.

There are, however, other elements to this particular tale. The father does not spend his time overseeing the honest son's work on the farm; rather, he is waiting and watching for the return of the absent son. When the son returns, the father welcomes him as though he had become a successful warrior. When the faithful son complains, the father chides him for not being more generous, saying, "My boy, you are always with me, and everything I have is yours. How could we help celebrating this happy day? Your brother was dead and has come back to life, was lost and is found." Then the story ends.

What is the reader to make of this tale? With whom can we identify? We may hesitate to place ourselves in the position of the generous parent, thinking that we would not want to squander our wealth so freely on an errant son. Most of us would also resist identification with the prodigal, preferring to be counted among the children who honor their parents. However, the good son is chided for simply doing his duty, rather than surpassing his obvious responsibilities. To be virtuous in this story is not simply to do one's duty, nor is it to hold onto what one has; rather, the story implies that we must give away what we have, prodigally. This story does not use the word *soul* once. It does, however, evoke the potential of soul by awakening the consciousness of the reader to two distinct kinds of self-transcendence. The first is the potential for being generous with one's goods. The reader, like the son who stays at home, is challenged to see the fulfillment of responsibility and obligation as merely a minimum.

The second has to do with the way in which the reign of God is likened here to a particular kind of parental love. The only way to win divine favor, in this tale, is to learn how to give away one's goods and one's love as the father does. In other words, there is no way to succeed by one's own merits in possessing the mystery of existence. The only way in which one can achieve genuine soul is by constantly giving oneself away—constantly allowing oneself to be drawn to what is beautiful, good, and true. The story, like Caravaggio's *Sacrifice of Isaac*, announces a threshold through which one might pass or not. If one does not enter the world of prodigality, one will only have the outer shell of the self to manipulate; if one does, then one can access and pursue one's own soul.

Chapter 6

Sitting by the Well

MARION WOODMAN

Marion Woodman began her professional life as a high school English and creative drama teacher. After twenty-five years, she left her position to reenter analysis in Switzerland, a move that led her to study at the C. G. Jung Institute in Zurich and to become an analyst herself. She has authored numerous books, including Addiction to Perfection *and* The Ravaged Bridegroom. *Her most recent book,* Leaving My Father's House, *cowritten with three other women, focuses on and interprets the fairy tale "Allerleirauh," the thematic thread for the authors' stories, which are told through dreams, images, and journal entries.*

A strong proponent of embodiment and body work, Woodman values the elemental nature of soul. In her essay, she focuses on the connection of soul to water.

G uided meditation: Imagine that you are walking through a desert or some very hot, parched place . . . As you walk, your feet are scorched; you long for a drink . . . You walk . . . You see a well. Is there a pail? Is there a ladle? Have you anything to help you get a drink? Look into the well . . . What do you see? What treasure is there? Do you leave it, or do you bring it up? Will you keep it for yourself, or will you share it with others? Try to fasten an image so strongly in your mind that you can draw it, dance it, sing it, or write it. Do what is right for you at your well . . . In your own time, come back into this room.

This meditation to look in our well is an important one because in the sacred moments of life—the soul moments—water is always with us. Without water there is no life. Think of how cold our lives would be without the waters of our bodies—without saliva, without sweat, without tears, without the juices of sexual passion. Without connection to our inner waters, we do not feel. Connecting to our well in meditation opens us to the possibility of drinking from the water of soul that gives meaning to life.

I realized just how great the connection between water and soul is when I set out to examine the soulful moments of my own life. I decided to draw a picture of the necklace of my life. I was trying to see the thread, the essence that was the soul continuum. On a large sheet of drawing paper I drew sixteen oval cameo shapes in a circle and joined them with gold chain.

For weeks, I thought about the threshold moments of my own life. As I sorted them out, I realized that they were all moments when the eternal swirled across my daily path, when the divine intersected the human. They are all as real to me today as they were when they happened because they are moments of soul. I have painted fifteen of them; one is yet to be filled. Reflecting on my cameo necklace, I realized that all but four of the moments are connected to water, both literal and symbolic.

I realized, too, that these soul moments often contain the paradox of agony and ecstasy. Everyone's life begins with that paradox and with water. During the birth of a child, the waters break. The mother is often in agony as the labor pains progress—tremendous pauses, tremendous tensions—and then the head crowns. The moment when the mother raises her arms and screams in agony and ecstasy is an eternal moment: one mother becoming Mother with every other mother of every generation. The divine has crossed the human threshold; from the waters that pour out of her, new life comes.

As the baby grows into childhood, water remains an important touchstone. The baby delights in its bath, loves mud and rain, loves the river and the sea. As a child, I loved to play in water because to be soaking wet was to be in touch with life's juices. I loved the luxury of "canning" in my playhouse—mountain ash berries, red peppers, and beets. My bottles were as colorful as my mother's tomato jars, and I was beet juice from top to toe.

Though in adolescence we may no longer literally play in water, the waters of creativity and of the soul's own truth flow strongly. I saw many examples of this in the twenty-five years I taught English and creative drama to adolescents. In the drama classes, we tried to stay in touch with the truth of our bodies, and from that place, we sang and danced and wrote, creating as we went. When it was time to create our annual show, things came, things went, and we allowed them to flow right up to the end of the last performance. Nothing was static.

We once attempted to act out a few lines from T. S. Eliot's *The Waste Land*. That poem is filled with images of our contemporary society existing without water. We were working on the section in which a lover comes to his girlfriend's bedsit for dinner:

> At the violet hour, the evening hour that strives
> Homeward, and brings the sailor home from sea,
> The typist home at teatime, clears her breakfast, lights
> Her stove, and lays out food in tins.
>
> . . .
>
> He, the young man carbuncular, arrives,
> A small house agent's clerk, with one bold stare,
> One of the low on whom assurance sits

As a silk hat on a Bradford millionaire.
The time is now propitious, as he guesses,
The meal is ended, she is bored and tired,
Endeavors to engage her in caresses
Which still are unreproved, if undesired.
Flushed and decided, he assaults at once;
Exploring hands encounter no defence;
His vanity requires no response,
And makes a welcome of indifference.
. . .
Bestows one final, patronizing kiss,
And gropes his way, finding the stairs unlit . . .

She turns and looks a moment in the glass,
Hardly aware of her departed lover;
Her brain allows one half-formed thought to pass:
"Well now that's done: and I'm glad it's over."
When lovely woman stoops to folly and
Paces about her room again, alone,
She smoothes her hair with automatic hand,
And puts a record on the gramophone.

My idea of teaching English was to bring the poem into the flow of
the soul by opening the mouth and letting it come through. I believe that
if poetry isn't resonating in the body, it is dead on the page, disconnected from soul. For Eliot's poem, we had three pairs of young people
playing the roles of the lovers. We were trying to convey a mechanical
way of life, an absence of soul. Each couple was going through exactly
the same gestures at exactly the same time. After three weeks of re-
hearsal—two weeks before the performance—one of the young men
said to me, "I can't do this, Mrs. Woodman. I am going to vomit." The
other young men said they too hated the charade. One of the girls said,
"Thank heaven somebody said something! Every night I go home with
a migraine headache." They all agreed, "We would do it if we could, but
we can't."

Now, I had known they were struggling, but I decided to wait, to let them bring their conflict to consciousness. Why were all six becoming ill? What they were experiencing was exactly what *The Waste Land* is about—loss of soul, demonstrated here in a total parody of lovemaking. Everything that would naturally flow from the sweet waters of soul is massacred in those lines. I was glad when these students said they could not do it. Their voices, their passions, their vibrant beauty—all were being blocked. They were experiencing the horror at the bottom of soullessness. They were healthy enough to react to the bleakness of a world without water; their own souls were asserting themselves in refusing to verbalize the nothingness.

The experiments of adolescents blossom for many into what is the next threshold: marriage. As two people work together to find the inner meaning of it all, they sweat, weep, make love, study, and pray—and if they are attentive, the waters of life flow. If partners cherish their own wells, the marriage can become a container in which both can trust their own maturing process. If the container is tempered to a degree of naked trust, then its strength not only contains the process, but also supports the birth of new consciousness by protecting it. Crossings into areas of new awareness often appear in dreams as the birth of a baby, a baby that needs the protection of a masculinity and femininity that honor each other. Another paradox: the deeper their love for each other, the more freedom they can allow each other and the deeper the well becomes. Of course, not everyone chooses a traditional marital situation. Many contemporary people choose not to marry; many divorcees choose not to remarry; many seek a same-sex marriage. But whatever the relationship between two people, each partner has to search within for his or her own inner masculinity or femininity in order to allow them to blossom into full flowering.

All of us will have to enter the final initiation of death. This is when all the bodily waters cease to flow. A swab of water over burning lips may be the last contact we have with the physical world. But as the soul strives toward its final Beloved, divine eternal springs gush into the well. Often, this activity emerges in seemingly nonsensical language. Many people dismiss the poignant searchings of those on their deathbeds as the effects of a morphine trance, a limbo created by drugs. But the liminal space between this life and the next, with or without morphine, may contain the sweetest yearnings, the most potent images, the most supreme moments of ecstasy and agony. To dismiss this last mile of the earthly journey as "crazed ravings" is to deny ourselves and the dying of the final paradox: that death, the ultimate loss, is also the ultimate gain. As with birth, one world is sacrificed, but another is born.

Whether the well work that engages us has to do with the big initiations I've referred to here or with daily life, one of our most important tasks is to keep the well wall strong. We need a safe container in which the soul can grow. This may sound simplistic, or even clichéd, until we look around and see people rushing pell-mell in every direction, rather than sitting still and enduring the often agonizing process of containing themselves. Most often, this occurs in people who have never experienced a container. Without a mother, a father, a grandparent, a teacher who loves who they are without judgment, they have no model for containing themselves. In silence, they become frantic to escape from their inner judgmental voices.

In any situation in which growth happens, a well-wrought container is part of the process. Recently, I had reason to recognize just how misunderstood the word *container* is. The poet Robert Bly and I, along with thirty workshop participants, made a videotape series called *On Men and Women.* Commenting on the films, many people have said to me, "You don't talk enough, Marion. You sit there and listen."

"I talk when I want to," I reply. "I get my turn, don't you worry."

What they don't realize is that someone has to be the container; someone has to sit by the well. In any vibrant workshop, as in any home, classroom, or psyche, participants have to feel that there is a still point of sanity at the center of all the wild emotions and possibilities that are erupting with new life. Otherwise, they unconsciously risk dropping into the "black hole." The perceiver is the container who can see them, hear them, mirror them, and hold that still point, whatever chaos threatens. In such a situation, the perceiver's consciousness contains the perceived until both become one. That is true of any therapeutic encounter or of any healthy classroom. If the sun doesn't shine, the plant doesn't grow. If the soul is surrounded by judgment instead of love, it cannot flourish.

Tragically, this happens to the souls of many children, who then cannot create their own strong inner container as adults. This lack of solid walls on the inside often results in an overprotectiveness, a rigidity on the outside, a refusal to allow any vulnerability. Unfortunately, though this may seem like a good protective device for the injured soul, it is in fact just the opposite of true strength, which can grow only out of the vulnerability of surrender. Without the courage to surrender ourselves to the potent archetypal forces that vitalize our inner springs, we cut ourselves off from our own wholeness. We slam the door on growing to our full stature. Then we choose to be victims; we blame other people; we refuse to take responsibility for our own gifts. We fail to grow up. To avoid such a fate, we must build our well walls strong so that we can contain and drink from the transformative waters. That is our task.

The consequences of refusing that task are all around us. When I look at our culture as manifested in the media, I think of a wild, undisciplined brat running around doing whatever it pleases, acting out in whatever violent way it chooses. Recently, I was reading about Helen Keller. She, too, was a wild, undisciplined brat, until her teacher, Annie Sullivan, grabbed her and said "No!"—until someone loved her enough to discipline her. Annie Sullivan dragged Helen to the water pump, pumped water over her hand as hard as she could, and wrote *water* in her hand until it got through to the child that what was being written on her hand was the word for what was coming out of the pump. Incredible moment! The little mind that had never understood anything and the little body that frantically reacted to everything suddenly broke through deafness and blindness. Water was a word; water was what was pouring over her hand. There was order in chaos; words could be connected to objects to give meaning. Later she learned that words could be connected to thoughts and feelings to give meaning. Water was the metaphor that brought light to Helen Keller's darkness.

Our culture is teetering on the brink of blindness and deafness, in part because we have lost our sense of metaphor—our sense of how one thing is parallel to or like another, our sense of the connections between different realms of experience. The word *metaphor*, at root, means to carry over or cross over; what Annie Sullivan taught Helen Keller was how to make that trip across. It is to be hoped that our culture will have teachers like her who love it enough to drag it to the pump and hold it under that water until it gets the message that it does have a soul and that it can comprehend metaphor. It doesn't have to mock myth, fairy tales, and Shakespeare; it doesn't have to act out in a frenzied, wild fashion. It doesn't have to exist on images from the blue tube of sheer, uncontrolled instinct: ten-year-olds in Liverpool deciding it would be fun to kill a two-year-old; adults wolfing down food, slurping alcohol, draining needles, and running from bed to bed because they can't tell the difference between instinct and spirit. Culturally, we are going through the breakdown of all our traditional images. All the more reason to love ourselves enough to attend to our wells and understand our own metaphors.

What does uncontrolled instinct have to do with our culture's losing its sense of metaphor? An instinct is a drive or energy that demands action. This action may take the form of immediate release, or it may be contained, carried into consciousness, and thus transformed. In most people, immediate release involves unconsciously acting out to dissipate the energy. Transformation, by contrast, is the conscious directing of that energy to a creative end—a creative, soul-making end. In the transformative process, the energy presents itself as an image that we can paint, dance, sing, or dialogue with. In entering into relationship with the image, we recognize the energy and try to integrate it as a part of ourselves. Thus, Othello's jealousy, blindly acted out, is transformed by Shakespeare's imagination into an inner, soul-making activity with which the audience interacts. The play in performance is the metaphor that allows a destructive intent to be raised to a level of moral and spiritual contemplation. It allows us, without acting out, to recognize and even redeem the murderer in ourselves.

Like Carl Jung, I believe that metaphor is a healer. Because we cannot pin down a metaphor, cannot define it precisely, it holds an element of mystery. That mystery requires that we contemplate the metaphor with our whole being, not simply our intellect. As we ponder it, very often there is a flash of insight—a moment in which everything comes into focus, in which we say, "Yes, that's it." We probably have goose-flesh, because even the cells of our bodies respond to that yes. For a moment, we are whole: emotion, imagination, and intelligence. In the contemplation of a metaphor, soul, body, mind, and spirit are working together. Such a moment reminds us what wellness is.

I once had a dream about a metaphor machine. In it, I was working with a presence who understood the subtleties of the machine far better than I. Together, we were deftly fingering the instruments that guided the energy coming in at one level through spires of wire and transformative nodes up to another level. At the time, I was ill, and it was crucial that instinctual energy be transformed into spiritual energy in order to facilitate my healing.

Often in fairy tales we find metaphors for the ways in which we have to work to transform our energies from one form to another. Think of how many fairy tales, such as "Cinderella" and "Snow White," begin in a kitchen and end in a marriage. When we look at this metaphorically, we can see that into the kitchen come raw instinctual energies—raw meat, raw vegetables. These are cleaned, cut, chopped, and put into the fire of passion—the oven—ready to be transformed into energy that the hero and heroine can bite off, chew, swallow, and digest. Eventually having integrated many divergent energies, the hero and heroine are mature enough to marry. Their wholeness makes the reader feel whole.

Assimilating healthy images is as important to us as assimilating healthy food. I watch my nephew when his mother enters the room. His metaphor machine works well. It signals, "breast, milk, mother, joy." He gurgles, bounces, and jumps; his whole body comes alive in the metaphor. Our adult bodies can be just as responsive to metaphor if we attend to our wells.

What I witness in my nephew and what I know is available to all of us is a transcendence through the body to a place where the soul resides. Most of us think of transcendence as moving through spirit, taking us out of our bodies. Making space for the divine to enter through the vulnerability of our bodies is a very different experience. To open to our own humanness and our own humility—from *humus,* or the earth—is to accept our own deepest wounds. That is where the divine enters. The images we find in our wells are our unique gifts from the divine source.

Jung realized how crucial such images are to our wholeness. In 1954, he wrote that it is "not only possible but fairly probable, even, that psyche and matter are two different aspects of one and the same thing." At that time, we did not have the research to validate his intuitive knowledge. Now, however, much research has focused on the influence of images on the chemistry of the body, as well as the influence of the chemistry of the body on dreams, fantasies, and meditation. Jung knew there was a connection, and he knew, too, that the health of the whole depends on the relationship of the parts. Increasingly, we are learning that that relationship is powerfully influenced by the metaphors that act as crossover points between psyche and soma. Metaphor is the literal language of the soul.

Few people in our culture understand that. Tragically, they sit dying of thirst in a wasteland, unaware of their own wells. They have no jug, no ladle, no understanding of the treasure that could be theirs if only they could receive. Those of us who know we have a well need to remember the words of the *I Ching* in the hexagram of The Well: "The all-important thing about a well is that its waters be drawn. The best water is only a potentiality for refreshment as long as it is not brought up."

A grotto containing a well or perhaps a spring is often sacred to the Great Mother, by whatever name she is called. I once dreamed of her sitting by a well. Her veil was made of spiderwebs fastened together with dewdrops. "Trust," she whispered.

Chapter 7

What the Soul Knows:
A Spiritual Approach to Dreams

ROBERT SARDELLO

Though based in archetypal psychology, Robert Sardello's approach to issues of soul and self breaks new ground. From the gently confiding tone of his 1992 book, Facing the World with Soul—*written as a series of letters to the reader, each beginning with the salutation "Dear Friend"—to his approach to dream material outlined in the following essay, Sardello seems as much poet as psychologist. He suggests that we should not only allow for but celebrate the mystery of our own individual psyches and resist being hemmed in by personal history. The result is an approach to psychology and spirituality that is both illuminating and liberating.*

Sardello is the author of several books, most recently Love and the Soul: A Guide to Creating a New Future for Earth *(1995). In 1993 he co-founded, with Cheryl Beckworth, the School of Spiritual Psychology, which offers an international program of intensive courses on that topic. He is also on the faculty of the Dallas Institute of Humanities and Culture, and of the Chalice of Repose Project in Missoula, Montana, a program in music thanatology.*

M y approach to working with dreams is different from what is assumed by nearly all of modern psychology—that dreams *mean* something. There is no question that dreams have meaning, but I want to suggest that meaning may be their most superficial aspect. Far more important for the psyche, and for the individual as well, is what dreams *do.* In getting closer to dream activity rather than content, we become initiates into the world of the soul.

No matter what technique we use, when we concentrate on the content of dreams, we easily become trapped by questions of meaning—what does this particular dream symbolize? How can I use the information from dreams in my life? What god, goddess, spirit, or mythical pattern is being expressed in dream imagery? But our dreams can be educators, actions that take us into a very different kind of world, the soul world. This world surrounds, interpenetrates, and informs our own but is fundamentally different from it. Dreams come, clothed in the events and experiences of waking life, so that we can gradually learn about their world rather than convert the soul world into some version of our own.

Our desire to convert dream material into something that it is not—the desire to know what dreams mean—can actually be seen as a defense against the soul realm. This realm is unknown to us, and as such its appearance provokes fear. Dream interpretation of any kind is a compromise that says we will go only as far into this world as the sort of thinking with which we are comfortable will allow us. Whether such interpretive thinking is cognitive, as with Freud; more mythical, as with Jung; more feeling-oriented, as with Gestalt approaches; or more dramatic, as with active imagination, we are all in such instances utilizing tools taken from the human world, not the soul world. I want to suggest that our tools for soul work be themselves soul instruments.

Another source of the tendency to convert dream material into something it is not has to do with the prevailing bias toward the past in psychology. Virtually all conventional dream work focuses on how the dream refers either to the collective past or to our individual past. What has yet to be recognized by depth psychology is that the soul is tremendously interested in the future. Soul is interested in what the human being can become, not just in what has happened in the past that seems to make us the way we are. Virtually all the words we use to describe individual psychological qualities indicate a gesture toward the future; desire, longing, anxiety, despair, hope, motive, fantasy, and much more of our psychological vocabulary is oriented toward what is not yet here rather than toward what has already occurred. If one feels desire, it is toward something; one longs for something not yet present; one feels anxiety about what might happen, even if this is imagined and not real. I have been a therapist for over twenty years, and not once has a patient come to me without an interest in the future. Unfortunately, what we are trained to say to our patients is, "Well, if you want to find out how to move into the future, let's examine your past for several years." Seldom does psychology recognize that psychological difficulties stem from trying to face the truly unknown of what we can become by utilizing only modes of knowing taken from the past. What needs to happen in such instances is the development of new capacities, new modes of consciousness through which it becomes possible to live in the realm of ever-changing possibility. Dreams take us nightly into realms of constant change.

In order to begin working with dreams as actions rather than contents, it is first necessary to recognize how converting dream life to ordinary consciousness occurs long before the moment of formal interpretation. There is the actual activity of dreaming, which occurs in the environment of sleep. We wake and remember a dream. We write it down. Then, the dream is brought to the analyst. We are already three steps removed from the actual activity of dreaming. What happens in this three-step translation process is that the dream is converted into a narrative sequence, which is really a story about the dream, not the dream itself. Dreaming does not occur sequentially. For example, a dream might be told in the following fashion: "I dreamed I was walking near the beach, and as I was walking in the beautiful white sand, a huge crab came up to me and told me I need to stay away from the water. I ran away afraid because I had never heard a crab talk." The dream-as-image has been converted into a narrative structure, which is itself already an interpretation of the dream. Because this translation goes unrecognized, everything further that is done with the dream only extends an interpretation that has already begun.

In order to sense the qualities of dream life, it is not enough to write dreams down and begin dream work. Rather, one can become a researcher into dreaming and into the realm of sleep. One can, for example, begin to pay attention to the quality of a dream at the moment of waking. The result of such careful attention is that more and more the dream will be felt as a simultaneous occurrence, something that happens all at once rather than one event after another. The order that we supply upon waking is the ego stepping in and structuring the dream so that the unknown soul world is quickly veiled. The first step in crossing the threshold into the soul world is to give up the need for sequential order.

There is an analogy for this way of paying attention to dream life in visual art. A painting cannot be described as starting at one place on the canvas and proceeding linearly over the whole of the canvas; we cannot say of a painting that it starts here and ends over there. The painting occurs all at once. Dream images happen more in this manner. All one need do is to begin paying attention to the qualities of the dream upon waking, rather than to its content. Then one can go on and write the dream as a narrative, recognizing that recording the dream is a fixing technique that must then be undone.

Here is an example. First, I will tell the dream as a narrative:

I am waiting in line at a clinic to see a doctor who reads the body clairvoyantly. I am at the head of the line, but other people keep moving in front of me. I become frustrated and angry. More and more people are getting in line and pressing me. One person points to a window on my left hand that is filled with Egyptian hieroglyphs. He says the doctor got his skills in Egypt. There is also a strange wooden toy next to the window—a circle of wood with a little wooden monkey hanging from the ring. This monkey begins to move, as if alive. More people come. Finally, the doctor says he will see me along with two other people. When he looks out over the crowd, he is making a sandwich and says, looking pleased, that it is going to be a long day.

To describe the dream now in its activity—to get closer to the dream quality—we have to find a way to write or speak the dream that suggests the whole thing happening at once. For example:

When I am in a clinic to have my body read, I am closed in and pressed by other bodies. When the doctor says he will see me along with two other people, then he is making a sandwich. When the doctor makes a sandwich, I am frustrated and angry, and he is pleased that it will be a long day and more people come. When a clairvoyant, sandwich-making doctor appears, then there is a window into Egyptian writing. When an Egyptian-trained, clairvoyant, body-reading doctor makes a sandwich, then there is a wooden monkey-toy that comes to life when hieroglyphs appear at the window. When a wooden toy becomes alive, I lose my place in line and become frustrated.

The actual dreaming in the night appears more like this kind of layering than a narrative story. The intention of taking the narrative and working it back into image is to thwart the impulse to make day-world sense of the dream. We want to be true to its phenomenology rather than try to make it conform to the laws of logic to which we are accustomed. We want to honor the soul world rather than use it to find out more about ourselves. The result of honoring the dream in this way is a gradual freeing of our own fixed modes of consciousness.

When dreams are worked with in this new manner, we also begin to learn some new things about the nature of the soul world and of the psyche through which this world is perceived. For example, we begin to suspect that the content of a dream is highly arbitrary. We notice that beneath what seems to be very different kinds of content, the soul activity of various dreams may be identical. Soul can present itself in many different pictures and still portray the same essential movement.

Here are two dream stories with very different content but the same essential qualities of action. In the first dream I am walking up a mountain, and as I am walking, I gradually leave the greenery and the landscape becomes more and more rocky. I come to a ledge, and as I walk onto the ledge, part of it falls away and I am standing, looking into an abyss without a way to get back. I'm stuck, and suddenly I am tremendously afraid and wake in fear.

In the second dream, I am walking in the mountains, and I suddenly come to an entrance to a cave. I walk into the cave, exploring it, and find that the cave goes deeper and deeper along a winding path. I come to a place where it is completely dark. I realize that I am in a circular chamber with no way out. Everywhere I turn, I bump into a wall. I become afraid and wake up.

In terms of their content, these dreams are very different. If I were to work with them archetypally, for example, I would treat them very differently. With the latter, we might become interested in going into the underworld and the Earth Mother; with the former, we would work with the consequences of a solitary pursuit upward, of what it means to rise above the earth, toward the sky, and the paradox of how the higher we go, the more we come to an abyss.

However, if we work with these two dreams with the procedure I have described, attempting to get close to the dream activity, we feel the soul engaged in a very similar motion in both dreams: the process or the activity of coming to a halt. The soul makes use of dream content to express itself as motion. These dreams, from the viewpoint of soul activity, can initiate the dreamer into a certain kind of soul action or soul quality. However, the moment we become more concerned with the content than with the qualitative action, we are really theorizing about the dream, trying to make it mean something, rather than letting it work into our day consciousness and bring more flexibility to the way we imagine, know, and perceive others and the world. The content of our dreams is connected with our past, personal or archetypal. But if we can learn to look through the content, symbols, and myths in our dreams rather than looking at them, we can get closer to the current of time that is creating possibilities in our lives—the current of our lives that implies uncertainty and unknowing but also creativity.

The need to know what our dreams mean is a way of trying to have more control in our lives. What the dream wants to offer us, by contrast, is a step into the soul world. There is no one who is not truly, deeply interested in that world. We are, however, afraid of moving into the different modes of consciousness that that world requires. Dream work often handles that fear by saying, "Well, I'll work with that realm, but I won't step into it. I will talk about it with the tools and habits of consciousness that are familiar."

There is yet a further step that can be made in coming to the soul world through dreams; we can go even further than moving from dream story to dream image. Our description of the dream utilizing the analogy of painting still implies a certain distance from the image. In saying a dream is more like looking at a painting than reading a story, we still have taken up a stance outside the image, though we do see and feel more of what is actually there rather than making up an idea of what is there. The next step is more difficult: we work toward dissolving altogether the boundaries between ourselves and the image.

Imagine that in the first step—in going from the dream story to the dream image—we have made a painting in which everything happens simultaneously. If we remain here, we would have a kind of aesthetics—dream work as image making. We would simply become aesthetes, gourmets, epicureans of the soul world. Rather than feeding on this new feast of the imagination, we must let ourselves be devoured by the soul world, be taken into soul, even if for just a few moments. The task here is to step into the painting itself. We do this by imagining: not just looking at the painting, but going into the painting in such a way that our bodies and our ordinary consciousness dissolve. Our consciousness now becomes the image.

This step is more than walking around in the landscape of the image; this is dissolving into it to the point where we cannot say where it ends and we begin. When we step into an image this way, the image, as a picture, disappears. We move from the picture into picturing. What is experienced is the particular mobility of that picturing—the movements; the tensions; the ups and downs; the musical, dramatic activity of the dream, no longer pictured, but now fully felt and experienced. By entering into the dream, we let the soul world enter into us, but consciously, not unconsciously as it does when we are sleeping.

In this step of dream work, we allow ourselves to fully feel the activity of the dream in all its complexity of movement, and then try to re-speak the dream from out of the immediacy of experience. Almost always, this re-speaking comes out as something that looks like poetry. The object here is not to be a poet; it is as if, with this step, we come to the very source of poetry itself. In the case of our earlier example of the dream of waiting to be read by the clairvoyant doctor, re-speaking the activity came forth in the following manner:

> An Egyptian-trained physician
> prepares a sandwich for a long day,
> a line of bodies pressing into each other
> waiting to be read like hieroglyphs,
> wooden monkeys brought to life.
> I bring frustration and anger
> to be clearly seen by a healer.

A most interesting aspect of working with dreams in such a way is that when doing so, the initial impulse to want to know what the dream means disappears. The impulse to want to know stems from fear. But fear is entirely appropriate regarding the soul realm. The world of the soul is very unfamiliar, and what goes on there is not all lightness and beauty; it holds tremendous darkness and confusion as well. The intention is not to tame the soul, as if it were a pet. Rather, the intention is to honor the soul world and, further, to let it do its productive work of changing us. Gradually, the ways in which the soul world informs and illuminates our own waking consciousness becomes felt as we find our fixed ways, our ingrained habits of consciousness changing.

Dreaming does not occur only at night, during sleep. The soul is dreaming all the time and creating within us a sense of the unknown. It is creating a possibility of movement into the unknown future. This creating activity of soul is felt in waking consciousness as a vague sense of destiny, which is quite different from fate. Fate concerns what cannot be avoided in life. Destiny concerns the individual, creative way in which we can take up fate and make something entirely new from it. Approaching dreams as content has more to do with fate, whereas approaching dreaming as activity helps make us aware of destiny. People seek knowledge of their destiny—from the astrologer, the psychic, the psychotherapist—as if it were content, a bit of unknown information available to those with special powers. But destiny does not express itself as a form of information. We are our destiny, and it can be felt in every act to the extent we are present to our actions in their creating, improvisational qualities.

We lose the sense of destiny when we live out of habits from the past. The questions we have about the content of our destiny disappear when we can feel in our actions, when those actions are imagination-filled rather than repetitive literalizations. Coming into connection in a conscious way with the active qualities of dream life, and letting those qualities enter into our bodies and our consciousness, restores destiny as an ever-present guide into the realm of unknown possibility.

If we learn to pay close attention to the moment of waking, we notice that there is always a definite mood upon waking up. Sometimes we feel very content, or even invigorated; at other times, we may feel a twinge of sadness or even of guilt. These moods seem unrelated to what might be happening in daily waking life. These moods verify, at least indirectly, that something very significant has occurred during sleep; it is as if we have had a consultation in the cosmos.

If we wish to become researchers into dream life, and to begin to make discoveries of our own rather than accepting the theories and techniques of professional psychology, it is as simple as beginning with the processes outlined above. What I have presented is not intended to become a new method, but rather to be an encouragement to find out for ourselves the way the soul functions. If we step away from the linear, dream-as-story approach, we do something wonderful as far as accessing the dream realm where the soul lives.

The major benefit of this approach is that we can do it on our own and it is perfectly healthy. This approach is healthy because we have done nothing more than create an artful imitation of what happens every night when we go to sleep and when we wake in the morning. We, in essence, follow the dream from the waking state back into the soul world with the first step, and then follow the dream further back to the point where we have a real impression of the source of the dream. We feel the active quality of dream life; we feel how the dream activity is creating the particularity of our consciousness and the particular style through which soul enters the waking world.

When we instead turn our dreams over to the analyst, we learn more about the therapist's soul life than we do our own, but the power of the therapeutic relationship does not usually allow us to see that this is the case. In therapy, work with dreams cannot be separated from the relationship between therapist and patient. I do not propose that what is created in such a relationship is without benefit, for it can be helpful. But there is a difference between the soul of a particular kind of relationship, such as therapy, and coming into connection with the individuality of soul life. The former runs the risk of dependency on another for a sense of soul, while the latter also has its own risks, the main one being that we do not learn anything truly new, but impose our ego in yet another domain.

The soul dreams in order to bring its world into the body as a teaching that each and every one of us is an incredible creating being. If we can bring such a realization into daily life, it will dramatically change the sense we have of our individual identities. We will discover that who we are changes every moment, while who we think we are is something that comes solely from the habits of the past. What would happen if we could begin to sense our individual identities, not from the limiting perspective of our personal histories alone, but from the liberating current of the soul's concern with the future, with what we can be? What could happen is that we would begin more and more to acknowledge that we are, at least in part, beings who create the world through soul.

As I have tried to show elsewhere, the life of the soul is not something that belongs to individuals alone but more like a drop of soul within the far larger ocean of the soul of the world. However, as long as dream work concentrates on content alone, it is not possible to find the way from our own soul life to the ensouled world. Because it changes our ingrained modes of literalized consciousness, working with dreams in their action initiates the possibility of perceiving that the world—which is ordinarily veiled or perceived as content—is also actually in the process of becoming. The aim of the kind of dream work outlined here is to see that soul work is not for our own benefit alone, but for the sake of the world.

Chapter 8

Between Grief and Joy: Soul as the Way Between the Worlds

DAVID WHYTE

Poet David Whyte was born with traveling shoes. A native of Yorkshire, England, he has lived in Wales, worked in the Galápagos Islands, and now resides on Whidbey Island, near Seattle at the north end of Puget Sound. He regularly takes groups on trips that combine hiking and poetry, including journeys to the Himalayas, the English Lake District, and, most recently, County Clare in the west of Ireland. He also gives readings and workshops throughout the United States.

Whyte not only travels the outer world, he also navigates the soul's territory. His poetry reflects his love of the earth and his understanding of the interior landscape of the soul. He has published three books of poetry: Where Two Rivers Meet, Songs for Coming Home, *and* Fire in the Earth. *In 1994, he authored* The Heart Aroused: Poetry and the Preservation of Soul in Corporate America.

Working in the tradition of the bards, David Whyte not only brings to his listeners and readers the music of the soul but, as in his essay here, also actively encourages people to give voice to the soul's complexities.

I am certain of nothing but of the holiness of the Heart's affections and the truth of Imagination.

John Keats

We know intuitively that the word *Soul* represents energies and qualities in human beings that defy categorization. *Soul* stands for both a life bound and held by time and a life outside of time. Contemplating soul, we might imagine simultaneously both the worm burrowing through damp, close-packed soil and the hawk forgetting itself on a keen wind. We live between two worlds, both equally difficult to embrace: the first and most familiar, a life struggling through the everyday grit and grime of incarnation, and the second, perhaps more fleeting because of the stressful nature of our time, an experience of complete participation and joyful self-forgetfulness. We have, on the one hand, the devil in the details—the trash, the washing up, the necessities of bill paying and earning the money to do so—and, on the other, a numinous experience of existence where all our strategies melt away in movement and encounter.

Raised for the perfect lifestyle with which to live out our lives, we find it hard to believe that human existence involves such an untrammeled degree of participation. Life itself, to our amazement, shows very little interest in choosing between those qualities we normally see as mutually exclusive but seems to flower and fruit from the very meeting of opposites. Joy appears amidst the worst losses and disasters, while certain griefs appear only when we are at the height of our success. Any understanding of soul or of the voice that can carry soul must emulate life's seeming refusal to choose between opposing worlds. If the tradition of poetic imagination teaches us anything, it is the impoverishment that comes through our own refusal to slip through the hairsbreadth gap between the worlds.

There are clear images of this poignant gap etched in the human literate memory. I think of Basho's *Narrow Road to a Far Province* celebrated in haiku, the ghostly visitations that appear so masterfully in Dickens's *A Christmas Carol,* and Yeats's Irish vision of the gateway to

Tir Na Nog, The Land of the Young. There are coded references to gateway states of numinous involvement through all the world's religions—the Kingdom of Heaven, Nirvana, Paradise, Eternity—whose true nature always speaks of a state of heart and mind rather than a location in place or time. Our children's stories, films, and mythologies are full of characters who slip between or around worlds, through hedgerows, under fences, past and beyond the immobile adult world we continually insist on presenting to them. The intuitive grasp of these stories takes children away from an impoverished choice between the difficulties and the joys of existence and gives them a momentary glimpse of something larger and quite miraculous that embraces both.

In the instant when we embrace both sides of any experience, we are stepping through a gateway, a threshold moment that initiates us into the world as it is, a cross-current of emerging patterns rather than a tamed creature amenable to doing our bidding. Yeats touched it most closely when he spoke of "a terrible beauty" being born, his description of the new Ireland then arising from the ashes of the past. A world that changes and transforms us in the very instant of contact.

As participants in this terrible beauty, we find to our amazement that we belong in one way or another to almost everything we encounter, but in ways our social inheritance could not have prepared us for. The experience has the sense of joining, as if a circuit has now been made that allows an invisible current to flow. The current, like electrical potential, remains unrealized so long as we do not put the two terrible edges of any given experience together. The spark of laughter itself usually arises from two irreconcilable opposites brought together through a previously implausible image. The agony and ecstasy of love comes through the dissolution of the smaller self into the greater self we feel in the presence of the beloved. In love we feel the painful stretch between self and not-self at its most physical.

But the self-forgetfulness of laughter is the merest touch of what awaits us on the other side of our daily mechanical choices; the emotional roller coaster of romantic love is only an indicator of what awaits us through the disciplines of not choosing. We could walk through the graduated importance of various conundrums we are presented with on a daily basis, beginning with the absurd trivia of advertising—Sprint or AT&T? Pepsi Cola or Coke?—nonquestions that preoccupy us when we have lost sight of what is essential. Then we could walk through our choices of this school or that to attend, this kind of person or that to marry, this kind of life to live or not, until finally we come to a particularly fierce kind of attention in which the question is allowed to live inside us. Out of this vital place, we could find ourselves saying or doing something from the depths of the question itself. In the question of marrying, I would put aside my "choice" of whom to love in order to be found by love itself. I would put aside the question of this life or that in order to be found by the new life now arising from the agony and exuberance of the question.

The very attempt to put the hidden urgencies of the soul into written form makes the writer hesitate, because simply talking about the soul's daily attempt for freedom through that kind of belonging—where the personality disappears to make for something greater and more alive— seems to bring as much grief and joy as any writer's frame could stand. It causes people to ask themselves how much they enter this timeless and blessed experience of the numinous on a given day. And how to create this experience in the voice? In the pressures of today's world, to feel anything in the span of a day would be marvelous for many; it has far more often been a span of *years* since people may have felt ecstasy in their lives. Real joy is almost always both a recognition of something precious and a grief-filled reminder of the depths we have refused to enter. At the bottom of this well of grief we find disturbing images.

The Well of Grief

Those who will not slip beneath
    the still surface on the well of grief

turning downward through its black water
    to the place we cannot breathe

will never know the source from which we drink
the secret water cold and clear

nor find in the darkness glimmering
the small round coins
thrown by those who wished for something else.

In the very act of writing this poem, I caught the image of something glimmering at the bottom of the dark well, and my first reaction was to swim round the image. I sensed something deadly to a personal identity I had been so carefully arranging for myself, and because I knew the image would bring the poem to a sudden and disturbing end, the strategic part of my mind was much more comfortable writing a longer poem on the *subject* of grief than celebrating the physical experience itself. But another, deeper current swept me toward the glittering itself. Forced to look, I found in those small round coins all the tokens I had thrown into the well to make my heartfelt wish come true—the wish being that I would not have to go down into the water myself, would not have to face what must be faced. We throw anything down there in the hope that we will not have to go down into the darkness, in the hope that we can go straight to one light-filled half of existence called happiness, in the hope that the universe will suspend for us the complementary nature of creation. When we see our attempts to buy our experience with some currency other than our true participation, we come to terms with everything we have sacrificed over the years, and sacrificed in vain. The well water in some ways is the physical body, the place where all real joys and griefs are felt and find a home. There is always a part of ourselves that would like to keep aloof from the physical experience of pain and loss and the poignancy of a felt joy, a part of us that would like to *think* our way into our life.

The embrace of joy and grief as one indivisible whole comes when we reach the end of our thinking and find ourselves no farther along the road. Our real entrance is the body itself and its refusal to ignore any of the qualities it encounters in the spectrum of experience. For instance, almost all of the great contemplative traditions stress the simple human ability to breathe as a doorway to a more vital existence. The breath itself is the physical encapsulation of all the cycles of life, giving and taking, coming to fullness and dying away. The voice *is* the breath made visible in sound. All the rhythms of song and poetry come from a celebration of the body and the intellect carried live on the alternating give and take of the breath traveling out to meet the world on its own terms. The voice is alive when it brings both these expanding and fading sides of experience into words or song. I think of Aretha Franklin's voice dropping to a dead hush from full-throated passion, Luciano Pavarotti moving effortlessly from grandeur to tenderness. In the vital voice we sense the courage not to choose but to live fully between the powerful urgencies of death and rebirth.

> A word is dead
> When it is said,
> Some say.
> I say it just
> Begins to live
> That day.

> *Emily Dickinson*

With a real connection between the intellect and the physical senses we can begin to experience the ability not only to represent ourselves truly in the world but also to call out for what we desire—a state of heart and mind where the sounds and images that people form of their world are also a representation of the way they fit in that world. In other words, we begin to cultivate a faith in our deeply personal images, aspirations, and hopes, not only as an indication of our path in life but as the very touchstone and representation of our destiny in the world. Our destiny is the possibility of fitting exquisitely into the constellation of experience we call life—not in a way in which we are held in place, but more as participants in a great communal dance. As we find a way of belonging, so are we able to find the satisfactions and celebrations of being alive. Even as we learn to discriminate what is good and right for us, so we learn not to make choices that impoverish us. Our refusal to choose between our joys and difficulties and our ability to embrace life as a constant act of meeting is the touchstone of our participation, a true *breath* of fresh air and the measure of *soul* in our lives.

The Individual Soul Journey

Chapter 9

Walking the Mystical Path
with Practical Feet

ANGELES ARRIEN

Angeles Arrien is an anthropologist, author, and teacher whose field of research is indigenous spirituality and shamanism. Her focus is on introducing and integrating ancient wisdom into contemporary culture. She is a faculty member of both the California Institute of Integral Studies and the Institute of Transpersonal Psychology; she is also a corporate consultant who works to bring indigenous approaches to community into the business world.

The material Arrien presents here is part of the Four-fold Way Training, a cross-cultural educational program she designed; parts are excerpted from her book The Four-fold Way: Walking the Paths of the Warrior, Teacher, Healer, and Visionary *(1993). She is also the author of* Signs of Life: The Five Universal Shapes and How to Use Them *(1992) and* The Tarot Handbook: Practical Applications of Ancient Visual Symbols *(1987).*

Recently I witnessed a moment of deep soulfulness between two strangers. I was at a bus stop, sitting next to a woman reading a newspaper, but I was totally engrossed in the performance of a fourteen-year-old boy on a skateboard. He had his baseball cap turned around with the bill in back, and he was skating beautifully and very fast. He buzzed by us once, then twice. When he came by a third time, he accidentally knocked the woman's newspaper out of her hands. She said, "Oh, why don't you grow up!"

I watched him glide down to the corner of the block, where he stood talking with his buddy. The two of them kept looking back over their shoulders at the woman. She hesitated for a moment, then rolled up her paper, tucked it under her arm, and walked into the street, motioning to him. "Won't you come here?" she called. "I want to talk to you."

Very reluctantly, he skated over to her, turned his cap around with the bill in front, and said, "Yeah?"

She said, "What I meant to say was that I was afraid that I might get hurt. I apologize for what I did say."

His face lit up, and he said, "How cool!"

In that moment, I witnessed what is called in Spanish a *milagro pequeño*—a small miracle. This small miracle was a holy, healing moment between generations, between two human beings who had just become important strangers to each other. The woman chose to shift the shape of her experience by moving out of reactivity into creativity. This kind of shape shifting is possible when we allow ourselves to speak directly from our souls.

Part of the business of soul, in fact, is to be a shape-shifter. When we are in touch with the deepest undercurrents of our lives, we have no choice but to act honestly, to speak soulfully. Our soul work is, quite simply, to find and remove whatever gets in the way of our being who we are.

In our culture, we don't have many aids to tracking our souls, to keeping in touch with the things that make us who we are and recognizing and eliminating those things that deter us. Indigenous cultures have important information to offer us about maintaining soulfulness in our lives. Just as they have outer tracking devices—for locating such things as food and water—indigenous peoples of the world have internal tracking devices that enable them to integrate their experiences, learn from them, and move on.

I have found, among a variety of indigenous cultures, four central tracking devices. We can think of them as four "rivers" that we must learn to navigate in order to keep our souls fed and healthy, in order to keep our true selves alive. One is the river of inspiration: I know I'm still alive if I can be inspired, expanded, and uplifted by events, by beauty, by other people. Another is the river of challenge: I'm still alive if I can bring energy to the experience of being tested and challenged. This river is about being able to accept an invitation to stretch, to move beyond the familiar, to grow.

The third river is the river of surprise. Children love surprises; as adults, unfortunately, we often lose that love. Navigating the river of surprise means being able to be shaken out of our need for control and reawakened to the awe of the unexpected. The last river or tracking device is the river of love: I know I'm still alive if I can be deeply touched and deeply moved by life. If I'm not easily touched by life, my heart has begun to close. Native peoples believe that the heart is the bridge between father sky and mother nature and that, therefore, if we are to stay in contact with both the mystical and the practical in our nature, we must stay healthy and open in our hearts.

The open heart is one that can both give and receive love; an open heart also recognizes that love does not always come to us in the ways we expect. I thought of this recently as I watched a mother and her son, who must have been about seven years old, walking though a public garden. The boy plucked a rose from a bush, brought it to her, and said, "Mommy, you're as pretty as this rose." She took the rose, thanked him, and then said, "Why don't you ever tell Mommy that you love her?"

That mother's heart was closed to the variety of ways that expressions of love might come to her. Perhaps only the actual words would have made sense to her. How sad for both her and her son that she could not hear the "I love you" underneath his statement.

When, whatever the reason, we find ourselves incapable of navigating those four rivers—inspiration, challenge, surprise, and love—we have begun to lose touch with our souls. We miss out on the beauty and opportunity of the world; we find ourselves caught in the prison of our own consciousness. And often we don't take soul sickness as seriously as we do sickness in the body. Again, we can look to older cultures to help us find the medicines of soul retrieval.

If you were suffering from the symptoms of soul loss—if you were depressed or dispirited—and went to an indigenous healer or shaman, it is likely that he or she would begin to work with you by asking one of four questions. One of those questions is, When in your life did you stop singing? If you can remember a time when you stopped singing, you might remember feeling that you were beginning to lose your voice; you might remember some circumstance or idea or person that made you feel it was no longer safe to give voice to your own truth.

Another question is, When did you stop dancing? When you stopped dancing is when you began to lose touch with your body. Children dance spontaneously all the time; they simply respond to music. As adults, we need to ask ourselves when and how it was that we lost that ability to respond; we need to look at how it happened that we stopped dancing.

The third question is, When did you stop being enchanted with stories? Stories are the greatest healing and teaching art that we have. Through stories, we transmit values, ethics, traditions, memories, and identity. One way to retrieve our souls is to ask ourselves what our favorite stories are, to repeat the ones that we find most healing and comforting, and to remember which ones we especially want to pass on to others.

The last and perhaps most difficult question that an indigenous healer would ask is, When did you stop being comfortable with the sweet territory of silence? Silence is recognized by all cultures as that place where we can connect to mystery, where our individual souls reconnect with the soul of the world. In order to allow ourselves adequate contemplation and reflection, we need to be comfortable with silence and solitude.

These four universal healing questions seem simple, yet they hold the keys to many of our soul-sicknesses. Despite all the obvious differences among cultures and peoples, there is not a culture in the world that doesn't sing or dance or tell stories or recognize the mystery in silence. In our culture, silence is often impossible to come by, and this is a tragedy, for silence allows us to replenish ourselves so that we can then give back to the world around us. The lack of generosity that we often experience in the world may be due to the fact that so few of us have adequate solitude within which to replenish ourselves.

One image I find useful for describing the necessity for replenishing ourselves is that of a well with buckets around it. Our soul—our deep source—is the well. We fill our buckets from that well and then pour out to others what is needed from our buckets. In order to protect that source, we have to be sure that we give from the buckets and not from the well itself, and that when those buckets are empty, there is a time for replenishing—a time to refill before we give again. Unfortunately, the frantic pace of our lives often requires that we begin to give not just from the buckets around the well but from the well itself; some of us, I'm afraid, are squeezing the last few drops of liquid from the moss at the bottom. Soul work requires that we give ourselves adequate time for replenishment—time to deepen and integrate, time to come back to the center of our lives.

Meditation is a powerful way to provide our souls with adequate solitude and silence. Though many of us think of meditation as happening in one posture—sitting down, legs crossed—there are actually four universal meditation postures: standing, sitting, lying down, and walking. Each of these postures is appropriate for certain kinds of problems or issues.

Standing meditation is useful if you feel victimized or helpless. It can remind you of what it feels like to stand up for yourself, to have, literally, both feet on the ground. In standing meditation, you can most easily access your authority and power. Sitting meditation gives you access to your own wisdom; sitting is the best posture for suspending judgment, for becoming a fair witness to your own processes. When I feel my self-critic gathering too much strength, I know it is time for sitting meditation.

If you are struggling with fear or anger, or any overwhelming emotion, lying-down meditation can help that emotion move more easily through your body. The lying posture is the most healing posture the body can assume; lying down, you can most easily access the nurturing, loving energy within you. Walking meditation encourages creative problem solving and helps you to reignite your own creative fire. If I find myself in periods of stagnation or inertia, I reenergize with walking meditation.

Recently, I discovered that Albert Einstein arranged his study to accommodate all four of these meditation postures. He had a tall table designed so that he could stand while writing his formulas. He had a favorite chair—an old wingback—to sit on. He kept an army cot in his study, too, so that he could lie down from time to time. And he wore a circular path into the wood floor of that room—just outside the perimeter of a circular rug—from pacing. Though he might not have called it meditation, it is revealing that a man so deeply involved with both science and spirituality structured his work room so that he would have standing, sitting, lying, and walking opportunities. On some level, he must have known that each of these postures allowed him to access different kinds of information.

It is becoming more and more important that we not only access such information but bring it into the world. That is our task, in this decade. We can no longer continue to support the "either-or" world—the place where we either put all our energy into our own individual paths or into the larger community—but must move into the "both-and" world. Many of us have spent a lot of time doing inner work, in a sense hopping on one leg in the internal world. Our task now is to put the other leg in the outer world, to combine spirit and action. It is absolutely essential that we learn to walk the mystical path with practical feet.

That can be a daunting task. But again, indigenous peoples have wisdom to offer us. In many indigenous cultures, you can find some variation on the following rules, which are intended to make living a life very simple. The first rule is, Show up. Choose to be present to life. Choosing to be present is the skill of the warrior archetype, an old-fashioned term for leadership abilities. The warrior in us chooses to be present to life.

Once we show up, we can go on with rule number two, which is, Pay attention to what has heart and meaning. This rule is associated with the archetype of the healer, the one who recognizes that love is the greatest healing power in the world. When we pay attention to what has heart and meaning, we are opening the arms of love.

When we show up and pay attention to what has heart and meaning, then we can follow the third rule: Tell the truth without blame or judgment. This is the path of the visionary, the one who can give voice to what is so. Telling the truth without blame or judgment is not necessarily being "polite," but the truth-teller does consider timing and context as well as delivery. Truth telling collapses our patterns of denial and indulgence, keeps us authentic.

When we are able to tell the truth, we can go to the fourth rule: Be open to outcome, but not attached to it. This is associated with the archetype of the teacher, who trusts in the unexpected and is able to be detached. Often, in the West, we define "detachment" as "not caring," but detachment is really the capacity to care deeply but objectively. If you've taken the other three steps, then the fourth rule should come naturally, if not always easily: if you have shown up, paid attention to what has heart and meaning, and told the truth without blame or judgment, then it should follow naturally that you can be open, but not attached, to outcome.

None of this is necessarily easy to do. But one of the great joys of soul work is that whether or not we are able to be fully present to life, life keeps calling out to us. No one is immune to the pull of the natural cycles of the universe; no one is immune to love. And because it requires just as much energy, if not more, to stay out of life as it does to be fully engaged in it, why not be engaged? Octavio Paz, a Latin American poet and Nobel Prize winner, realized when he was in his forties just how much of himself he had spent staying away from the deep currents of his life. He wrote this prose poem describing that experience and describing, too, the persistence of the world in spite of it all:

XII   After
    After chopping off all the arms that reached out to me; after
    boarding up all the windows and doors; after filling all the pits
    with poisoned water; after building my house on the rock of a
    No inaccessible to flattery and fear; after cutting out my tongue
    and eating it; after hurling handfuls of silence and monosylla-
    bles of scorn at my loves; after forgetting my name and the

name of my birthplace and the name of my race; after judging
myself and sentencing myself to perpetual waiting and perpetual loneliness, I heard against the stones of my dungeon of syl-
logisms the humid, tender, insistent onset of spring.

No matter how we try, soul calls out to us. We may have become so
injured in our instincts, so wounded in our souls, that our demons
threaten to overwhelm us, that we cannot quite hear the call of spring.
But spring calls to us anyway. The center of our soul work is ensuring
that the good, true, and beautiful in our nature is at least as strong as
the demons and the monsters; put another way, it is ensuring that my
self-worth is at least as strong as my self-critic. That issue is central to
all of the indigenous peoples that I have studied. If I am living in a way
that feeds the good, true, and beautiful in my nature—as opposed to
feeding the self-critic—then I can heal myself. I can stay in touch with
my own deep source, my soul. And I can also be a healing agent in my
family, my community, my nation, and the world.

I said before that the basis of soul work is really to eliminate everything that gets in the way of my being myself and to feed that which encourages me to be myself. I want to suggest a simple exercise—two
simple questions—to help you track that. Each morning, before you step
out into the world, ask yourself, "Is my self-worth as strong as my self-
critic?" Be sure you can say yes before you go out the door. Then, using
your name, say, "Jim, are you Jim?" or "Sally, are you Sally?" and be sure
that you can say yes to that, too, before you go out into the world.

All of us carry, within ourselves, an original healing medicine that is
not duplicated anywhere else on this earth. If we say yes to those two
questions every day, then we can bring our medicine fully into the
world. We can, as the woman at the bus stop did, move out of reactivity
into creativity. When we live soulfully, each of us can be a shape-shifter;
each of us can create holy, healing moments. Each of us can be fully engaged, moment to moment, in the great gift called life.

Chapter 10

The Shamanic Journey: A Way to Retrieve Our Souls

SANDRA INGERMAN

Sandra Ingerman holds an M.A. in counseling psychology from the California Institute of Integral Studies and is educational director of the Foundation for Shamanic Studies, which is directed by Michael Harner. She also teaches workshops on shamanism both nationally and internationally and has a private counseling practice in Santa Fe, New Mexico, where she uses shamanic healing techniques with individuals, couples, and families.

Some of the information presented in this essay comes from The Way of the Shaman, *by Michael Harner, and from Ingerman's first book,* Soul Retrieval: Mending the Fragmented Self, *which was published by HarperSanFrancisco. She is also the author of* Welcome Home: Following Your Soul's Journey Home, *which builds on the material presented in her first volume.*

Many of us move through our daily lives feeling as though something is missing, as though we have lost an intangible but nonetheless real part of ourselves. Unconsciously, we may spend a great deal of psychic energy trying to retrieve what is missing—through dreams and daydreams or through exploring a number of spiritual paths. Around the world, in a variety of cultures, there have traditionally been healers whose work it is to help us locate and bring back the missing parts of ourselves. These healers are known as shamans.

The word *shaman* comes from the Tungus tribe in Siberia, but the practice of shamanism exists cross-culturally—in Siberia, Lapland, parts of Asia, parts of Europe, Australia, Africa, and North and South America. Definitions of the word vary from anthropologist to anthropologist, but in all shamanic cultures around the world, part of the core definition is that a shaman journeys outside of time and space into nonordinary reality to access spiritual information and do healing work. In nonordinary reality—which we can think of as a parallel universe—there are helping spirits with whom the shaman or the one being healed can communicate. This is the oldest healing practice known to humankind.

There are two basic approaches to a shamanic journey. In one, you go for yourself: you take whatever problem or question you have and enter into a nonordinary realm to learn what you can. In the other, more traditional approach, you go to a shaman, and he or she makes the journey and retrieves information for you.

This information is often relayed through what we call power animals and teachers in human form. In shamanic cultures, it is believed that when a child is born, the spirit of an animal or animals takes pity on that child and volunteers to be its protector—a kind of guardian angel. We can assume that each of us has at least one, and perhaps two or three, power animals who want to help us. We can learn to work with our power animals, not just in a shamanic journey, but in all aspects of our lives, so that we don't necessarily have to travel into a state of nonordinary reality to access their help.

When a person comes for shamanic healing, we don't differentiate among the physical, the emotional, and the spiritual realms, unlike in our culture, where we have kept these areas separate for so long.

Whether an illness primarily manifests itself in a physical, emotional, or spiritual way, there are, according to shamanism, three major causes of illness. One is the loss of a power animal. Over the years, our power animals come and go: one might teach us what it has to teach us and then move on, to be replaced by another. Occasionally, however, an animal will go away and not be replaced by a new one. In that circumstance, the person is left without power.

Loss of power often manifests itself in chronic conditions. It could be a chronic physical complaint—such as always getting a cold or the flu—or a chronic emotional state, such as depression. Another sign could be chronic misfortune. We all know people who seem unlucky: they fall down and injure themselves a lot, their cars get broken into, their pets die, and so forth. What we think of as a string of bad luck could be a symptom that a person has lost his or her power animal, because part of the role of your power animal is to protect you from misfortune. To treat power loss, a shaman has to journey to look for a missing power animal and return it to the person's life.

Another cause of illness is spiritual intrusion, or misplaced energy that has entered your body. Spiritual intrusions often manifest themselves in very specific, localized ways. For example, a person might come to me complaining about an ulcer. When I go on a shamanic journey to look at that person's body, I might see something ominous—maybe a big black snake with its fangs showing—that clearly does not belong there. Spiritual intrusions can take on a variety of faces, but they are never pretty: I might see swarms of insects, a rusty knife, or black sludge. In such a case, it is the role of the shaman to take that intrusion out of the person's body and put it back into nature again.

Spiritual intrusions are created by negative thought forms. But any discussion of dealing with these forms is tricky because it is so easy to misinterpret. Shamanism does not advocate the repression of anger, sadness, or any other troubling emotions that we might consider "bad." In fact, no emotions are bad. What we have to learn is not to repress our negative emotions but to deal with them responsibly.

We deal with our emotions responsibly when we remember that they create real conditions for other people on the planet. If I am very angry at someone and don't work with that anger or take responsibility for it, I can send a spiritual intrusion into that person. Intrusions can come from strangers as well as people we know—when I walk down any populated city street, intrusions constantly float around; if I'm not aware of the danger of those intrusions and do not call on my power animals to fill me with power, I can be very vulnerable to their assaults. Or I can also create an intrusion in myself. If I have a lot of anger and completely repress it, I can create an intrusion within my own body.

It is important to remember that spiritual intrusions are not evil, just misplaced. As an analogy, if a spider crawls into your bed, the spider is not evil; it is simply in the wrong place. What you need to do is put it outside—back into nature, its real home. In most shamanic cultures, spiritual intrusions are put into water, a natural element that is believed to be a neutralizing agent.

The third and most common cause of illness is loss of the soul. I am defining *soul* here as our essence, our life force, our vitality. It is our soul that keeps us engaged in our lives, and its loss is usually the result of a trauma.

The psyche has a survival mechanism to deal with emotional or physical trauma: a part of you goes away in order for you to survive the experience. The shamanic term for this is *soul loss;* the psychological word for it is *dissociation.* In psychology, we talk about dissociation constantly, but we don't talk about what part of us dissociates or where it goes. In shamanism, we recognize that a part of the soul dissociates and goes into the realm of nonordinary reality I referred to earlier.

Any trauma can result in soul loss: sexual abuse, physical violence, accident, surgery, war, divorce, the death of a loved one. In such cases, soul loss is actually a useful protective device: the last place I want my soul to be in a moment of trauma is in my body, because that would be too painful to endure. From the shamanic point of view, the problem is not that the soul leaves in traumatic moments but that it usually doesn't return on its own.

Another cause of soul loss is the soul's being stolen by someone else. This is actually a very common event in our culture. For example, if I don't want to break my connection with you but you want to leave me, I might take a piece of your soul in an attempt to stay psychically connected to you. Or if I'm a mother who is very depressed, and my child is a bundle of energy and light, I might try to take some of that energy, some of that light. None of this is necessarily done on purpose, or with the deliberate intent to harm; it may in fact be done out of complete ignorance. But either way the result is that something is stolen and put into a place where it cannot be used.

One thing we need to remember is that you cannot use another person's life energy for yourself, so when you steal another person's soul or when another person leaves a piece of his or her soul with you, it's a lose-lose situation. The person whose life essence has been taken away is now open to illness, whether emotional or physical. Meanwhile, if you've stolen someone's soul, you're stuck with unusable energy that becomes a tremendous burden.

Symptoms of soul loss can be seen in people who complain of feeling that they observe life rather than participate in it. Soul loss mimics many of the symptoms of power loss, such as chronic illness or immune deficiency problems, but the symptoms of soul loss tend to be much more severe. The cure is for a shaman to journey into nonordinary reality, find the soul, and bring it back.

For people suffering from soul loss, I would suggest that, rather than taking the soul-retrieval journey themselves, they have a shaman do it for them. Often, the soul blasts out of the body so far and so fast that it gets lost. Also, there is always the possibility that the soul does not want to come back. In the case of an adult who was abused as a child, for example, the soul might not know about adulthood. It might not be aware that the person doesn't live with the abuser anymore, that there is now a safe place to go. Part of the job of the shaman would be to negotiate with that soul and update it, assure it that things are different now. That kind of negotiating is complicated—you can't bribe a soul or hurry it if it is reluctant—and, again, someone trained in shamanic healing may be able to do a more effective job of it than you could do for yourself.

There is also a kind of power that comes from not being alone in your journey. When I interview clients who have had soul retrievals about their experiences, one thing I hear again and again is that a great deal of healing comes from knowing that someone else cares so much about you and your condition that he or she is willing to go search for your soul. Having someone who is willing to intervene in the spiritual realms on your behalf, to track down the soul you lost and to negotiate for its return, can, in itself, provide an extra impetus for you to work hard on integrating what they bring back to you. I find that most people journeying for themselves, though they can sometimes find their own lost soul parts, cannot successfully bring them back into the body.

Lost souls can usually be found residing in one of three realms of nonordinary reality that the shaman or you can explore: the Lower, Middle, and Upper Worlds. In traditional shamanic literature, the Lower World is most often referred to as the Underworld, but because Underworld has too many negative connotations for people in this culture, *Lower World* is a safer term. We reach the Lower World through a passageway or tunnel into the earth, such as a tree trunk or a cave, or through a body of water, such as a lake or a river. The Lower World is inhabited by the spirits of animals and plants, as well as by any human spirits who are particularly connected to the earth. Though it is definitely a part of nonordinary reality, the landscapes you might find in a journey to the Lower World are recognizably earthy—forests, fields, streams.

The Middle World is the location of nonordinary reality related directly to the here and now. Middle World journeying is traditionally used in looking for lost and stolen objects, because it allows us to see things just as they are but outside of time. I have also used Middle World journeying to gain access to a client who is unconscious. It is unethical to embark on a shamanic journey on behalf of someone who has not given you permission to do that; yet there are many cases, such as when someone is in a coma, when a soul retrieval might be in order. If I had a client in that condition, I would take a Middle World journey to ask that person's permission to work on his or her behalf.

The Upper World is, for some of us, more ethereal in nature. In that world we may be unsure just what we are standing on or where whatever light we can see is coming from. In the Upper World, as well as the Lower World, we might find teachers in human form.

The most common way to enter into any of these worlds is through the use of a drum. In almost all shamanic cultures, percussion is an essential part of any other-world journey. Scientists have discovered that listening to a repetitive beat actually alters brain waves: they slow down into a very deep meditative state of consciousness that allows the shaman to travel into these other worlds. I like to think of the drum as the path out of the body and back into the body again. The Siberians call the drum the horse that takes the shaman on his or her journey. If you are journeying on your own, you can use tapes of drumming or have someone else do it for you; if you're working with other people, you may be able to have live percussion, which is ideal.

There are a few things that can get in your way when you're beginning to do this work. One question that people often ask me is, When I'm journeying, am I making this up? How do I know this is real and not my imagination? From a shamanic point of view, the answer is no, you're not making it up. We believe that you are traveling into a hidden reality and meeting with spiritual helpers who exist. Because most of us don't have that kind of spiritual foundation, you might not be able to believe that at first. I feel it's absolutely useless to fight yourself on this question. After you've had some experience, you'll know that the journey is real.

Many people are insecure because they are afraid they might be doing something wrong. One of the beauties of shamanism is that there is no right or wrong way to journey; your experience is your experience. There are, for example, different styles of journeying. In the Lower World, some people actually become their power animal, some are with the power animal, and others observe the whole interaction. One style is not better than the other, and everybody has his or her own style. As you work, you may find that you flip back and forth between various styles.

Another stumbling block can be a fear of journeying into nonordinary reality. I have been asked, for example, if there is any danger in doing shamanic journeying. Again, the answer is no, but I think it is helpful to think about the experiences of nonordinary reality that you are already familiar with—dreaming and daydreaming—and compare them with what happens in the shamanic journey.

Unless you have been studying lucid dreaming and developed some skills in that area, you have no control over what happens to you in your dreams. When you are having a nightmare, you're stuck in that nightmare—you just have to hope that you'll wake up or that the dream will take a better turn. In a daydream, on the other hand, you control everything: you control what you do, who you meet, what you say, what who you meet says back to you. In a shamanic journey, you have control of yourself. You can choose to move to the right; you can choose to move to the left; you can choose to go to the Lower World; you can choose to go to the Upper World; you can choose to move toward a particular animal; you can choose to move away from a particular animal. You cannot, however, choose what that animal does or says with you. You can only control your own actions; you cannot control the actions of the spirits. But in any given situation, you have control over what you do and say, even if that means that what you decide to do is to leave.

For example, I cannot choose whether a bear, elephant, eagle, mouse, or dolphin will be waiting for me when I enter the Lower World. The animal I meet might tell me that she has appeared to answer my question; the animal might take a stance to show me his power or love; the animal might actually perform a healing on me. It is important to note, too, that it is the whole species of the animal that is lending its support. One does not have a bear as a power animal; one has *bear*. Though the animals one meets on a shamanic journey often appear with a particular personality—one might be very soft and loving; another might be very humorous—you in fact have its whole species behind you lending its power.

It is also important to note that in shamanism one journeys between nonordinary reality and ordinary reality at will. A journey is something that is performed with discipline. Someone who is practicing shamanism would not flip into a journey while at a party or while driving; rather, such a person would make a decision that it is time to journey, allow his or her soul to enter nonordinary reality at will, and at the journey's end, come back fully into his or her body in a centered and grounded way.

Another important aspect of such a journey is the results you get. In shamanism we are very goal oriented: we want to see results. So the fundamental question, whether you've been embarking on your own shamanic journeys or whether a shamanic practitioner has been journeying for you, is, Does your life move in a positive direction from doing shamanic journeying?

One of the challenges for me as a shamanic practitioner is that often people come to me thinking that I can provide a kind of spiritual aspirin—I'll go retrieve a part of them that has been lost, and life will be miraculously wonderful forever. But each of us is responsible for making those changes in our lives, and that is no different in shamanism than in anything else. Each of us needs to take what information we can gather from nonordinary reality and use it to create life-supportive situations for ourselves instead of life-destructive situations.

Here is an example. Lorraine came to me while she was trying to cope with chronic fatigue syndrome. When I journeyed for her, I saw that I was to bring back a part of her self that she lost when she was three years old and felt emotionally abandoned by her parents. I also saw that I was to remove a spiritual intrusion that showed itself to me as black sludge in her solar plexus. I performed these healing rituals on her behalf.

After I did my part of the healing work, I continued to see Lorraine as a client. I taught her how to journey to the Lower World and the Upper World and to meet with her power animal and teacher in human form. The helping spirits in nonordinary reality began to give Lorraine a program that taught her how to participate in her own healing process.

While her power animal continued to perform healing work for her in nonordinary reality, her teacher advised her on dietary changes and slowly started her on an exercise program she was to include in her daily life. Both her power animal and her teacher taught her how to create better boundaries in her relationships with others so that she would learn not to give her power away. Through my encouragement, she consulted with her helping spirits about what would bring passion and meaning back into her life. She decided to take a class in painting—something she had always wanted to try but was afraid of failing at. She learned that by using her creativity she could begin moving the blocked energy in her body. Lorraine's healing was not a quick fix. Through maintaining the spiritual practice of journeying, she was able to find ways to feed herself physically, emotionally, and spiritually, which led to her recovery.

Obviously, discovering what changes we need to make in our lives takes time. Once we access the information available to us in nonordinary reality, it may take a lot of time and work to integrate it into the lives we live here and now. We may find that we have to make changes in our relationships, jobs, families, even our diets. Most of all, what we have to do is discover and hang onto what has heart and meaning for us, what we feel passionate about. That is a big job. The shaman's role may be to provide the "cure," but it is the clients' job to change their lives afterward, and that's what really matters.

In my opinion, one advantage traditional shamans have over Western shamans is that they work on the same land that they were born and raised on. Shamans in traditional cultures know the spirits of the land they live on. Also, they have their own, rooted communities. One of the most important concepts in shamanism is that of community: one works, not just for individual healing and good, but for the good of everyone. If you come for healing in a shamanic society, the whole community also comes. It is a group process. This concept is particularly hard to remember in this culture, because we often feel so isolated. But this is also why the concept of community can be so healing for us.

For me, nourishing the soul means reminding ourselves that we are welcome in the community of this planet—that we have a right to be here, and it is our birthright to express our souls fully in our lifetimes. We are important members of a community of living beings; we really matter. There is a whole world of help for us out there, in that other place where we can learn to travel. There are spirits there waiting to help us; there are parts of ourselves there, perhaps, who are longing to be returned. When we learn to access that world, we acquire a whole new way of approaching our lives that respects and feeds the soul.

Chapter 11

Ensouling Our Embers: Recovering the Tradition of Ember Days

MERRILL WARE CARRINGTON

Merrill Ware Carrington is a teacher, writer, lay preacher, spiritual guide, and mother. She teaches adults in parish settings, leads retreats, and has been a member of the faculty of the College of Preachers at Washington Cathedral. She is also a freelance writer and a contributor to Common Boundary *magazine.*

Carrington's approach to spiritual matters is down-to-earth. She brings a practical eye to the problems and pitfalls of maintaining a soulful life in contemporary culture and offers sensible prescriptions for taking time out for replenishment and self-care. In her exploration of the tradition of Ember Days, she gives us a plan for ways to incorporate reflection into the cycles of the year. She is currently at work on a book that expands on her idea for reviving the celebration of Ember Days.

A decade ago, professional burnout was a hot new topic. Books, workshops, and popular jargon were full of assessments of the problem, while every street corner held an expert touting relief. Although nowadays the phenomenon remains an ongoing threat, especially among helpers and healers, the topic elicits noisy yawns. Programs aimed at reducing stress and promoting self-care sound just a bit stale. After all, don't we already know everything there is to know about protecting ourselves from the perils of overwork?

Yet despite the familiar ring of warnings about burnout, we seem more vulnerable than ever to its demoralizing impact. As a culture, we have gone a long way in addressing the effects of the problem, but we still understand relatively little about its roots or prevention. Even astute and experienced individuals find that the zeal they once felt about their work can dwindle to ashes. Nurses find they are no longer able to nurture; managers lose all motivation to excel. The flames of eagerness can disappear with frightening rapidity. Meanwhile, in the domestic sphere, those who spend their days caring for others—children, aging parents, or the chronically ill—look with desperation for renewable reserves of energy and patience.

Burnout is not just a matter of physical exhaustion, nor does it resemble the fatigue that follows a period of intense but meaningful labor. It unquestionably shares certain characteristics with anxiety and depression and often wears the masks of addiction, yet in many cases, the symptoms of burnout elude conventional diagnosis. Though it is always good to get away from the workplace and calm the weary synapses, burnout is rarely remedied by two annual weeks of rest and relaxation.

Burnout is, at root, an affliction of the soul—that elusive aspect of our being whose very existence is debated by philosophers and physiologists alike. Though we may never locate soul amid the brain's neural firings, we can know its reality, paradoxically, by its hungers. We can recognize, too, the dangers of allowing the soul to remain too long untended.

However hackneyed the public discourse about burnout, the reality continues to grow in direct proportion to the barren soullessness of our age. For all its efficiency and vast range of consumer choice, America in the 1990s is a soul-starving place. Noise pollution and information overload are more than sensory irritants: they rob the soul of its need for spacious silence. And for all the efficiencies of our technological age, disposable time is a scarcer commodity than ever—time to "dispose of" through long walks or long, companionable conversations, or simply long looking. The pace of life and the speed of change are almost universally bemoaned, but they persist nonetheless as central features of contemporary American culture.

Meanwhile, one wonders if "less developed" societies may have something to teach us in the realm of soul. Whatever their shortcomings—in communications, health care, education, and physical infrastructure—traditional societies remind us of things the soul yearns for and finds in short supply in more "civilized" cultures: beauty, ritual, mystery, and connection to the earth and its creatures. More significantly, these forms of nourishment for the soul not only exist in the segregated realm of formal religion but are woven throughout a community's dailiness: women in India and South Africa painting and repainting their houses in explosions of pattern and color, tribal peoples reverencing a totem animal by refraining from eating its kind, field laborers joining voices and hearts in a generations-old refrain. These practices, often judged from without as quaint or backward, are in fact the soul's daily bread.

Though one must always guard against sentimental idealizations of the developing world, the burnout we find in industrial democracies doesn't turn up with the same frequency elsewhere. The worker who prepares corpses for cremation at the ghats by the Ganges may experience fatigue at day's end, and certainly copes with all manner of deprivation, but it is hard to imagine him suffering burnout as we know it. His work holds him in community and connects him to life's universal rhythms. If a mother's work is never done in Houston or Topeka, how much more so in Tegucigalpa or Kinshasa, where there are more children and more chores—done without labor-saving devices (not to mention 7-Elevens). But however weary, hungry, and economically oppressed that mother may be, her soul seems less imperiled somehow than that of a Chicago management consultant with his or her "billable hours." Burnout in America seems to be an inevitable feature of our higher standard of living.

When we are faced with the threat of burnout—in individuals, families, or institutions—we experience acute helplessness. The ugliness of our cities, the disembodied conversation of the information highway, and the tell-all confessionalism of the talk-show era strike us as vast, monolithic, and suffocating. We are challenged to address the soul's hungers on a very small scale indeed: in the arena of everydayness, in the small decisions we make about where and how we will spend our time. We cannot change the culture, but we can at least take ourselves to what the poet William Wordsworth called "spots of time," whose "renovating virtue" offers nourishment and repair for the soul. Given an authentic willingness, such moments are actually not that hard to find; they are "scattered everywhere, taking their date/From our first childhood." However hostile the culture to our soul's health, we have memory, desire, sensation, and imagination to lead us to the rich veins of soul fuel.

Not long ago, during a three-and-a-half-year sojourn in Britain, I happened upon one small-scale but potent form of burnout prevention: the neglected but centuries-old Christian tradition of Ember Days. An invitation to cyclical replenishment, the Ember Days are a cluster of three days, occurring four times a year at the turn of the seasons. The dates of the Ember Days were once held in the memory of religious orders by means of a rhyme—"post-Lent, post-Pent, post-Lucem, post-Crucem"—which refers to the Wednesday, Friday, and Saturday following the first Sunday in Lent, the feast of the Pentecost, Holy Cross Day (September 15), and Saint Lucy's Day (December 13). Like a bell calling us to attentiveness, this ancient and nearly extinct custom of setting aside a few days, four times a year, for reflection and contemplative awareness can nudge us away from daily demands toward a focus on simple being. That focus, in turn, can reconfigure the rest of our lives.

Whatever our life's work, our effectiveness and our levels of satisfaction are very much tied to where that work is anchored. Whether we are involved in healing others, developing sales projections, or designing cities, if our psychic energy is ego-based we will inevitably run out of steam. But if our work has some direct connection to our essential being-in-God—not just the readily apparent, role-related dimensions of our personalities but our very core—or if we at least experience that connection regularly during the 120 or so hours each week we're *not* at work, our reserves of energy will prove to be both limitless and self-renewing.

The challenge of keeping one's work closely allied to one's core identity is especially crucial for those involved in the helping professions; individuals drawn to those fields are paradoxically often the most prone to burnout, because their draining labors are likely to draw not only on their doing—their education, training, and skills—but on their being as well. More than that, those they serve frequently look to their healers to provide access to Being itself, the ultimate source of healing, energy, and transformation.

It is not just healers, though, who need an open line to the transpersonal core of their identities. In all of us, the soul yearns for the fruits of this connection: an abiding awareness of one's potential, value, and uniqueness; a spacious inner freedom; a calm but clear sense of one's own authority; an ability to be compassionately, unambiguously present to life in all its multiplicity; and a capacity for apprehending otherness, whether in another creature or in an animating, inner other.

Possessing conscious access to the mystery of Being is like having, in a pocket of the psyche, a trustworthy compass for guidance and reassurance. A healthy, resilient ego rests on and is made possible by our awareness of this fundamental matrix. What we need in order to slow the onset of burnout—or to relieve it when it strikes—are simple but compelling reminders prompting us to tend the embers of Being within. In the monastic tradition, such tending is referred to as recollection, a process that has less to do with remembering the specifics of one's past than with recollecting oneself around a nucleus that knows—and some say even partakes of—divinity.

It was not just the Ember Days that came into my field of vision in Britain, but also the evocative image of burning embers. Ever since real fires were outlawed to minimize smog, Londoners have "burned" simulated ceramic coals in their fireplaces. These coal fires burn on for hours, but, like Moses' burning bush, the coals are never consumed.

While recovering from my own case of Stateside burnout, I sat before their radiance. The glowing lumps in my fireplace provided an example of a form of energy that is moderated and usable, plenty hot but not raging out of control. (For some of us, burning up can be as much of a threat as burning out.)

Interestingly, the Ember Days do not seem to share the same etymological root as that coal midway between flame and ash. Experts disagree about the name, citing sources in the Latin *quattuor tempora* ("four times") and the German *Quatember,* as well as the Old English *ymbrene* (the circuit, or "running around" of time). But one thing is clear: throughout their history, the Ember Days have been associated with spiritual renewal. Unfortunately, ecclesiastical trivialization and cultural entropy have done their worst. We are left with an empty form, stripped of its rich associations and severed from its origins.

The Ember Days now exist mainly on the pages of liturgical calendars, prayer books, and, interestingly, certain farmers' almanacs. Some current calendars deem them important enough to include, but only in parentheses. Rooted in Jewish agricultural festivals and also in pagan practice, the Ember Days were abandoned, along with much of the texture of the church year, during the Protestant Reformation. Roman Catholicism retained traditional Embertide observance until Vatican reforms of the 1960s opted for deemphasis in the name of simplification. The impulse toward streamlining was no doubt a worthy one—the few Catholics who now remember the Ember Days do so with a burdened air. But, as with much else in liturgical reform, it was a baby-with-the-bathwater loss.

Though the origins of the tradition are obscure, references appear in Church documents as early as the third century. Since that time, the Ember Days have occasioned various emphases: prayer, fasting, and almsgiving for the soul's benefit; gratitude for Creation's abundance; and a specific attention to the sacrament of ordination, embracing both those already ordained and those considering such a path.

Rites of ordination are still often performed at the Embertide following Pentecost. In some branches of the Church, postulants en route to holy orders are encouraged or even required to write Embertide letters to their bishops detailing their unfolding ministry and the state of their spiritual health. In the Church of England, the current prayer book expands the focus of the tradition to include all Christians, lay or ordained, who are exercising or pondering intentional ministries of service. Over seventeen centuries, Embertide has invited the individual to address vocational questions: What seems to be calling me at this time? What experience of transcendence prompts my sense of call? Where will I find the energy to sustain that call and other callings?

The notion of reviving this tradition speaks to the soul's sense of aridity and depletion in our current milieu. Though those involved with nurturing—by circumstance or vocation—may well have the most to gain from Embertide observance, anyone could benefit from the energy-generating potential of the Ember Days. Any line of work is enlivened by a periodic plugging into the incandescent Source. By setting aside sacred time four times a year for such recharging, we replenish ourselves not only as professionals but as participants in the cyclical mysteries of life.

The quarterly rhythm here seems significant: Embertide occurs less frequently than the weekly Sabbath (and what remains of genuine leisure in American weekends) but more often than an annual vacation or retreat. In the space of three months, sufficient time elapses to make visible the inner and outer shifts in our lives, but too little time for us to have irreparably disconnected from the coals at the core. Like the spokes in a spider's web, the Ember Days create a framework for gathering the soul nourishment we need. Spiraling from radius to radius, we have an orderly, dependable pattern to work with.

As we move through the year's quarters, the Ember Days invite us into discernment. Following the metaphor, we might ask ourselves, Where am I in the cycle of ash into flame into ash? Is it more fuel I need, or more oxygen, or perhaps a better container for my coals? Am I moving toward inertia or toward frenzy? Where are the sparks in my life?

The questions are crucial ones for us all, and examining them can be life-changing. In my experience, however, the most fruitful use of the Ember Days has less to do with reflective analysis than with a kind of naked perception. We tend the embers best by simply paying attention, by calling on our childlike, wide-eyed powers of observation to take note of sparks of possibility we have missed. The Ember Days invite us to look for the mica embedded in our quotidian granite.

But whether our Embertide observance entails rumination or sensation, we may find that the process of recovering the original fire is not always about glistening mica. It is also about obsidian, shale, and mud. Ember energy is extinguished not only by inattention but by deadening habit, unrealized sorrow, eviscerating betrayal, and quiet self-betrayal. Some Ember Days may renew us not through fresh air and sunshine but through arduous descents into painful memories. Spiritual renewal, to be lasting, must involve periodic journeys to the center of our psychic earth, however difficult or terrifying those journeys might be.

Whatever our instinct when Embertide cycles around—descent, ascent, or circumambulation—a variety of practices suggest themselves as aids in honoring both the tradition and our souls' yearnings:

• Gentle conversation with mentors, soul-friends, and spiritual teachers or guides, exploring, for example, the fragments of grace discovered at the supermarket or on the commuter train

• Rites of reconnection with the earth—such as weeding the garden, drawing in a city park, slow-walking a nature trail, or backpacking on a mesa—that are informed by an attitude of mindfulness and enjoyment rather than task-oriented improvement or earnest groping after meaning

• Regular gatherings with colleagues or soul mates, especially those aimed less at problem solving than at simple availability to the sacred presence in our midst

• Letters, mailed or unmailed, to individuals—be they inspiring teachers, old flames, or beloved grandparents—who brought our fading embers to life in the past. These people may be either living or dead; what matters is that they evoke a special vitality in us or assist us in bringing to birth facets of our identity

• Extended time spent with the fruits of creative imagination—the ore mined from Emily Dickinson's solitary depths, the choreography of Martha Graham, the chorales of Bach

- Experiments, timid or bold, in one's own creative path
- Contemplative silence, whether in a formal retreat setting or in one's own living room, awakening to the fact of existence and savoring the balm of stillness

For Christians, Embertide will have a particular significance if observed on the days traditionally appointed; historical resonance will add texture to ember tending. The ever-changing juxtapositions of the liturgical year with the natural seasons gives each Ember Day a fresh nuance. The flavor of Lenten Embertide, for instance, will vary depending on whether Lent begins amid the frozen earth of February or the melt of mid-March.

For those in other religious traditions, or those with no formal religious practice, it may feel appropriate to balance whatever is feasible schedule-wise with a nod to the turning of the seasons. Celtic practice, for example, would suggest honoring such days at the hinges of the solar year. Precise dates aside, it is accomplishment enough for many of us to set aside four days of the year, if not all twelve days, for unapologetic self-replenishment. The goal is to keep those quarterly blocks of time on the engagement calendar open and inviolable.

For some of us, especially those involved in parish ministry or supported by spiritual communities, it may be possible to honor Embertide for three full days a quarter. For others, such as those with small children, hallowing one Ember Day each season, or even an Ember afternoon, may be as much as can be managed. But whatever the form or duration of our observance, the simple fact of doing it can reconnect us with renewed sources of motivation. In hallowing the Ember Days, we signal to the Source that we take seriously its potential to renew us.

The crucial issue is to tailor our observance not only to our schedules but also to who we are. Though *The Book of Common Prayer* provides specific, carefully chosen prayers and scripture readings for the Ember Days, we can devise our own practices and methods. For example, each of us has our own sacred texts and hymns—from Augustine to Auden, from plainchant to jazz—that would suit these days of spiritual renewal. For some of us, Embertide will, by definition, have a solitary timbre; for others, companionship and accountability will be more important. To make the observance of Ember Days truly nourishing to our souls, our rituals need to be idiosyncratic, expressive of our particular temperaments and circumstances. Our forms of hallowing need to be homegrown.

Embertide invites us into unreserved subjectivity: only I can remember which sparks originally ignited my embers of enthusiasm, and only I can determine what rekindles my energy and sustains my soul. However, subjectivity need not mean self-absorption. We blow on the coals not merely for our own well-being but also to regain our capacity to nourish soul in the workplace and in the larger culture. If all goes well, our Ember Day doings—combined with our mode of Being—will banish burnout as well as generate the kind of radiance that can enliven others. Most significantly, ember tending will spare our colleagues, clients, families, and friends the damaging experience of being fed upon by those who haven't managed to keep their own coals glowing.

Chapter 12

Awakening a Sacred Presence

JACK KORNFIELD

Jack Kornfield is one of those fortunate individuals for whom a personal inner journey became his life's work.

Following his graduation from college, Kornfield joined the Peace Corps to study Buddhist meditation in Southeast Asia. As part of the Public Health Service, he was sent to an area in Thailand where many of the oldest forest monasteries were located. There he studied meditation and later lived as a monk for several years.

In 1972, Kornfield returned to the States and became one of the senior teachers of vipassana meditation in the United States. In 1974 he cofounded Insight Meditation Society in Barre, Massachusetts, and ten years later cofounded Insight Meditation West, north of San Francisco. He has earned a Ph.D. in psychology and has coauthored and authored several books, the most recent of which is A Path with Heart.

A psychologist, meditation teacher, author, husband, and father, Kornfield is primarily involved in applying meditation principles to everyday life. In his essay he talks about the value of being present in each moment.

The essence of Buddhist teaching can be found in a story that takes place just after the Buddha's enlightenment.

Buddha was walking down the road and encountered a man who recognized that he was extraordinary. Intrigued, the man stopped him and asked, "What are you? Are you some kind of angel or deva?"

Buddha replied, "No."

"Are you some kind of a god?" the man inquired.

"No."

"Are you a wizard or a magician?"

"No."

Obviously, this person is someone special, the man thought. He asked, "Are you a man?"

Buddha replied, "No."

"Then what are you?"

"I am awake."

In three words, all of the Buddhist teachings are summarized. The word *Buddha*, in fact, means "awakened." It refers to someone who is awake in his or her life.

In all the world's religious traditions, meditation and spiritual practices aim to remind us of our capacity to be truly present in life. The founder of Soto Zen in Japan was a Zen master named Dogen. He taught that enlightenment is never found in some special state or other place. He said, "To be enlightened is to be intimate with all things." To awaken this intimacy means to make the whole of our life sacred. In 1971, Ram Dass published a book with the essence of this message as its title, *Be Here Now.* Yet often we are not "here now." If it is such a good idea, why don't we do it? Because when we're "here," we end up having to deal with the messiness of human life. Spiritual life can never be fulfilled in compartments, or by avoiding life.

A wonderful Burmese monk I knew set up a temple for refugees on the border of Thailand. He had been through a bloody revolution in Rangoon and had marched through the jungle with people who were escaping the carnage wreaked by the Burmese dictators. It was a very difficult situation. Many refugees were dying of malaria. One day I learned that he was considering immolating himself on the steps of the

Burmese embassy in Bangkok. I was upset to hear this and went to ask him why he was going to do it. He said, "No one listens to the pain of the people of Burma. I have to make a statement."

As we talked further, however, it turned out that there was more to the story. He was forty-five years old. A young Thai woman from a nearby village had come to offer her assistance at the refugee temple, and he'd fallen in love with her. Because he'd been a monk since he was a young boy, he couldn't imagine not being one. But he also couldn't imagine living without her. Finally he decided to immolate himself. I looked at him and said, "You mean you've been through a revolution, worked with people dying all around you; you've walked through the jungle, survived malaria; but when it comes to being close to a woman, you decide to burn yourself? It can't be that bad, can it?" I chided. As the conversation went on, he discovered that this was a dimension of life he'd never dealt with, a dimension that he *had* to deal with. The young woman and he talked, and they decided to separate for a time to sort things out. Now they're friends. He stayed a monk, and she married a man from her village.

I had a similar if less dramatic experience. After studying meditation for ten years—during which I had wonderful visions, understanding, and insight—I came back from monastic practice, got a job, started graduate school, and became involved in an intimate relationship, only to discover that I was almost as emotionally immature after my meditation as before it. The relationship triggered all my old patterns of insecurity, grasping, fear of abandonment, and unresolved pain that had been put on hold in the monastery. The worst thing about it was that as I reenacted all these old habits, I now saw them even more clearly. So for the next ten years, I spent time working with the opening and transformation of my emotions. I practiced compassion and loving-kindness meditations, worked in personal therapy, and explored body work. I followed these paths to reclaim feelings that had been shut down since childhood, to learn to open my heart as well as my mind.

To be present in the moment requires us to accept what Zorba the Greek called "the whole catastrophe of life." It takes courage to awaken. If one wants to enter a spiritual path, to explore soul, a certain warrior quality is needed. I'm not speaking of defeating someone, but of having a courageous heart. We need courage to be with what is, to say what is, to tell the truth.

A dear and respected friend and Buddhist teacher, Joanna Macy, works with meditation and empowerment as applied to nuclear problems and issues. She visited the city closest to the Chernobyl reactor disaster that is still inhabited. It's a city of fifty thousand at the edge of very beautiful, old mountains. The people used to walk in the mountains, collect firewood, pick mushrooms, take their families for picnics. Now they stay in their apartments because the earth around them is poisoned. The windows and doors are sealed, as are the windows and doors of their workplaces. They have only pictures of the forests on the walls. When Joanna met with the mayor and some of the townspeople, she asked, "When will you be able to go back into the forest?" The mayor said, "Not in my great-grandchildren's lifetimes, and not in their great-grandchildren's lifetimes."

One of the women in the room became very angry and said, "How dare you come from America where you're so comfortable, rub our noses in this situation, make us talk about it. It's so painful, there's so much loss . . . " Joanna didn't answer; she just sat with that statement. Finally one old man said, "Well, at least we can tell our children that we told the truth about it." And another woman spoke, "We must be able to tell our story and bear witness to our suffering. We must ask others to tell it, to warn them not to let it happen to their forests and their children." This is what is asked of us if we want to awaken in an authentic way: We must bear witness and open to the truth.

The night of his enlightenment, Buddha sat under the bodhi tree. He opened his eyes and ears, opened his senses and his heart to the world as it was. He saw unspeakable beauty and an ocean of tears. He said, "Greater than the four great oceans of the world are the tears of human beings for the sorrows of the world." In the midst of that great beauty and great sorrow, he found a place of rest and compassion.

Paying full attention in the midst of life is a sacred practice, a practice of the soul. Actually, the Buddhist tradition doesn't use the word *soul*. This is because usually the concept of soul refers to some unchanging part of us, separate from our body and mind. In Buddhist practice, we directly experience that everything in life is changing, that what we are is a flowing process, interconnected with all life. There is no separate soul because there is nothing separate. So when we use the word *soul,* it refers to a quality of sacred presence in any moment when we are able to be with life as it is. There's a sign in a casino in Las Vegas that reads, "You must be present to win." It's true in Las Vegas, it's true in therapy, and it's central to one's spiritual life: to be present is to awaken. There are many things that can begin to awaken us. Playing with our children, walking in the mountains, listening to great music, making love, or getting a call from our physician that says, "Your tests show that you need to have a biopsy for cancer." All these events awaken us, but then all too soon we go back to sleep. The good news is that through spiritual practice it's possible to train our capacity for awakening.

For example, at some point, I realized that I used my body, but didn't really inhabit it. I identified with the character of whom James Joyce said, "Mr. Duffy lived a short distance from his body." I realized that I had to come into my body as a spiritual practice. Being aware of walking, eating, and moving is the ground of our awakening. People speak of out-of-the-body experiences, but what we begin with in meditation is something more difficult: an in-the-body experience.

To be attuned and fully present in our bodies can turn the simple activities of our lives into sacred practice. For example, we spend a lot of time buying food at the supermarket or growing it in our gardens; bringing it home and putting it in the cabinets; taking it out, chopping, seasoning, and cooking it; placing it on the table; eating it alone or with family and friends; then cleaning up and putting all the things away. We do this two, three, four times a day. Yet we often do it on automatic pilot. It's as though we're sleepwalking. We do it, but we're not there. The quality of awakening, when brought to our connection to food, first requires that we pay attention, that we notice the entire act of eating.

This is how the eating meditation in a monastery goes. You have your plate or bowl, and you sit in front of it without doing anything for a while. Instead of eating something the minute you're hungry, you honor the sensation of hunger before acting. Is the hunger in your tongue, your belly, or your eyes? Where do you feel it? Maybe you're salivating, maybe not. Then you look at your food. If you look carefully, you'll see certain shapes, colors, and forms. You touch the food, feeling the crinkles, the softness or hardness, the stickiness, the temperature. These are the direct elements of experience. You do a blessing of gratitude for all the labors of others, for the gifts of earth and rain that bring you this food.

Then you eat slowly and mindfully, with full presence. You are aware of lifting your arm, of opening your mouth, of placing the food inside. You don't chew yet but lower your arms and close your mouth. Then, with your eyes closed, you begin to chew and taste. You notice also, when you swallow, how the food goes down your esophagus into your belly. The direct experience is always new and unique.

There are times, especially if you have a family life, when you must do two or three things at once. But it's still possible to be present. A Zen master I know likes to speak of Zen and spiritual practice in the simplest terms. He says that when you walk, just walk; when you eat, just eat; and when you sit, just sit. One morning, however, he was sitting in his Zen center eating his breakfast and reading the morning paper. A couple of students came in. One was quite upset with him and said, "What kind of example is this from a Zen master? You say when you eat, just eat, and when you walk, just walk." He looked up at them and smiled, "When you eat and read, just eat and read."

Whether you're doing only one thing, or involved in a dance with several things, it's the same basic principle: be there fully. Of course, this simple goal can be quite difficult to achieve, because our society is terrified of discomfort. If pain comes, we usually try to run away from it. When you're a little bit uncomfortable, you move. If it's too cold or too hot, you change your clothes or get a different car with better air conditioning. When things get worse, you get a divorce or a face-lift or change your job. But there come moments when you can't avoid pain or discomfort. Everyone experiences pleasure and pain, no matter what modern society says. Then the question is, When pain comes, what do you do? One strategy is to avoid and resist; another is to bow to it, to acknowledge it, to feel the pain, to bring your full attention to it. In meditation, you get to practice being with what is wonderful and what is difficult. So when pain comes, you might ask, Does the pain feel like needles, pinpricks? Is it hot, twisting, throbbing? Let me feel it and make space to allow it to be. As we do this, we learn a new art: to be with what's uncomfortable with the same ease as what's comfortable. A simple way to acknowledge your discomfort is to name it: pain, tingling, throbbing. As you name it softly to yourself, see what it does.

Let's say you are sitting in meditation and you get lonely. Instead of calling a friend, sit there and be lonely. Loneliness is neither good nor bad; it is a point of intense and timeless awareness, a beginning that initiates new sensitivities. You sit and you name "lonely." What does it feel like? Does your heart have a hole in it? Do you feel it in your belly? What is it like in your body to experience loneliness?

Many states come in meditation. You may feel restless; sit and name it: restless. Feel it. You may feel desire, longing, fear. When fear comes for the first time, it's frightening. But if you name it, listen to its story, feel its contraction, breathe gently with it, then after fifty or two hundred times the fear will come, and you will say, "Oh, fear, I know you." It's as if you've made friends with it.

I once saw a poster of Swami Satchitinanda, a Hindu guru with a long, flowing beard. He was wearing a little orange loincloth and was balanced delicately on one foot in the yoga posture called the tree pose. He did this atop a surfboard riding a big wave! Underneath the picture it said, "You can't stop the waves, but you can learn to surf." It was a perfect image for meditation: to rest in the middle of what arises, to bow to it, to name what's there, and in that way to become intimate with all the parts of ourselves.

In the life of the Buddha, there was a very important moment in his discovery of his sacred attention. After leaving the palace and deciding to discover the secret of freedom in the midst of birth and death and to teach that freedom to all beings, he undertook the most intense yogic and ascetic practices that were available in India. He said, "Whatever could be done, I did it. I held my breath, sat up all night under an icy waterfall, slept on beds of nails." He was trying to beat his mind and body into submission through his will. But it didn't work. Finally he was exhausted; he realized that there was no more he could do without actually dying. Then there came to him, unbidden, a memory of his youth: being a boy of eight or nine sitting under a rose-apple tree in his father's garden. He remembered that morning in his father's garden, feeling absolutely peaceful and whole, completely at one with all things in the world. He realized that he'd practiced the wrong way, that the spiritual life is not about fighting the self, but sitting in the midst of all things and letting the self open to them with the heart of compassion and the beginner's mind of a child.

So how do we open our hearts? First we must start with ourselves, because if we can't love ourselves, it's hard to love others in an honest way. The Dalai Lama was amazed, working with a group of Western teachers and psychologists, to hear that one of the biggest problems in Western spiritual life is people's sense of unworthiness and self-hatred. He said, "Self-hatred? Would you translate that?" He could not understand the word. He said, "You mean people hate themselves? They don't like themselves?" He couldn't understand it. Yet for us in the West, I think half of our spiritual life is our need to learn self-acceptance.

A poem by Galway Kinnell, "St. Francis and the Sow," describes what I'm trying to convey:

> The bud
> stands for all things,
> even for those things that don't flower,
> for everything flowers, from within, of self-blessing;
> though sometimes it is necessary
> to reteach a thing its loveliness,
> to put a hand on the brow
> of the flower and retell it in words and in touch
> it is lovely
> until it flowers again from within, of self-blessing . . .

Your sacred attention can lead you to whatever area of your life needs blessing. There are times in spiritual life when you need to replenish your source of self-blessing. There are times when you need to serve others, and then there are times when you need to be alone. For all the riots and political turmoil in India before the great Salt March, Gandhi still took two months in meditation. The politicians were tearing their hair out. "When is he going to decide?" they asked. He just sat and waited quietly until the right moment came. Only then did he act. Just as we breathe in and out, we have to honor the times of contemplation and the times of service. Just as most flowers open in the daylight and close at night, our hearts too have their own rhythms.

In *Zorba the Greek,* Nikos Kazantzakis wrote, "I remember one morning when I discovered a cocoon in the bark of a tree just as the butterfly was making a hole in its case and preparing to come out. I waited a while, but it was too long appearing and I was impatient. I bent over it and breathed on it to warm it. I warmed it as quickly as I could, and the miracle began to happen before my eyes, faster than life. The case opened, the butterfly started slowly crawling out, and I shall never forget my horror when I saw how its wings were folded back and crumpled. The wretched butterfly tried with its whole trembling body to unfold them, in vain. Bending over it, I tried to help it with my breath. It didn't work. It needed to be hatched out patiently, and the unfolding of the wings needed to be a gradual process in the sun. Now it was too late. My breath had forced the butterfly to appear all crumpled before its time. It struggled desperately, and a few seconds later died in the palm of my hand."

There is a season to everything. Our practice of soul has a sense of those seasons, which should never be confused with withdrawal from life. A wise heart does not move away from life. Even in the monastery, there are all kinds of interpersonal relations going on. You don't escape from living by going into a monastery.

Once, when I was having trouble teaching retreats, I went to see a well-known Tibetan lama. After three or four ten-day retreats, I would be exhausted; I didn't want to hear another person tell me about his or her life. I went to this Tibetan lama for help. First he asked whether I kept my vows not to harm others.

I said, "I do my best with that."

He said, "That's your basic safeguard; you are protected because you care for the life of others." Then he said, "Tell me more about how you teach and how the interviews happen."

I gave him the details. He was very respectful. Finally he told me, "I can give you practice that will help you."

I was thrilled. I thought I would be visualizing the Buddha in white light and surrounding myself with it; then, I thought, I can be with people's problems forever and never be bothered by them.

He said, "What I recommend is that you teach shorter retreats and take longer vacations."

This was the advice of this great Tibetan tantric master. It was practical. It meant that I should respect this body and mind that I have been given, that there are times for quiet and times for service.

In Zen, it's said that there are only two things: you sit and you sweep the garden. You make time to connect with yourself, and you go out with that spirit of sacred attention to assist others. Just by being still, you remember who you are. Remembering who you are, you honor others.

Chapter 13

Feeding the Demons

TSULTRIM ALLIONE

Tsultrim Allione is a former Tibetan Buddhist nun who has studied, practiced, and taught Buddhism for over twenty-five years. She has been a member of the faculty of the Naropa Institute, where she was invited to teach by the poet Allen Ginsberg, and is the author of Women of Wisdom, *a collection of biographical studies of six Buddhist women teachers, as well as a work-in-progress,* Places She Lives. *She is the founder and director of Tara Mandala, a nonprofit religious educational organization and retreat center in Pagosa Springs, Colorado.*

As her essay indicates, Allione is particularly interested in exploring the areas of intersection between psychology and Buddhism. In these pages, she offers a practice that can help us deal with the more negative aspects of our psyches—what might be called the shadow side of soul.

From a Buddhist point of view, the struggle with our demons—the parts of ourselves that we don't see but that drain our lives of vitality—is a result of our incorrect view of reality. Unless we are enlightened, we believe that things are solid and separate from one another, or that it is possible to make things permanent. Such beliefs create suffering and a feeling of entrapment; if we cling to them, they create demons.

Tibetan Buddhist teachings on demons were developed by Machig Lapdron, an eleventh-century Tibetan woman teacher. Her family roots were in Tibetan shamanism, not Buddhism, so as she evolved in her spiritual development, she incorporated both pre-Buddhist Bön teachings and Buddhism. Before she began to develop her teaching on demons, she asked her teacher how she could help sentient beings. He replied,

> Confess all your hidden faults!
> Approach that which you find repulsive!
> Whoever you think you cannot help, help them!
> Anything you are attached to, let go of it!
> Go to places that scare you, like cemeteries!
> Sentient beings are limitless as the sky,
> Be aware!
> Find the Buddha inside yourself!

Shortly after that, Machig was in a meditation hall, preparing to receive initiation from her teacher along with a few other women practitioners. In the Tibetan initiation process, the teaching often goes on for several hours, until everyone is completely exhausted, and then comes the point where the wisdom is actually transferred. In this process, wisdom comes from whatever deity has been evoked through the lama and to the recipients. At that point, Machig rose a foot off the floor and performed the twenty-four dances of the *dakini*.

Then she went out through the wall and up to the top of a tree, took off her clothes, and stayed there all night. This tree was a tree that no one else would even dare to look at. In Tibet, a single tree is often thought to be inhabited by a demon, and this tree was not only singular, but by a pond, so it was thought to be ruled by a *naga*, or water spirit.

People were so scared of this water spirit that they wouldn't even look at the tree, yet here was Machig sitting up in the top of it.

The spirit got very angry and also a little bit afraid, so he conjured up a huge army of demons. They came at her full force, and there she was alone and naked in the tree. When they got to her, she offered herself to them. In fact, because she offered herself to them so completely, they had nothing to get hold of, so they offered her their hearts.

This process of surrendering to the demons is the basis of *chod* practice, which is what Machig taught. Chod practice is very complex, and one could spend an entire lifetime on one or two aspects of it. But there are elements of chod practice that can be adapted to working with our own demons, to discovering the sources of our own destructive inner voices. There are two steps: first, bringing your demon into consciousness by visualizing it, by giving it a form; second, feeding or surrendering to it whatever the demon wants.

I first used this process when I was in Tibet, traveling with a group of about eighty people. The journey we were on took thirty-two days, and you can imagine what it is like to be on a bus with that many people for that long. Also, because we didn't have permits from the Chinese police for some of the places we were going, we had to take a very treacherous, mountainous route—we were going to seventeen thousand feet above sea level and then below sea level. A lot of people were getting altitude sickness, which creates incredible pain and headaches; you can even die of it. Also, no one was sleeping very well; in one instance, we were actually chased all night by Chinese police.

That day, I noticed a woman sitting by herself toward the front of the bus, sobbing. I sat next to her and said, "Susan, what's wrong?"

She said, "This is the most difficult thing I've ever done in my life. It's the most difficult thing I've done emotionally, and it's the most difficult thing I've done physically. And I feel like I'm going to die today."

"Why?" I said.

"There's too much pain in Tibet from all the killing and destruction the Chinese have done here," she said. "Then there's the pain in my head from the altitude and my emotional pain from my mother, who was horrible. I can't handle it anymore. I think I really am going to die of all this pain."

I said, "Susan, let's try a little experiment. Let's gather all the pain that you feel in your body and in your head and take it outside yourself and give it a form. Give it any form that you want to give it."

She closed her eyes and said, "Oh, God. I see a monster with a huge mouth."

I said, "What does the monster want from you?"

She began crying even harder. "It wants to devour everything that I have," she said. "It wants my whole life force."

I said, "Okay, let's give it everything that it wants."

She looked at me as if I was crazy and said, "What? I've been trying to avoid giving it what it wants for my whole life."

I said, "Well, has it worked?"

"No."

I said, "Let's see what you can do to completely satisfy this monster. Find a way to picture your life force and hand it over."

She was silent for a while. Then her sobs subsided, and she began to breathe deeply, and she said, "I created a strong woman who took her heart out and fed it to the demon. After that, the demon disappeared, and my mind relaxed into a spaciousness that I never thought was possible for me."

Susan's case was a very dramatic one, because she was in such strong physical and psychological pain, but the principle can be understood through it. Through our own clinging and trying to escape our own demons, we actually make them bigger. When we offer them whatever they want, the dualistic struggle is relaxed, and, ironically, they disappear. There are other, less extreme examples I can offer, as well as a few that involve physical healing. But first, I want to emphasize that there are two elements of this practice that are essential for it to work.

First, you must take your demon outside of yourself and give it form. Demons are usually the result of either a hope or a fear; we become attached to the hope or the fear to such an extent that it seems to take over our lives. It is essential to disentangle the demon, to give it a shape and an identity of its own. Because demons generally work on a subconscious level, it is particularly important to make them conscious by giving them a form.

One of the best ways to illustrate the subconscious level of the operation of demons is through the example of addiction. I used to smoke, and when I stopped, I realized how clever the tobacco demon was. As it began to starve, it knew just when to attack me on an unconscious level. I might be at a party, not thinking at all about smoking, but drinking a glass of wine, chatting with someone who happened to be smoking, and all of a sudden I would find myself with a cigarette in my hand. I didn't buy the cigarette; it just seemed to appear in my hand. When heroin addicts say, "I have a monkey on my back," this is what they mean.

The demon gets in by waiting until you are slightly distracted, and then planting little suggestions: "Oh, just one. Don't be so uptight," or "Everybody else is doing it. Why shouldn't you?" Then the little suggestions get stronger and stronger, until finally they win: you grab a cigarette and light it. If, in a moment like that, you can actually lift the demon out and see how it looks, talks, and acts, you bring it to consciousness. It won't be able to slip in the side door anymore; you eliminate its power to surprise you.

The second crucial point is to feed it to complete satisfaction. If the demon is completely satiated, the struggle is over. This process varies from person to person and situation to situation. For Susan, the change was so extreme that just one encounter altered the rest of her life. Some of us may have to return to the same demon a few times to feed it to satisfaction. But either way, it is essential to this form of chod practice that you ask the demon what it wants—don't be sure you already know, ask it—and then visualize whatever the demon wants and feed the demon until it is full.

I saw this practice work in my own life. I had a tremendous fear of abandonment, and the demon of that fear manifested itself very painfully. If, for example, my husband was not home when I thought he would be, I'd think, "Where is he?" Then the abandonment demon, feeding on my unconscious fear, would say, "He is probably with someone else." Then, seeing that I was listening, the demon would continue, saying, "Well, not only is he with someone else, he's probably actually in bed with someone else." I'd think, "Well, yeah, probably."

Then all of a sudden many little, unconnected facts would start feeding into that possibility, and a picture would come together in my mind of how I was being betrayed. That picture seemed to make perfect sense, and I would go off on a long, painful journey into it with this demon guiding me. Finally, the demon would say, "If he is going to leave you, you might as well get it over with and leave him first." When my husband came home, I would say, "I don't think we should be together anymore. This isn't working." Then he would get angry that I didn't trust him and was so worried about what he was doing.

In these situations, the abandonment demon would often say to me, "Don't worry. When he's gone, I'll still be here with you." This is common. There's almost a kind of coziness with the demon—the smelly nest syndrome—in which you feel really comfortable with your pain, with the fulfillment of the demon's worst predictions. When I actually manifested the reality of my husband leaving, the demon said, "You see, I'm still with you; I was right, wasn't I? I'm the only one you can really trust."

The smelly nest is made up of our neurotic patterns, which are horrible but familiar—obsession, addictions, and fears. We get attached to these "problems" to the extent that we return to them even when alternatives are available, the way abused women go back to their abusive lovers or addicts go back to their addictions. We all have our smelly nests; each one is different, but they give us a feeling of familiar pain.

When I became involved in a new relationship, I decided that unless I wanted this one to be equally painful, I had better work with my demon of abandonment. When I took it outside myself and gave it a form, it turned out to be a little girl with fangs who was very lonely and very scared. When she appeared, I fed her love. At first, I noticed that her fangs got smaller and smaller, until they were more like normal teeth; she seemed to be less and less scared, too. Then she disappeared after being fed. One day I noticed that she wasn't coming around anymore; those little suggestions about who my husband might be with or what he might be doing weren't coming into my mind. I love the man I'm with now very much, and I don't obsess about the possibility of his leaving me all the time. It is a big relief and a kind of liberation to be free of that demon. It feels miraculous, in fact, that after all those years of struggling with my abandonment demon I don't have those fears anymore.

In a sense, feeding one's demons is the opposite of the hero's journey. In traditional heroic stories, we hear about overcoming obstacles—killing the dragon, rooting out the enemy—by destroying them. This chod practice approach could be seen, in some ways, as an alternative path. Not only are you not destroying your enemy, you're inviting it in for dinner. You're nurturing it to the point that it disappears. This is not an easy path. For most of us, our natural tendencies run much more in the traditional heroic direction. When confronted with our demons, we fight, which is a natural reaction. Many natural reactions are the ego's attempt to affirm its existence through dualistic vision.

The problem is that the demons feed on our struggle against them. From the Buddhist point of view, the only reason we fight against them in the first place is that we believe that we must strive for our hopes and avoid that which we fear. We live by spending most of our time alternating between conditions of hope and of fear. Unfortunately, it's not as if one is a relief from the other. In the same way that our fears drain us, our hopes also drain us; there's an incredible struggle that takes place when we hope for something, a tension that drains our life force. This is the first noble truth of the Buddha: all existence is conditioned suffering.

Simply trying to avoid demons won't work, either. Our demons are like little kids. Everyone has seen what little kids do when you ignore them—they become louder and louder, they become really obnoxious. If we don't pay attention to our demons, they don't disappear. They get bigger and more destructive; they start taking over more and more of our lives. Working with demons in the way I have described provides a way to see them, feed them, and allow them to disappear.

This method can be used for physical healing as well. When there was a cholera epidemic in Tibet, the *chodpas*, those who practice the chod teaching that works with this principle, were called in to handle the dead bodies because they never got sick. I myself saw an amazing example of a way to use this practice for physical healing in a student of mine who came to me five years ago. He had been diagnosed as HIV positive, and he was starting to get sick.

Fred had done a little bit of Buddhist practice. When I met him, he had already begun the downward spiral: his T cells were falling, and he was getting sicker and sicker. He was afraid of the sickness and afraid he was going to die. When I suggested the chod practice to work with his disease, he said that he absolutely didn't want to work with AIDS as his demon. He wanted to avoid looking at this thing that he was completely obsessed with. But because it was so clearly the center of all his fears, I persuaded him to try it.

When he took his illness outside of his body, he saw a huge blob, green on the outside and yellow on the inside, that filled his whole field of vision. When he asked the demon what it wanted, he discovered that it wanted his fear. So Fred fed the demon his fear of the implications of being HIV positive. He fed it the fear that every time he got a rash or a cold, it was the beginning of the end. He fed it his fears about what he ate, what he drank, whether he was resting properly—everything.

Over the course of this process, the demon began to change size. Every time he'd call it up, it was a little smaller. Finally, it became very tiny. Simultaneously, he was involved in an AZT test—the kind of test in which one group is taking a drug and one isn't and the participants don't know which group they are in. His T cells were monitored regularly, and the doctors couldn't understand why Fred's T cells were going up, because he was in the group that was being given a placebo. After a while, his cells had gone up so significantly that the doctors running the test said that whatever he was doing, he should keep doing it. Now, every time Fred has been tested in the last year, his T cells have gone up, and he hasn't been sick at all.

One of the most significant aspects of Fred's story is how resistant he was to name his demon. He did not want to work with the demon of AIDS, even though it was completely obsessing him. But remember what the teacher said to Machig: "Approach that which you find repulsive." That means face the demons that you don't want to look at. There are certain demons that are almost socially acceptable—we can discuss them with our friends. Then there are demons so unpleasant and messy that we don't want to admit, even to ourselves, that they exist. Yet the teaching requires us to "go to places that scare you."

According to Machig, repulsive tendencies may continue to arise, but through love and compassion, we can bring them to liberation. If we were to look at this in Jungian terms, we might say that this process is about the shadow, about acknowledging the shadow side of the self. Most traditional cultures, in fact, have ways to do this. Though they would not call them by the names contemporary psychotherapy gives them, traditional cultures recognize the existence of darker forces that have to be fed and acknowledged. There are customs, for example, of putting out plates of food for the demons, or making visual representations of them that can then be dealt with. In Tibetan Buddhism, at the beginning of a ceremony, small *formas*—forms made of barley flour, butter, and water—are offered outside the shrine room to feed the disturbing spirits. Outside every home in Bali, plates of banana leaves hold rice and fruit offerings for the spirits so they will be fed and leave the family in peace.

Many of our hopes and fears—the material from which the demons are made—stem from our fight against the nature of reality: that things are empty of individual existence. In truth, everything is interdependent, and there is no solid self; there is nothing separate and nothing permanent. It is not enough, however, to simply say, intellectually, "Well, now I know the nature of reality. Now I see dualism is an illusion. I am enlightened." That knowledge has to manifest itself on an experiential level so that you are living it, all the time, every day. That is enlightenment. We all have innate wisdom. On some level, we already know the nature of reality, but somehow we've forgotten. We've made, in fact, a habit of forgetting. By recognizing the Buddha inside yourself—by realizing that you actually have all the knowledge you need inside yourself—you can begin the turning-around process.

By "confessing all your hidden faults," meaning making the demons conscious, you do "approach that which you find repulsive." This creates a compassionate attitude toward oneself and others. In order to do this, you must, as Machig was told, let go of attachment,

face your fears, and through this "find the Buddha inside yourself."
This process requires effort, both at changing the familiar patterns of
clinging to our smelly nests and at nurturing the parts of ourselves that
we find most objectionable and frightening and that we try to avoid.
However, the result can be, at the least, relief from endless internal
struggles, and at the most, an understanding of Buddha nature and liberation.

Chapter 14

Food: Connecting Spirit to Body

ANNEMARIE COLBIN

Annemarie Colbin is the founder and director of the Natural Gourmet Cookery School in New York City, the oldest cooking school in the country devoted to natural foods, as well as the associated Natural Gourmet Institute for Food and Health. The latter is an educational organization aimed at a general audience and offers courses on vegetarian cooking as well as the uses of food in physical and emotional healing. Colbin is also the author of two cookbooks, The Book of Whole Meals *(1979, 1983) and* The Natural Gourmet *(1989), as well as* Food and Healing *(1986), which examines the relationship between our diets and our health. She gives presentations and workshops at the New York Open Center and the Omega Institute and lectures internationally on the subject of health and food.*

Colbin's interest in food arises out of personal experience. Born in Holland, she emigrated with her parents and brother to Argentina after World War II. There, her mother put the entire family on a vegetarian diet that vastly improved their health. Since then, Colbin has devoted her life to learning about and teaching how vegetarian cooking can contribute to a healthy body and mind.

Nothing is more a part of everyday life than eating. Most of the time, we disdain the process—we eat on the run, skip a meal, scarf down a plate of something, restrict "bad" foods, punish ourselves for not eating "right." We don't notice that the conversion of leaves, grains, roots, and meats into the substance of a human is nothing short of miraculous.

To nourish our souls properly, we must pay attention to the nourishing of our bodies. Body and mind are not two: they connect, interweave, and speak with each other. Psychosomatic illness, which occurs when the troubles of the soul affect our physical structure, is a scientific fact; so is what I like to call somatopsychic illness, when the troubles of the body impinge on the functioning and expression of the mind.

Food is the substance that connects our body and mind. Without food, the abilities and expressions of both soon cease. When we pay attention to our diets—when we choose foods that nourish and support us—the entire bodymind is content.

I am always amazed to see how well people communicate, make decisions, implement plans, and in general go about their everyday lives, given that it all depends on a fleeting neurotransmitter, a capillary that remains open, a couple of neurons that speak to each other. Our hold on the mind can wobble with a simple fever; it trembles with lack of food, with the absence of sufficient nutrients, proteins, and carbohydrates; it shakes with stimulants and drugs, with an overdose of sugar, an excess of caffeine, a chocolate pig-out. Even the well-intentioned drugs of our medical system disturb the finely calibrated pathways of neurons and neurotransmitters. It seems only logical to assume that everything we allow into our bloodstream—food, drink, medicines, drugs—influences, for better or worse, how our minds work.

For a long time, the relationship between body and mind was only intuited—accepted as obvious only by holistic thinkers. In the 1970s and 80s, however, Western medicine discovered neurotransmitters—chemical substances, made by the brain and other organs, that transmit nerve impulses across a synapse. Mind-body studies took off like a rocket.

The Western Model

In Western nutritional science, it is agreed that food is made up of nutrients, which include protein, carbohydrates, fats, vitamins, and minerals. In this essay, I will focus primarily on protein and carbohydrates. These two macro-nutrients are instrumental to the manufacture and transport of neurotransmitters. When neurotransmitters were first discovered, it became evident that the brain communicates with other organs and tissues by manufacturing them; later on, it became clear that, in fact, all the organs of the body can manufacture them as well, and that these organs all talk to one another through electrical impulses and neurotransmitters. As Deepak Chopra says in *Quantum Healing,* "Neurotransmitters are the runners that race to and from the brain, telling every organ inside us of our emotions, desires, memories, intuitions, and dreams."

Regardless of their monumental role in our humanity, these "runners" are simply chains of proteins, manufactured from some of the basic amino acids found in the foods we eat. Three of the many amino acids in protein contribute to making these neurotransmitters: tyrosine, phenylalanine, and tryptophan. The first two are involved in the building of the "alertness chemicals"—dopamine and norepinephrine—which cause us to be mentally energetic and alert. Tryptophan is the precursor to the "calming chemical," serotonin, which makes us more relaxed.

All the amino acids are present in protein foods. Because there are many different kinds of amino acids, they compete with one another for access to the brain, thus preventing the tyranny of any single one, with its inevitable imbalances. Among the three amino acids that affect neurotransmitters, tryptophan seems to be the laggard and is usually last to be absorbed by the brain—unless it is consumed with a carbohydrate food such as a sweet or a starch.

When we consume a small amount of protein food by itself, without accompanying carbohydrates—for example, a hard-boiled egg, a piece of chicken, or a plain falafel—the brain will make more energizing

brain chemicals. However, a large amount of protein food does not increase that energizing effect, but instead creates the opposite: sleepiness
and lethargy. When we eat a carbohydrate food with some protein—a
grain-and-bean combination or a chicken sandwich—the carbohydrate
stimulates the production of insulin, which encourages the cells of the
body to absorb most amino acids from the bloodstream. As tryptophan
is the laggard, when the competition disappears, this amino acid has
better access to the brain and can make enough serotonin to create a
calm, relaxed mood.

If the carbohydrate is complex and comes with its natural comple-
ment of fiber—as in whole grains—it can set up a steady supply of energy: the fiber slows down the nutrient absorption into the bloodstream,
so insulin is released more gradually and the production of serotonin is
more measured. But if we eat a large amount of low-fiber or no-fiber
carbohydrate food—particularly white flour and simple refined
sugar—without any protein around it, the lack of circulating amino
acids may swing the pendulum too far and also cause sleepiness and
lethargy.

Here is how we can use this information to manage various energy
states:

For a comfortable, calm, alert state with steady energy, I have
found that combining protein and carbohydrate seems to be the best.
Grain and beans, bread and hummus, fish and rice, or a turkey sandwich will stimulate the production of all three of the brain chemicals
in a balanced way.

For a strong energy sprint, protein with vegetables and no carbohydrates (no starch or sugar) works well. Beans and vegetables, fish and
salad, Chinese stir fry with chicken or scallops and broccoli (but no
rice), or similar combinations will do the trick of producing dopamine
and norepinephrine.

To calm down and relax, a carbohydrate (starch or simple sugar)
with no protein will help kick in the serotonin and promote feelings of
comfort. Bananas, anything sweetened with maple syrup or other unre-
fined sweeteners, whole grains with vegetables, plain pasta with garlic

and oil, dry breakfast cereal, and crackers will all have a similar calming, relaxing effect.

White table sugar fits into the last category, but I do not recommend it. Too many people find it addictive or experience unpleasant aftereffects. Often it will stimulate so much serotonin that the consumer falls asleep at the wrong time or may have a hard time waking up in the morning.

THE EASTERN MODEL

In addition to the neurotransmitter paradigm, I have found two Chinese models—expansion/contraction and the Five Phases—to be useful in understanding the mind-body connection. These models are complex, so I will state their basic tenets as simply as possible.

The *expansive/contractive* model is based on the Theory of Opposites, or yin-yang. Here are its principal components: In the visible universe, everything is part of the force and energy of nature. That force and energy have two aspects, called "yin" and "yang," which are opposite yet complementary; the movement or swing between the two is what keeps balance. This concept says that every event or phenomenon in nature has an opposite and that the two are inseparable, like the two sides of a coin. Examples would be night and day, up and down, in and out, male and female, hot and cold, expansion and contraction, wet and dry. Even the opposites good and bad are complementary and cannot exist separately. If we favor one side of the pair over the other—if, for example, we want to eliminate the bad and keep the good—trouble always arises, because nature does not permit imbalance.

The most responsive set of opposites, when dealing with the mind-body phenomenon, is the set of expansion and contraction. In the area of health, we can easily work with this set, because it manifests itself throughout the body: the lungs, the heart, and all the blood vessels are continually expanding and contracting.

In addition, certain symptoms, such as headaches and moods, can be classified as either expansive or contractive. Foods may have an expansive or contractive effect on how energy moves in the body and may affect the physiology as well as the emotions. A symptom or mood of one kind can be counterbalanced with a food of the opposite kind. The following is a list of food categories from the most expansive to the most contractive:

Alcohol
Fruit
Land vegetables
Sea vegetables
Root vegetables
Beans
Grains
Fish
Fowl
Meat
Salt

According to this model, moods and attitudes can also be classified as expansive and contractive. Expansive moods and attitudes, when experienced in excess, we might call "spaced out," "out to lunch," or, less idiomatically, unfocused or depressed. Contractive, in excess, is equivalent to rigid, uptight, unyielding, even enraged.

Expansive foods promote expansive mind-sets and counterbalance the contractive ones; contractive foods promote contractive mind-sets, and counterbalance expansive ones. A well-balanced meal, therefore, focuses on the center of the aforementioned list—grains—and brings energy from both sides of the spectrum. For example, such a meal might involve brown rice (center), poached salmon (contractive), salad (expansive), and baked apples (expansive); or miso soup (contractive), barley croquettes (center), stir-fried zucchini and broccoli (expansive), and pitted dates (expansive).

Another concept from Chinese philosophy and medicine is the Five Phase model. This is a system for charting energy flow in both the inner and the outer worlds. It sets up relationships and correspondences among seasons, colors, foods, organ systems, and moods. It also relates peripherally to the expansion/contraction model in that it charts energy that goes up (Wood), reaches maximum expansion (Fire), flattens (Earth), goes down and hardens (Metal), and reaches maximum contraction (Water). (Water is considered the most contracted substance in the world because nothing can squeeze water—it can't be made any smaller or more compact than it is.) This cycle of energy flow repeats itself. I have found this model to be particularly useful for both meal planning and managing mood states.

Fear, anxiety, anger, worry, sadness, grief—these are all emotions and therefore are thought to reside in our minds. All body workers know, however, that there is a correlation between our organs and our moods. The Chinese theory of the Five Phases ascribes specific negative moods to organ systems. In order to balance unwanted moods, you first note the overactive emotion. Then note what types of foods and flavors you are eating in abundance, cut down somewhat on those, and add ones that are the opposite or that are missing entirely.

- Anger, impatience, irritability: related to the liver and gallbladder; known as the Wood phase. Dominant flavor: sour (lemon). Opposite flavor: spicy.
- Anxiety, hysterical laughter: related to the heart and small intestine; known as the Fire phase. Dominant flavor: bitter (chicory). Opposite flavor: salty.
- Worry, overactive imagination: related to the spleen, pancreas, and stomach; known as the Earth phase. Dominant flavor: sweet (yam or sweet potato). Opposite flavor: sour.
- Grief, sadness: related to the lungs and large intestine; known as the Metal phase. Dominant flavor: spicy (ginger, cayenne). Opposite flavor: bitter.
- Fear, lack of vitality: related to the kidneys and bladder; known as the Water phase. Dominant flavor: salty (salt). Opposite flavor: sweet.

There are a few rules to keep in mind when using these guidelines. Although a little of the dominant flavor in a given emotion is strengthening, a lot of it is weakening. In dealing with any of the Five Phases, a little of the opposite flavor will help to counter an excess, but a lot of it will weaken the organ in that original phase and create the chronic negative emotions associated with it. Trouble arises from either excess or deficiency of energy. To get at the source of a given problem, assess the components of your diet in terms of flavors, then add what is missing and/or diminish what is dominant.

For example, a little lemon strengthens the liver, while a lot of lemon weakens the liver and brings up anger. A little of the opposite flavor—spicy—keeps the liver in balance, while a lot of it weakens the liver and brings up anger and impatience. A little sweet flavor strengthens the spleen, stomach, and pancreas; a lot weakens those organs. As this flavor is also opposite the kidney, in excess it may indirectly exacerbate fear.

In my experience, food is an extremely effective tool for working with emotions, one that can be used, for the most part, without having to consult an outside professional. An exception, however, occurs in the case of food allergies. The most common food allergies are to wheat, milk and milk products, eggs, tomatoes, corn, soy, and peanuts. In an allergic person, the consumption of one of these foods can bring about headaches, swellings, and mood swings. If you suspect that you have a food-related allergy or even a food sensitivity, you should arrange for testing to determine the specific nature of your condition and follow a diet appropriate to it.

Barring that, however, most of us can bring our bodies into dietary balance through the avoidance of stimulants on the outer edges—such as sugar, alcohol, and coffee—as well as the regular consumption of nourishing, nutritious foods such as vegetables, whole grains, and sufficient protein of animal or vegetable origin. What follows is a list of emotional extremes and the foodstuffs and other elements that can help you deal with them. These are intended for both children and adults and have no negative side effects unless used to excess.

Anger, crankiness: In Five Phase theory, these conditions are classified as a disturbance in Wood energy. To counteract this disturbance, first note what you have eaten in the last two hours. Usual causes include excess meat, fat, salt, or other dry, contractive foods; the overuse of alcohol also contributes to this condition, as it damages the liver.

Remedies include soft and sweet foods—especially bananas and other sweet fruits—as well as curries, cinnamon, and low-fat foods, and abstention from alcohol.

Hysterical laughter, anxiety: The former is a fairly frequent expansive behavior in children. Sometimes it is no problem; at other times, the wildness of this expansive mood can lead directly to injury. The latter condition manifests itself mostly in adults. In either case, the condition is classified as an excess of Fire energy and is remedied by eating something salty, such as olives, anchovies, or umeboshi plums (pickled, salted plums available in health-food stores and Japanese markets).

Overactive imagination, worry: These are a result of an excess of Earth energy. To interrupt the imagination or to calm down, try either something salty and hearty—beef stew, Chinese stir-fry with soy sauce, or black beans and rice—or something sour, such as a salad with vinaigrette or, if your diet is very low in fat, some extra-virgin olive oil or butter in your meals. In general, this condition can be the result of excess sugar and other sweets.

Sadness, depression: These moods result from a disturbance in Metal energy. To prevent such a disturbance, make sure your diet has enough protein foods, including beans, chicken, fish, and organic meats, as well as oatmeal, brown rice, and other whole grains. Undernutrition may be a contributing factor. If you have a tendency toward depression, obtain sweet flavors from yams, squashes, carrots, and fruit, but eliminate sugar completely. Chocolate, often recommended for temporary relief from depression, may cause it too, as it creates a pendulum swing once the stimulant effect wears off. To bring someone out of a depression quickly, offer hot apple juice, fresh strawberries, umeboshi plums, or olives. Regular daily exercise is an excellent countermeasure to this difficult and damaging mind-set.

Fear and panic: This is an imbalance in the Water phase. Eliminate sugar and milk products. If there is no salt in your diet, add some; if there is a lot, reduce it. Miso soup or salted chicken soup can be useful to counteract this condition. If you are prone to nightmares, make your dinners vegetarian and eliminate all sugar.

Managing our moods by monitoring and adjusting our diets may seem like a small act, but it can be empowering. There is a certain satisfaction in calming down a temper tantrum with a piece of umeboshi plum. In a sense, it doesn't matter how or why it works; the fact that it does work is enough. You may discover your own ways of dealing with emotional ups and downs through food. Moods and emotions may be "real"—based on events and facts—or the result of body imbalances unrelated to the events of our lives, or a combination of both.

By correcting an imbalance with simple foods—some Greek olives for energy, a banana to calm down, a good dish of Indian curry to deal with an upset—we can often defuse the emotion. Then we can deal with the real issue, if there is one, without distortion. Food is a simple tool that we can access every day. By balancing ourselves through appropriate food choices, we can bring our mind states into focus and correct many minor problems. Let us find what works for each of us and then put it to good use—for our benefit, and for that of our friends, relatives, and children—so that we can improve the quality of our lives and those of all who are near us.

Chapter 15

Behind the Scenes in Therapy

NOR HALL

Nor Hall brings an interdisciplinary approach to the study and practice of psychotherapy by combining elements of mythology, poetry, and drama. She maintains a private practice, leads women's groups, and collaborates with artists in various media on projects that explore the intersection of therapy and the creative arts. She is also the author of several books, including The Moon and the Virgin: Reflections on the Archetypal Feminine.

Her essay reflects Hall's devotion to the literary arts. It can be read as a sequence of prose poems, in which the life of the soul is not so much discussed as it is reflected in a series of images drawn from the therapy room.

W inged souls in psychotherapy long *to be seen* by another, not to be pinned to the wall by the eye of a clinical diagnostician. Instead of writing traditional case studies, I want to simply describe moments, to capture the soul of the exchange between us, *in camera*. Because these scenes are expressly about very particular instances in relationship as perceived by the artistic supervisor (in me), they tend to be more about the therapist than the one who sits opposite. Such scenes are at once fiction and painstakingly, essentially real—but it is a reality deeply imagined and only occasionally shared. I cross the border into the realm of transference-countertransference this way for the love of the poet H. D., whose analyst inspired the thought "The soul of each hour can be named."

MIRROR OUTFITS

As the hour approaches, I frequently move ahead of myself to the door to see how he's changed. His appearance always changes dramatically between our sessions. There is admittedly something that disturbs me in the degree of his changing, but for now, fascination has the upper hand.

He is young and slender and sways like a graceful willow when he walks. His hands are shy animals that hold completely still when you are watching, yet dart and dance in some invisible bee-flight pattern when you are not. Even without makeup, he has a stunning face with features perfectly drawn. His ears and eyes and lips all turn delicately upward, giving the impression of a lightly satyric smile. He loves being regarded as beautiful and one day dresses for his fellow bus passengers wearing a flowing cape to match his flowing hair, carrying a book with Lauren Bacall on the cover. Another day his hair is in hennaed dreadlocks. Or it is short and slicked back to display the antique glasses of a scholar. He came with one tattoo the first time we met. Later a second one appeared. And then the first one was filled in with intricate color. Some days he looks like a small boy in suspenders and sturdy shoes. Another day he is twice that size in huge, heavy, black leather boots and chain bracelets. His hair color goes from sandy to red to black—and his accessories likewise range from lovely to terrifying. These kaleidoscopic transformations continue, unbelievably, for months.

Talking to me is difficult for him. Sometimes he floats above the chair, feeling as if he is barely in the room. Other times it must be that he can hardly connect to me, because the world I live in is totally unlike his. Sometimes he brings me music he regards as "his" or a Patti Smith poem that haunts him.

I worry that the gap created by our differences is too great to be spanned—until the morning he arrives as my double.

He looks surprisingly like me—not intentionally, because he has never seen these new cropped pants or this long-tailed shirt. We glance down and up again in unison—down at our fronts and up at each other, registering pleasure in the similarity of our costume. His hair is parted on the side, straight, chin-length, and brown. Our black pants look alike. Our short black cotton socks and low boots with pointed toes are identical. We move closer to each other, extending arms the way girls compare tans, elbow to elbow, to examine the black printed design on our olive shirts.

This confirmation of our sameness links us unexpectedly. We go more easily into the hour, joined a little by laughter and a lot by the love of dress-up.

WANTING TO GIVE PERSONAL ADVICE

When she won a settlement for the partial loss of an arm, her friends encouraged her to start therapy, which she could finally afford. After buying a car and a hot tub, she put the bulk of the money into a trust fund, where she had ongoing problems with the officer. First she needed to draw money out for school, then for leather clothes and going to the bars; now, I suspect, for cocaine.

Today the dream is about a sky-high conflagration. A barn full of boxes is bursting into flame. All of her stores of goods—everything is going up in smoke.

I want her to register the disappearance of the goods. She has these resources that shouldn't be squandered. She needs to be told that the concept of "holding onto the capital" is as sound in the psyche as it is at the bank, that she should not blow it all away at once like this. But these words in my head instantly conjure up the father whom she hates.

Anyway, it is not my role to decide that she shouldn't expend all her resources. Nonetheless, the giveaway syllable ("hmm") of concern slips out into the space between us.

Instantly her eyebrows come together like the wings of a thunderbird, straight before arching sharply down. Her throat constricts to shape an audible growl, an animal sound suggesting that I keep out. The patient is poised for flight now, one foot pointing past my chair to the door, and I am in danger of losing her. Father? Wolf-mother? Trust-officer? Who am I in these flickering seconds? The image in my heart is of putting my paw down hard on her, to hold her in place until all her wounds can be licked.

WHITHER DESIRE?

There is a chorus of women chanting or drumming up accolades with their voices whenever this woman comes into my office. Rider-of-tornadoes, burner-of-bridges, lover-of-lightning, she is one of those people who brings the experiences of others trailing on their own.

Today she stabs her finger onto the photo of herself as a fat little girl. She calls herself "ugly" (not really) and "glowering" (actually, withdrawn). She wants to know where her desire has gone. Who stole it? When did it leave? *Being* desired is nothing to her. She wants to *feel* desire. Men want her, but she instinctively backs away into the frame of a still life.

Her dream repeats itself in response to her demand for an answer: a man who attracts her is physically handicapped, chairbound. Like Aphrodite's choice, he is lame. She is in no danger of this man's moving over to her, up behind her, or onto her. She can come and go. She can come to him, over to him, up against him, under him. He is just there, doing his work. His skillful hands are occupied rather than groping. As her desire requires, he is fixed. His immobility moves her. Passion pulses through her bloodstream.

She grips the arms of her chair, grits her teeth, seething with the recognition of how hemmed in that little girl in the picture is. No man will pin her down and fatten her up. The sparks of her desire flash in all directions, kindling the extinguished candles of other women's stories lying about the room. The effect is a spontaneous combustion that lifts her into radiance. Carried by this wildfire, she moves on up and out of the room.

SMILING TOO SOON

She is telling me that her daughter has had a baby. As soon as labor was announced, they came in from their country place to be present at the birth.

A floodgate opens in my head, releasing a torrent of images that belong to her: dream after dream of babies, human and animal, born hurt, deformed, occasionally older than their years, but always with the attendant question, "Will she take care of this one?" Before I can register the history of ambivalence about the newborn, I am smiling in response to her news of an actual grandchild. This simple smile is a strong indicator of my feeling. It is an immediate personal response—more true to my feeling in general about childbirth than to her specific feelings about this child's birth. Her manner is gently effervescent. The corners of my mouth could be rising to meet her mood. But I am smiling too soon. A smile like this that spreads before the whole picture is painted lends its color to the process. I've not yet heard how she is distilling the event. Is her detectable sparkle a reflection of her daughter's experience, a sign of her own spirits rising, or an anticipation of my response?

A moment of minute adjustment follows in which my expression of pleasure evens out so that I am not beaming as much as receiving. I watch her face—tracking a mood—trying to see if she has taken a detour into happiness for my sake.

SORROW

We sit in the ordinary way, across the room from each other, but I am seeing her face in "close-up." The delicate hue of her skin has been overtaken by a deep rose mask of sorrow. This color is intense, red-to-bursting, like that of infants when they hold their breath, wet-faced against the coming squall. Her weeping imbues the air with moisture so palpable that condensation could form on the ceiling. Soon it will begin to drip, then rain. I am awash in this grief with her.

Birds returning to clear-cut forests are not able to find their nesting trees anymore. She weeps for the bodies littering the old forest floor. Her children will not have fields to play in, in the future, unless she changes something. She weeps for having no time.

She has no time, hardly any money, little help, inadequate husbands. She has a tremendous store of energy—but still there is not enough. She is overwhelmed by the specter of want, fatigued by giving to so many. She gives peerless attention, devotion. Her questions are like gifts to a conversation. I think of her laughter as climbing the steps of a canyon, warming them like the sun. Now her tears rain down like pearls. I am pelted with shimmering images: Pietà, Mary Maîtresse, Erzulie, Mater Dolorosa. Theirs is the weeping that causes weeping, making even the servitor rich in sorrow.

She is so close to me that I can no longer see her in her entirety. She is calling me to come in behind her grief. Any words I try to form sound utterly inane. It seems cruel to only nod and receive. I want to do something. I want to change the conditions of poverty. I want to reduce her fee. I want to help find her another teaching position. I want to install a bathroom in my basement so she can move in with her children.

My frantic "general assistance" thoughts are impotent. They do nothing to assist her and do not affect the sickness in my heart. It feels as if the only proper response would be a prayer. As the scholar said, "The only response to poetry is poetry" (N. O. Brown).

Our work goes on because sometimes we reach that place together. She comes here, not for aid but for beauty—because sometimes there are these pearls that fall, getting stuck in our hair, in the seams of the chair, on the carpet, rolling to the edge of the room. They leave little trails of incandescence, spots of luminosity that light us up.

BURDEN OF BEAUTY

I am taken with the turn of her foot, like a dancer's about to dance. Freud's fascination with the ankle of the young woman in bas-relief passes through my mind. This woman is so fair that she blends into the shaft of sunlight falling across her chair. Her sisters have so teased her about her fine, golden hair—how straight, how helpless it is—that she believes them and tries to hide it under a challis scarf. Even in mud boots her ankles turn gracefully. It's as if there are very delicate, invisible wires connecting her feet to her wrists, keeping a musical cadence going between them as she speaks.

I note that her beauty makes me a man. Seeing her through the camera lens, matter-of-fact about the priceless blue crystal of her eyes, I am Bergman. Light plays so softly at the nape of her neck that I need a shadow falling across this scene for contrast, to make her distinguishable from the light.

Another time I am the mortal and unsuspecting Anchises. As she talks, she draws the light out of the sun into her shining self. Light leaks around the edges of her disguise, dazzling the eye. I am the solitary shepherd coming into his cottage stunned by this apparition that reveals itself to me. This beauty is so bold that it makes the ground give under my feet. Her divinity is fully lit. It could carry her up. She could float to Olympus, were it not for the gravity of a single image that brings her back to earth. This terrible beauty is a drag.

In dreamtime, she drags her bounty behind her like a sack of rocks. Burdened by beauty, she is slowed to an agonizing crawl. I already love her and am unable to help. I sense the truth of those contents and am afraid that my slips into awe have added two more stones to her burden.

THE RETURN OF THE IMAGINATION

She explodes into the room in a kind of ecstasy. Her fantasy was that she would run up the stairs and throw open the door to announce her spectacular dream. Instead, she completes her entry by becoming more compact, pulling her feet up close on the stool. She is as contained as usual, but *un*usually vibrant. There is something happening around her, a glow that extends out beyond her face for several inches. This is in stark contrast to the melancholy that her body ordinarily hosts. The dream *is* spectacular, one of the big ones—about a statue of a goddess falling from the sky . . . split in two . . . into a small pool in her back-yard. But what takes my breath away is the way the dream answers our question: Where does imagination come from?

Hers was stolen from her when she was very small by virtue of being placed in a hypervigilant position at the center of her household. Literally perched on a couch so she could watch both entrances, she guarded the doors for sibling activity and neighborhood intrusion that would disturb her depressed mother. She stopped drawing, reading, playing, even sleeping, when she was six. Childhood imagination was witched away and recast as obsessive anxiety.

In therapy, she gradually reconstructed a painful litany of neglect, the kind of neglect that impoverishes a child's aesthetic: no one ever held her or told her stories, no one sang or played music for her, no one presented food in a pleasing array, no one delighted in helping her dress up, no one gave her a birthday party, no one asked her about what she did at school, no one told her where her mother had gone, no one put pictures on her wall. No one was curious about the pictures in her mind, so they grew tight and small and congealed into a mass of apprehension.

Now, from "out of the blue," that which had been hers from the beginning is returned to her. When she picks up the broken goddess to take her into the house, she finds that there are already indentations in her floor exactly proportioned to cradle the statue.

No exegesis is necessary to greet the dream text that returns her imagination. The moment itself is resplendent. We are in the presence of one of the psyche's dazzling epiphanies, showered by joy.

Chapter 16

Angels of the Wound: Re-visioning the Crucifixion as a Lesson in Soul

SHAUN MCNIFF

At the age of twenty-three, Shaun McNiff, a committed but struggling artist, applied for a job in social work at a Massachusetts state hospital. The personnel director informed him that such jobs only went to social work graduates but added that with McNiff's background in painting he might be qualified for an art-therapy position instead. A few hours and one interview later, he walked out of that hospital as a budding art therapist.

Today Shaun McNiff is recognized as one of the leading innovators in the field of creative-arts therapy. He is a professor of expressive therapy at Lesley College in Cambridge, Massachusetts, and lectures internationally on the subject of the arts and healing. He is also the author of several ground-breaking books in the field, including Art as Medicine *(1992) and* Earth Angels *(1995).*

In treating physical injuries or illnesses, we know that symptoms, however uncomfortable, often function as messengers. They have stories to tell about how we live our lives and how sensitive we are to the body's needs. The pain in my stomach is a messenger that comes to help me look at the way I eat or how I handle stress; a broken ankle and its resultant condition of dependency may force the "in control" person to sit back and accept the assistance of others.

I distinctly remember how my childhood illnesses and accidents changed the pattern of daily life. I was a constantly active little boy, but when suddenly forced to lie down and miss school, I would have a completely different kind of contact with my parents, based not on checking in to ask permission for various adventures but on conversations about my physical state as well as on quiet time together. The wounded condition made it clear to me that people need one another; it taught me how to ask for help, how to receive and appreciate it. My wounds also taught me how to minister to others when they were injured.

According to folk wisdom, the disease contains its own remedy—the toxin is the antitoxin—and wounds generate what we might call the agents or angels of their transformation. It seems to me that the same is true when we suffer a wound to the soul. In my work as a therapist, I see that when the soul is injured and vulnerable, and when the person involved openly accepts this condition, an angel of transformation often appears. This angel might take the form of another person who offers support and guidance; it might manifest as an inner feeling or vision from which we draw sustenance or an artistic expression that suggests another way of imagining our lives.

The key to this approach is that the person who has suffered the soul wound must admit to the injury. This seems paradoxical, and perhaps even counter to instinct: our tendency is to deny our wounds, to resist the emotional loss and suffering that they bring. However, when a wounded person denies the affliction, it does not diminish; it grows. Unable to reach the person in whom it resides, the demon of denied pain turns its energy and need for attention onto others. This is how cycles of soul wounds work their way through families and generations of families, through dysfunctional societies, and finally through nations.

My most vivid experience of denying a soul wound came when my grandmother died when I was a teenager. We were very close, yet I did not cry. Perhaps the loss was too much for me. At that time in our culture, boys were not supposed to show their feelings. In fact, denial in men and boys was considered the basis of our survival. Yet I remember, after my grandmother's death, sitting for hours, staring out of my bedroom window.

Years later, immersed in a love relationship, I often burst into primal tears when my feelings were touched. Although my expression resembled madness, I felt that I was finally purging what had been held inside since my grandmother's death. This release was only possible within the sanctuary of a love relationship where I could feel the depths of my loss and the wounding of the soul. In this case, my beloved functioned as the angel of my wound, recognizing the pain and helping me to feel my repressed emotions.

When we admit to our wounds, we elicit such angels, who assist the soul in preparing for transformation. The creative work of angels is paradoxically dependent upon the conflict-inducing demons who prepare the soul for change. Though, as an art therapist, I am accustomed to encouraging others to examine and give expression to images of their wounds, however uncomfortable this process might be, a recent experience reminded me of the importance of such an approach in my own life.

I was asked to give a lecture on this idea of angels of the wound and decided to use images of suffering from art history as a way of making the idea tangible. Going through the slide collections of various Boston museums, I was stunned to see how frequently the Crucifixion motif appeared and how often the figure of the dying Christ was surrounded by angels who cared for his wounds.

When I began my search, the Crucifixion never occurred to me, nor did I expect to see angels ministering to the wounded Christ. I imagined people on sickbeds, perhaps injured animals or soldiers. I thought that if I showed such pictures of wounded, vulnerable figures, my audience would respond with an angelic sensibility—as in group therapy, when a wounded person expresses pain or fear and others empathize with the condition and offer support. I had also observed, in art therapy, that someone who is suffering might begin by expressing the hurt in a picture, but then in subsequent pictures treat and transform the condition. In this way, the pictures themselves could function as angels who minister to the wound.

I saw both of these patterns displayed in the Crucifixion pictures I uncovered. I found pictures that formed a sequence, with the dark, isolated, and agonizing images of the suffering Christ followed by images of Him surrounded by angels at the moment before death or just after He was taken down from the cross. In addition to the winged figures, who are often portrayed holding goblets or cups that collect the blood running from Christ's wounds, the Crucifixion motif also frequently involves another kind of angel: sympathetic human figures surrounding the cross or the figure of Christ after He is taken down.

Collecting these Crucifixion images triggered a complex of emotions in me that I did not readily understand. Although the images I uncovered were perfect illustrations of the points I wanted to make about soul wounds and their angels, I found myself reluctant to show them in my lecture. Initially, I thought this hesitance stemmed from a fear that Crucifixion images would be offensive to many in the audience—they might think that I was proselytizing or that religious images should be kept out of public discourse on psychological topics. But I realized, too, that I have no trouble showing images from religions other than the one in which I was raised. It was this image, drawn from my own Catholic upbringing, that was causing me trouble.

I began to think back over my own first encounters with the crucifix, looking for the source of the problem. I was raised in a Catholic household with a crucifix over every bed. As a child, I simply accepted this as the way things were in our home. As an adolescent, however, I decided that I didn't want a crucified Christ watching me at night, so I took it down.

My mother respected my personal things and in general tended to stay away from my room, but the crucifix was another story. It seemed only a matter of hours before it was back on my bedroom wall. I took it down again, and she put it back up. I tried hiding it in my closet, but somehow she managed to find and restore it to its former position.

My mother and I never spoke about this. If I were more inclined toward the supernatural, I might say that the cross kept returning itself to the wall. Perhaps it did communicate to my mother in ways that were beyond my comprehension, for no matter how well I hid it, the crucifix always reappeared.

Finally, I made an unspoken truce with my mother and stopped trying to restructure the sacred things in our house. The crucifix stayed out of my closet, but I took it down from the wall at night and put it back up again in the morning. When I moved out of my parents' house, I made a decision to keep crucifixes out of my own homes. Today, it is apparent to me how actively involved I was with the image. Rather than living passively and unconsciously with the crucifix, I had a complicated set of negotiations with it, an indication of how much it affected my soul.

I repeatedly tell my students that what disturbs you most has the most to offer: that's where the spirit is most vital. Yet I offered this idea to them over and over without consciously making connections to my own childhood religious experiences or to my own struggles with what were to me the most disturbing aspects of Christianity. As I looked through the history of images of the crucifix and recalled my own responses to it, I was reminded of what Samuel Beckett once said: "I see that the darkness I have been fighting is the purpose of my life."

I remembered, too, that I had broken my earlier vow and currently had, in my home, a crucifix I had bought in Mexico. Examining the object told me something about the nature of what I had been fighting in the earlier image. In the Mexican crucifix, both the cross itself and the Christ figure are made of straw; I like the lightness and the texture. I also like the way Christ and his cross are one: there is not such a horrible dichotomy between the person and the wood and nails. The Mexican cross lightens up the ponderous image of my childhood. There was too much emphasis on suffering in those images of Christ fixed to the cross that I remembered from adolescence.

I also find the Mexican cross preferable to my childhood images of the Crucifixion because it has specific, handmade qualities strong enough to distinguish it from the impersonal, mass-produced symbol I grew up with. I love it because it is "particular." I see now that my earlier rebellion probably had to do, in part, with the emergence of my artist *imago* (an idealized concept of the self or another that is formed in childhood and carried into adult life). My dislike for the machine-made crucifix over my bed was aesthetic, and this specific dislike of the image corresponded to my feelings about impersonal religious practices. It never occurred to me that my conflict with my mother over the cross embodied the shaping of my personal religious and artistic vision. My difficulties with institutional religion, then as now, are aesthetic.

The conflict was also related, I'm sure, to how I associated Christ with the repression of sensual life. As an adolescent, I was beginning to enter into an adult sexuality inspired by a mystical imagination of the world. It seemed perverted to have Christ hanging over my bed. It suffocated my reverie. Now I realize how the essence of the Crucifixion, and of Christ's teachings in general, has been obscured by institutional interpretations. I had to go to the cross as an adult and find my own interpretation; only then could I welcome the image of the Crucifixion into my home.

As an adult, I am also able to find meaning in other interpretations of this image of soul wounding. In the novel *Mr. Noon,* D. H. Lawrence embraces the image of crucifixion and reframes its meaning. The title character, Gilbert Noon, is traveling on foot through the Austrian countryside when he comes upon wooden crucifixes carved by villagers and displayed along the side of the road. In the roughly made icons, Gilbert feels the presence of pre-Christian "tree-dark gods." Lawrence writes of his character's encounter with the crucifix, "Gilbert's heart stood still. He knew it was not Christ. It was an older, more fearful god, tree-terrible . . . dark mysticism, a worship of cruelty and pain and torture and death: a dark death worship."

The image of Christ on the cross has become so conventional that we are no longer moved by the details of the figure, by the soul qualities specific to the particular image. But Lawrence was able to feel the survival of the pagan past in the Christian crucifix. When Gilbert Noon reflects on the varieties of crucified images that he sees, a whole new world of belief and imagination opens up for him.

The painters of the Italian Renaissance imagined the Crucifixion in much more extraordinary and lavish ways than the simple wooden crosses described by Lawrence. Renaissance painters frequently portrayed the body of Christ with ideal, beautiful proportions being comforted by equally splendid bodies, all of them painted according to the highest standards of academic perfection. This idealization of the human form creates a sense of distance between the emotional horror of the event and its remembrance through art.

Without judging these representations as avoiding the "reality" of the Crucifixion, we can see how they express different aspects of the ways in which we might respond to soul wounds. The Renaissance versions idealize suffering, imbue it with beauty and grandeur. Such an approach can open us up to the sacred level of our own suffering, to the gods in our wounds; when we see that God the Son is not spared the agony of earthly pain, our own pain is elevated to the divine realm. On the other hand, the indigenous effigies encountered by Gilbert Noon portray the suffering Christ as a member of the particular, local community. The Christ on those crosses is both Himself and not Himself, both the Son of God and an extension of every villager, before and after Christ.

In the 1970s, I worked with the New York City "folk" artist Ralph Fansanella, who made a series of paintings of his father as a crucified figure. The elder Fansanella, who worked as an iceman, was portrayed nailed to the cross with the ice picks he used every day, his ice tongs clamped to his temples. The son felt compassion for his father's struggles and suffering and used the Crucifixion motif to amplify the pain to a transcendent scale.

Fansanella, D. H. Lawrence, my mother, and I all have our personal stories to tell about the Crucifixion motif. There are others, of course— the pietàs of men dying of AIDS being held in the arms of loved ones, the starving children in countries ravaged by war, grieving families everywhere. The wound expressed is individual and universal, mine and yours. Like all archetypal images, the Crucifixion is lodged in the personal and collective world psyche. With each individual interpretation and revision, we grow simultaneously closer to the power of the image itself and closer to an understanding of how our own souls have taken it in and understood it.

The angels of our soul wounds cannot flourish without individual imagination and freedom of expression. In my art therapy practice, I encourage everyone to see the images they create as angels and to access the specific qualities of their expression. This approach is particularly helpful when the images evoked are archetypal in nature. The more significant a symbol is within a culture, the more it can teach us about the need to individuate. In my case, the image of the Crucifixion comes alive when it is liberated from institutional interpretations and is intimately connected to my life. Reflection on the angels of our soul wounds might, if we are undeterred by such interpretations, lead us directly to the image of the Crucifixion—where the cruelest death is transformed into redemptive love and exaltation.

Yet negative feelings toward an image—such as I had toward my mother's crucifix—also need to be welcomed. Examining the full spectrum of my reaction to crucifix images, both positive and negative, helped me to access a deeper sense of the inversions and transformations that are the basis of the Christian mystery. The goal is not to find an easy, clear explanation—a "cure"—for our reactions to the images that most affect us. The goal is to continue to work with them deeply and imaginatively, in order to uncover what our reactions may be trying to teach us about our souls.

Archetypal psychologist James Hillman says that attempting to cure the symptoms of our wounds "may also cure away soul, get rid of what is just beginning to show, which at first is tortured and crying for help, comfort and love, but which is the soul in neurosis trying to make itself heard." Hillman suggests that "what each symptom needs is time and tender care and attention." Soul wounds cannot be denied, put aside, or easily cured. Rather, it is "the prolonged occupation with suffering," says Hillman, that can provide us with "a humiliating, soul-awakening experience."

The medicine of angels is a reimagining of the way we view our lives, a re-visioning of our chronic conditions, and an emergence of the spirit of renewal. I can see from my personal reflections that I hid and repressed the wound of the Crucifixion—I did not want it ruling my life—but the wound must be given its place within the life of the soul. We all will no doubt have periods when, for whatever reason, we stoically choose to deny our wounds. But we must also trust the healing opportunities that life brings us—such as when my search for images for my lecture led me to an examination of my own complex relationship to the crucifix—and rely on those circumstances in which the time is right to open to our wounds and receive angelic medicine.

Chapter 17

Stories That House Our Souls

DEENA METZGER

Deena Metzger approaches story through many lenses. As a novelist (The Other Hand, in progress; What Dinah Thought, 1989; The Woman Who Slept with Men to Take the War out of Them, 1981), poet (Looking for the Faces of God, 1989; Tree, 1981), playwright, and essayist, she has told innumerable stories using a variety of forms. As a psychotherapist, healer, and teacher, she has collected as well as shared them.

After years of story telling and story listening, Metzger is keenly aware of the significance of myths. "To live the myth, to live the story, is to know the image as the prima materia *of our lives," she states in her most recent book,* Writing for Your Life *(1992), a writers' guide and resource. In her essay, Metzger explores the idea that stories both house and create soul.*

S tories that house our souls. Just to speak these words is to enter into a mystery, for soul and story partake equally of the visible and invisible, the manifest and ineffable worlds. We experience a *frisson* when we say the words *story* or *soul* because we know we are plunging into the liminal space that exists at the edge of the knowable and unknowable, the real and the wondrous.

Some people believe that the soul resides in the body, and, without disagreeing, I also believe that the soul resides in the stories we live and tell. Or, to be more explicit, stories both house the soul and are the process through which we make soul. Stories nestle in the body, and soul comes forth. The reverse is also true: the soul inhabits the body, and stories emerge from the body. In a constant process of creation and recreation, one transforms the other: stories make soul, and soul speaks in story. By becoming aware of our stories and their complexities, we access soul because through story, we make meaning.

In many cultures, wisdom is transmitted through stories. If you ask a roshi, a rebbe, a mystic, a shaman, the wise old woman or man for a teaching, you are likely to get a story—probably an enigmatic one, one you can chew on for a long time because there is so much meaning in it.

The expression "that's only a story" is one in which we disparage a way of knowing. Instead we should say, "Oh, that's *really* a story," meaning that we not only recognize the inherent wisdom of that particular story but also that, in saying it, we form and validate a world in which story is a profound way of knowing.

The Old Testament says, "In the beginning was the Word." This means the world was created through story. It is as if Spirit imagined the entirety of creation and then the words became manifest. In the Jewish tradition, that is what we mean by the Holy Letters of Flame. We mean that, in the area of the sacred, word and manifestation are aspects of each other, are involved in a holy dance of transformation and manifestation.

Because the word is not separate from the thing-in-itself, finding words for something may be more difficult than creating it. For example, when you get an idea, it is through the precise choice of the particular words, and the exact placement of the words in relationship to one another, that meaning occurs. Meaning occurs in perceiving the totality in its particularities. Creation didn't result from Spirit thinking, "Let there be a world." That would be too vague, too abstract. Creation happened when Spirit said, "Let there be a blue jay, a stellar jay, and a pinion jay." This is perhaps one of the esoteric meanings of the naming of the animals in Eden. That story holds the process by which the wondrous distinctions that had issued forth were perceived. But then the pinion jay required a pinion pine and the pinion pine required particular altitude, weather, insects, soil, and microbes, and so those came into creation, too. Thus, in its interrelated particularities, the world came to be.

The task for those of us who are interested in writing and language—or who are interested in exploring our own lives—is to find the theme of our life and the language to hold it, so that there can be a dialogue between ourselves and our lives. We are learning from physics and the new sciences that nothing exists in isolation, that everything is in relationship to everything else. Each particle exists in dynamic relationship to other particles. Our story, similarly, has meaning in its relationship to other stories and because it sits within a larger story.

Stories bring different elements together and place them next to one another in such a way that we understand things in relationship to each other; we see things we couldn't see when we thought the elements were independent of one another. The problem with the way we usually organize our stories is that we tell them chronologically. That is, the relationship we perceive or establish is one of chronology. But chronology is merely a convention of our thinking process, not the ultimate meaning. In physics, for example, time flows forward and backward. Perhaps in *real* (not human) time all dimensions interpenetrate one another and everything is coexistent and coextensive.

In order to tell a story, we often bring things in from different places and place them alongside each other so that they and the story are illuminated by their relationship. We remember something from the past, we refer to a poem, we find an analogy; as we arrange these elements, we see their relationship, and the story is deepened and transformed.

When we tell a story that is based only on a chronological structure—this happened and then that happened—we can get caught in that story. We can become fixed in a linear structure that is as inflexible, unbending, and relentless as the events; it cannot be arranged otherwise, just as we assume that time cannot proceed in another manner. We are unable to see behind or under. We do not have another perspective. It feels inappropriate to add an antic element or to take something out. Unable to be informed by coincidence, simultaneity, contingency, similarity, opposition, contrast, or by the interpenetration of different time periods, we avoid the dynamic possibilities—especially the imaginal, the possible, the mythic. We are trapped by realism.

This is why people often tell the same story again and again and again. The story has become a prison; it confines them. They cannot get out of it, just as they cannot get out of time. Perhaps they tell the story again and again in a desperate search for a door.

Thus we can be either liberated or contained by our story. Either it can offer us enormous possibility or we can feel it is our terrible fate. Between these options, I prefer the former.

Another way to look at story is as dynamic arrangement of images that partake of several worlds. These images reflect physical, emotional, spiritual, and symbolic events. If we didn't have a story that unified these worlds, we might suspect that there were other dimensions but we wouldn't know how to reach them.

In this regard, we can think of story the way scientists think about mathematics: as a way in which other dimensions are known. The reason we can talk about six, eight, ten, or twenty-two dimensions is that mathematicians theorize that they exist. In fact, their calculations show that unless we presume other dimensions, this world does not exist. Their formulas cannot work in only the three dimensions (or four, including time) in which we live. The formulas depend upon the existence of other dimensions.

If we look at mathematics and writing as different cultures, then in my culture—the culture of the writer—I depend upon story to know that other dimensions exist. For example, I could say, "Yesterday I spent some time in the woods," or I could speak about it in story. When I am in story, walking in the woods almost always becomes walking down a *path,* or *stumbling* through briars, or getting *lost* in the woods.

When I am walking in the forest, I am subliminally aware that I am walking where others have walked, that I may also be negotiating a way, a spiritual road that of necessity winds through the dark and the wild. All these meanings and their history are implicit in the story.

Two weeks ago, I was walking in the woods when I heard a sound, a deep, breathy "mh, mh, mh." It was very loud and came from up on the mountain. What might it be? Then I remembered some lines from Judith Minty's book of poems, *The Yellow Dog Journal:*

> . . . Awake, sweat gathers in my palms,
> the moon opens on my ceiling and my heart
> beats as if I had been climbing the ravine.
> The mh, mh, mh from the bear's throat
> still echoes in the cabin. It is only
> draft from the stove as embers cool.
> When I was a child, I never dreamed
> I'd have to hold this bear inside.

That's a bear, I thought, as I continued on the path and prepared myself for a possible meeting. I told myself, "Keep your eyes down; don't look the bear in the eye. Do not come between a she-bear and her cub. Remember not to turn your back on the bear. And bow as if meeting a Buddhist teacher." The mh, mh, mh continued up on the slope as I walked below, and for a while we proceeded on our own separate but parallel paths. Then the sound ceased, and I was alone again.

That is the story of an event that happened in the real world. But in telling the story, I am referring to a poem and also to a spiritual and meditative practice. Given permission to use its entire capacity with regard to the poem, the mind understands a relationship between bear and fire. At the very least, it is that fire runs through all of us—people, bear, tree—as energy, as the life force. Or we could see the bear as a little furnace whose heat keeps it alive when it hibernates. Or there is some relationship of shape between a wood-burning stove and a black bear. In any case, within the mind and the imagination, many connections are possible. And the story is enhanced by each of us individually bringing our own idiosyncratic connective understandings to it.

Additionally, in this instance, when I was walking in the woods, I was also trying to learn something about nature and about myself. I felt that it was important to meet the bear if that was given to me to do. Speaking about meeting the bear in that way takes us to another level: walking through the woods becomes walking a path and confronting whatever I need to confront. The story is now about overcoming fear and meeting the Other. And/or it is about the parallel lives of the human and the wild.

Story is very simple. A story is "something that happened *and . . .* " That is all there is to it. But in the time and timing of the telling of the "something that happened and," and in the silences in between, other things enter in—perhaps surprise or expectation. The listener fills in the spaces, and we have a story.

I once asked a friend for a story, and she said, "I can't think of a story." Of course, it was not that she didn't have a story; she didn't *know* she had a story. So I asked her what she had done the day before.

"Really, nothing happened."

"Good," I said, "I like working with stories where nothing has happened."

She said, "I was driving along a very narrow road that wound its way along the sea, through fields of wildflowers and poppies. I was on my way to visit a friend who is in prison. On the way back I drove again through the same fields of wildflowers and poppies. And the tall grasses were waving on the hill."

I gasped in the presence of that story. Everything was there in her telling of it.

She is driving along a narrow, winding road on a cliff; danger and precariousness are implied. Then she goes through fields of flowers to visit a friend who is in prison. In order to get to her friend, she encounters danger but also beauty. There is a striking contrast between the beauty of the flowers—the brilliance of the orange poppies—and the dreary confinement of her friend, between the delicacy and mutability of the life of the flower and the dull, ponderous routine of prison life. And what is implicit though unspoken is, How can flowers grow when one's friend is in prison? Everyone knows that feeling. Something tragic happens in our lives, we feel devastated, yet the sun still rises. We depend upon the sun rising, but the fact that it rises is incomprehensible. A story can hold all such contradictions at once. And further, listening to a story about a woman whose friend is in prison, we realize that we may not be exempted from human suffering, even imprisonment. The moments and events connect, and we are connected to them as well.

The woman who said, "Nothing happened," links us in many important ways to other worlds, including the personal, emotional, political, and spiritual. That is what story does. And this was just one moment in her life.

If you ask yourself, "What happened yesterday? What did I see? What did I experience?" your answers can be given in stories. Then, if you recognize the story—if you can enter into its presence—you can live your life differently. Every movement you make can have a different quality because you will be walking in several worlds at once. It is like the path I was walking in the woods: I recognized it as a spiritual path, and I tried to learn to walk it.

Still, we must be careful so that our involvement with the mythic, symbolic, and spiritual does not overwhelm the most important path that we are walking—the one with real stones, real twigs, real traffic, and real bears. The symbolic has no meaning whatsoever without the reality of the body. The physicality of our life on this earth is what we must fully inhabit and embody. It is the *materia* from which everything is made.

In the kabalistic Tree of Life, spirit enters the world at the place of Kether, the crown, and it moves down to Malkuth, which is at the root. But it is also moving up, simultaneously, from Malkuth to Kether. There is a gesture in East Indian dance in which one hand, palm horizontal, moves up as one hand, palm vertical, moves down, and then they reverse. That is the movement, up and down, of the Tree of Life. Spirit comes down, and the world rises up at the same time. At the very heart of the tree is a place called Tepheret, the place of beauty. That is where world, form, and spirit come together. That is where story is. Buddhists say, "Form is emptiness, and emptiness is form." That koan holds some important teachings; namely, that there is a place where spirit and form are perfectly matched. That place is creation and story.

The ancients profoundly knew the domain of story. It is the basis of the mystery religions. In the mystery religions, one was called upon to live a myth fully for a certain period of time. One was called upon to live a story of the gods. By experiencing what the gods experienced—by feeling what they felt, by seeing what they saw, and by being open to what they knew—soul was made.

That is the way the Eleusinian mysteries, the great rites of Demeter, were observed. This is not very different from the way the Lenten story of the passion of Christ is celebrated. The story becomes real when one is willing to take on the injunction of living the story, of recognizing that through story everyone is Christ: we all carry the cross; we are all crucified. Living the story, and the way in which we live it, determines who we are.

In 1980 and again in 1990, my colleague and the theater director, Stephen Kent, and I led a group of people in the reenactment of the Eleusinian mysteries in Greece. These were, to the best of our knowledge, the only reenactments at the sacred sites in fifteen hundred years.

We spent over a year in research in order to recover the knowledge of the mysteries that had been lost and suppressed, realizing that many moments had been enacted in secrecy and were not ever to be or couldn't be spoken about. Often, secrets aren't told because they can't be told. If we try to tell what cannot be told, we reduce and trivialize the tale. How can one describe mystery?

When Steve and I did recover what we could about those mysteries, we created a ritual narrative that we could enact. In the process of researching, we came upon an astonishing, uncanny, but not unlikely relationship between the nine days and rituals of the Eleusinian mysteries and the observances of the Jewish High Holy Days, the days from Rosh Hashanah to Yom Kippur. Both of these occur at the same time in the lunar calendar. (The lesser mysteries, which were a preamble to the greater mysteries, occurred at the same time as Passover.) Among other similarities, both celebrations include fasting, purification in the sea, rites of the dead, the sacrifice of chickens, and the avoidance of certain foods. One can say that both rites, each in its own way, prepare one to be written into the equivalent of the book of life.

For the Greeks, participation in the mysteries, even if only once in one's lifetime, ensured that one would have a soul in this world and in the next. In other words, to live the story of the gods was to enter into the process of soul making. Anyone could take part—servants, slaves, children—anyone who had no blood on his or her hands. Someone with blood on his hands could perform the rites of the Kabeiri, another mystery, as a cleansing.

Because we understood the importance of living the story, and because we wanted to create authentic and effective contemporary rites of transformation and soul making, we included the stories of Demeter and Persephone and of Theseus and Ariadne as narrative stratae. We considered the story of Persephone the way of the feminine into the underworld and the story of Theseus as the way of the masculine.

Each day of the mysteries, we walked all the stories in all the dimensions at once. We made sacrifices, we purified ourselves, we experienced loss, we met the Minotaur, we were shattered, we fasted, we descended into the underworld, we asked for vision, and we lived the stories of the gods. Because we grafted the Theseus-Ariadne story onto the Eleusinian mysteries, I will tell only the story of Persephone's descent into the underworld here.

Demeter, the Great Mother, had a daughter, the young and innocent Kore. One day, she was dancing in the fields with the daughters of Ocean when the earth opened and Hades, god of the underworld, emerged on his black horses and took her down into the earth. Demeter (meaning mother, *materia*, earth) was inconsolable at the loss. When no one would tell her where or how her child had disappeared, she declared perpetual winter. The crops died. The gods were without offerings.

One day she was approached by the daughters of Queen Mataneira to become a nursemaid to the young Prince

Demaphoon. During the day, she performed the nurturing duties of the day world, but at night, she burned the child in the sacred fire of immortality. One night, the queen came upon her child being held in the fire and screamed in protest. Outraged, Demeter threw the child across the room and then, pulling herself to her full stature, let down her magnificent hair. "Mortals never see," she declared as she left.

A year passed. The gods demanded that Demeter restore the world, but she refused until she learned the whereabouts of her daughter and was reconciled with her. Finally the gods revealed that the Kore, the girl, was in the underworld.

The underworld is eternity, is the source, is the beginning. Pluto (the Roman equivalent of Hades) means treasure. Thus, the underworld or Hades is the place of seeds and treasure. Here the girl, through the process of descent, became the feminine partner of the god; she became the feminine presence, Persephone, Queen of the underworld.

The exoteric rape of the Kore by Hades means something quite different esoterically. It is a description of the moment when we are pulled down, when we are ravished by the descent into the psyche. Perhaps we would rather be the innocent one, the Kore, blithely dancing in the fields of perpetual springtime, but there comes a moment when we enter story, when we can no longer be innocent, when we must eat the fruit of knowledge, when we must make our soul.

In the underworld, we are stripped of the outer forms; we are made naked; we are united in a terrible and wondrous divine marriage with the god that simultaneously unties the opposites, reconciles the dualities of body and spirit, life and death, good and evil, male and female. All divisions dissolve. Boundaries disappear. Dimensions transform into one another.

Persephone returns to the day world, but only for half a year. Because she has eaten the fruit of the underworld—the pomegranate, fruit of death and fertility—has consumed six of its seeds, she must spend six months of the year every year in the underworld.

This is the cycle. Persephone returns. She is reunited with Demeter. Spring and summer come. But even as she is reunited with her mother, her preference now is for the company of Hekate, the crone. Hekate is the goddess of the occult, hidden knowledge, of the lunar vision on the cusp between this world and the other, between life and death. Now, when Persephone descends—as she must—Hekate follows her. As old knowledge follows the new, as wisdom follows experience, so they too enter into the dance.

In gratitude for her daughter's return, Demeter offers three gifts to the world. The first is the gift of grain, which nourishes both body and soul. When the *mystai*, or those whose eyes are closed, reached the temple at Eleusis, they drank the *kykeon* made from the fermented barley on which the hallucinogenic fungus ergot grows. Afterwards, they would have a vision. It was said that at the moment of vision, a great light appeared from Eleusis that could be seen for miles around signifying the advent of Persephone in her full glory.

The second gift is paradoxical. Demeter demands a temple be built in her honor, thereby assuring the people have a place of worship. Implicit in this "gift" is the understanding that people need a place to house their spiritual lives. As our domiciles house our bodies, we can say that our temples house our souls.

The third gift is the rites of the Eleusinian mysteries themselves. The goddess offered the way, the path, the story to be walked in the process of gaining a soul in this world and the next. As was said earlier, during the mysteries the *mystai* walked, fasted, prayed, danced, made sacrifices, and purified themselves. They crossed the bridge of jests where the ego was broken down through ridicule; they engaged in tournaments; they made offerings; they confronted death; they had visions; they heard the cry of the birth of the divine child. Also during these days of pilgrimage and ritual, the initiates took on the lives of the gods: Demeter's grief, Hades's longing for life and beauty, Persephone's transformation from innocence to knowledge and vision. For a moment they became, like the gods, immortal; they returned home ensouled.

That is what it means to live a myth. And each of us in our own ways can live myths. But first, we must take our myths seriously. When Christmas, Easter, Beltane, or Passover occur, we can enter the stories with similar passion so as to allow the stories to live in us and to live us.

Some years ago, when I was very depressed, I tried to explain the quality of the experience to Corey Fischer of the Traveling Jewish Theater. I spoke of the dryness of my spirit, the lack of water, moisture, and juiciness in my life. Nothing is growing, I said. Everything is barren. "Oh," Corey said, "you must be in the desert."

Suddenly my despair lifted. He had located me in story. I knew some of the dimensions of desert stories. I knew they involved forty days, as with Christ, or forty years, as with the Israelites. I knew the territory and how to proceed in it. I had a map. Though I was in the desert, I suddenly had hope.

I was still oppressed: the desert is hot and oppressive. I was still sometimes afraid that I would become lost, that I would die. But there were other possibilities to be experienced, as well. The desert is often a place of spiritual journey. It is a traditional place for retreat, the abode of hermits and ecstatics, the territory of solitude. In the desert, one confronts illusion, or learns wandering and faith as Hagar did, or wrestles with the angel as Jacob did, or wrestles with the devil as did Christ.

The metaphor of the desert came alive for me because I recognized it as intrinsic to a larger story and to my own story. As a Jewish woman, I come from a desert people. Though I was born on the Atlantic Ocean, the desert is in my consciousness, in my DNA, and is part of my history. When I found a house at the edge of sage, maguey, and manzanita, I recognized the land. When I was given the desert story, I was given a story I could live in, a story I could live out. Depression and paralysis were transformed into journey and soul making. That is what happens when one decides to walk a myth.

The gods teach us by giving us stories to live. If the theme of our life is freedom and danger, we will be given confinement and danger to struggle with. If our theme is loss, we will inevitably endure loss. The gods teach us through experience. When we perceive, understand, and accept the story behind our suffering—when we see that it is one of the terrible and wondrous gifts of the gods—we are transformed. We have a soul. Like the Kore, we gain an identity. Without a soul, we are no one with no name; with a soul, we have a life in this world and in the others.

Every path leads to the same place, and every path is different. It is not the place we seek but the path to it, the path chosen or given, that makes the difference. It is the particularities of the journey that shape the individual story, that bring knowledge in certain and distinct forms. In the abstract, teachings can be incomprehensible; in the particular, they are profound and complex. Our bodies know this because we cannot live a story except through our bodies, through the way we walk the path, through the brambles and leaves we pass. And still, this day, this night, this stone, this exhaustion, this blindness, and this sight are also the path. Each truth partakes of the universal truth.

For this reason, we have many different cultures, many different paths, and many different experiences. Story comes to each of us in its own form, but it also takes on our particular shape and the shape of our people and tradition. We hold the story the way the bank holds the river, and so the story resembles us. And still it is *the* sacred story, *the* way, wherever we are willing to enter it, to walk a path, to make a soul, to see.

The story of Demeter was a path for the Greeks for three thousand years. The Christ story is another path. The Passover—the journey from slavery to freedom, from Egypt to the Promised Land—is yet another.

Each one of us has the possibility of being awakened by our story. Living with it, musing upon it, and walking it offer us an alternative to what might otherwise appear a transient and meaningless life, and insight into the luminous meanings that shine about our soul.

Here, as a companion on this journey that is intrinsic to story, I offer you a poem that I wrote after I once ascended from the underworld:

> Return
>
> When you go
> to the dark place
> you must come back

singing
the note inscribed
on your palm
the song written
on your hand
the way trees
grow about the
shape of wind.

Soul and Community

Chapter 18

Business from the Heart

THOMAS M. CHAPPELL

Tom Chappell is cofounder and president of Tom's of Maine, a com-
pany that makes natural personal care products for the public and pro-
vides a caring and creative work environment for its employees.

His company's culture and his efforts to uphold ethical business
standards have garnered numerous awards. Tom's of Maine has been
named among the top corporations in the United States for working
mothers by Good Housekeeping *magazine and as one of thirty Great*
Companies for Dads by Child *magazine. In 1992, the company re-*
ceived the Corporate Conscience Award for Charitable Contributions
from the Council on Economic Priorities. In 1993 Chappell and his
wife, Kate, were presented with the New England Environmental
Leadership Award and the Governor's Award for Business Excellence.

An active member of the Episcopal Church of Maine, Chappell re-
cently earned a master's degree in theology from Harvard Divinity
School. His personal journey and accomplishments make him an excel-
lent candidate to discuss the soul of business, the subject of his essay.

For many people, the idea of bringing soul into a consideration of business practices might seem absurd. We have become accustomed to the idea that business is about using specific resources for specific gain—profit, market share, or some other kind of material incentive—and that it is, in fact, the desire for a specific gain that drives us into business in the first place. However, I am convinced that it is possible to be an effective competitor in the marketplace and still actively support and affirm human values. Our businesses can be structured and organized in such a way that they honor the dignity of human beings as well as the earth and its other creatures. In fact, I believe that there must be room in business for acknowledging the ultimate worthiness of life itself.

I have come to this conclusion through my own experience in running a business. In 1974, my wife, Kate, and I cofounded Tom's of Maine, a company committed to making personal care products from solely natural ingredients. By 1986, the signs of success were all around me: growth rates for the prior five years had been at least 20 percent every year; profits were increasing at even higher rates; we were expanding our retail markets from health food stores to supermarkets and drugstores. Materially, my life was certainly full: having started our business with a $5,000 loan, Kate and I now had a wonderful house, two cars, and a boat and were putting our children through school.

By conventional standards, all this success should have made me a happy man. Instead, I had begun to feel that something significant was missing from my life and from my business. I was confused by this thing called success; I could not understand why, despite my achievements, I was not happy. I began to question all the means by which we judge success—money, possessions, power—as well as the ways in which some of the professionals we had hired wanted to continue the company's growth. I even considered selling the company.

Instead, I decided to try to investigate some of the sources of my discontent by looking into what the great moral and religious thinkers have had to say, over the centuries, about what it means to be alive. Religion has always been an important part of my life—I grew up in the Episcopal Church, singing in the choir and serving as an acolyte, and

Kate and I had been members of the Episcopal church in Kennebunk ever since we moved there—and it seemed like the natural place to turn. I spoke with clergy I trusted, and with some wise friends, about the possible spiritual sources of my problem. Finally, I decided to take a rather unorthodox approach to resolving my dilemma. I applied and was accepted into Harvard Divinity School.

I had by then assembled a good, balanced group of experienced people on the board of directors, people who I knew would be more than capable of handling the business while I spent two days a week in Cambridge, thinking and reading about God. Fortunately, they were also open to the effect that my studies began to have on the company itself. No sooner had I begun the program at Harvard than I began to see the deficiencies in the way we had approached doing business. We had always been concerned with strategic planning—with the questions Where do we want to go? and How can we get there?—which requires that we focus on the outer life of the company. I became convinced that we needed to examine the inner life of the company, to ask ourselves questions about just what kind of company Tom's of Maine was and what values it manifested and promoted. The more I thought, the more convinced I became that these questions and their answers would be what would put the soul back in my business.

Together, the board of directors, the managers, Kate, and I began to examine the soul of the business—who we were as a company and what it was that we cared deeply about. We read and discussed literature about the value of human life and interaction, such as Kant's writings on freedom and Martin Buber's *I and Thou*. This must sound like an unusual endeavor for a board of directors to undertake, but the further we pursued this path, the more all of us became convinced that there must be some way, in business, to honor the dignity of human beings, nature, and animals and the ultimate worthiness of life itself. Our research and discussion culminated in a two-day retreat in 1989 by the end of which we had formulated answers to two questions: What do we believe? What, as an enterprise, do we think we're about?

That was the origin of what came to be our statement of beliefs and of mission. What I had learned in school, however, told me that the process couldn't end there. If we were truly going to live by our mission—which included an emphasis on respect not only for our customers, but for all of our coworkers—we needed to get ownership of the idea from everyone who worked at Tom's of Maine. We went through a process of sharing the draft of our statement of beliefs and mission with everyone in the company. Over a three-to-four-month period, we reworked and reworded sections of the statement so that it was a clear and adequate representation of the company.

Our statement of mission, however, is not a static thing. Though it represents where the company is now, it is also a guideline for how we do business, including some very specific decision-making processes. For example, we say in our mission statement that we want "to be distinctive in products and policies which honor and sustain our natural world." In order to be consistent with this aspect of our mission statement, we have to consider not only the ingredients in our products, but how our products are packaged.

Most packaging in this country is designed without any acknowledgment of the limitations or sustainability of the earth and therefore creates a huge amount of waste. We have always worked to create packaging that creates the least possible waste. We have also always believed in full and complete disclosure about our products, so we use our packaging to give a very complete description of whatever it contains. A few years ago, these two goals—to create minimum waste and to give maximum product disclosure—seemed to come into conflict. An employee pointed out that the outer box that our stick deodorant came in was using a lot of natural resources, and that the deodorant could just as easily be sold without it. Though it would have been simpler and cheaper to say, "We need the box to convey information to our customers," and let it go at that, what we decided to do instead was to come up with a way to get rid of the outer box and still provide information to our customers.

Through prolonged patience, interdepartmental teamwork, and creative thinking, we came up with an alternative that reduced our use of paper by 80 percent. The information that comes with our deodorant is now printed on an accordion-folded label. When you tear the label off, it opens up into a small booklet that actually holds a lot more information than the original package. We still honor our obligation to inform our customers, but we create 80 percent less waste.

We also reexamined the packaging of our roll-on deodorant and switched the container itself from plastic to glass. Though no one was selling glass for that purpose in the 1980s, we knew that when roll-on deodorants and antiperspirants first came on the market in the 1950s they were all in glass containers. With persistence, we were able to persuade our manufacturers to construct such glass containers so that our deodorant could come in recyclable material. When the container is empty, you have two environmentally friendly options: either buy a refill for the container or recycle it. In the case of our stick deodorant, we found an HDPE 2 plastic that was also recyclable—the first of its kind in the country—and so we were able to provide the option of recycling that container as well. Our commitment to honoring and sustaining the natural world is even reflected in something as comparatively small as our coupon strategy. Because the coupons that usually come inserted into the Sunday newspaper are not made of recyclable paper, we have chosen to advertise on newsprint itself, which is recyclable.

Another major influence on our company's decision making and identity is reflected in the part of our mission statement that states our commitment to "address community concerns, in Maine and around the globe, by devoting a portion of our time, talents, and resources to the environment, human needs, the arts, and education." Our policy today is to give 10 percent of our pretax profits toward these purposes. We also give 5 percent of our employees' paid time to volunteerism. These policies have a tremendous effect on the day-to-day workings of the company and on the attitudes of our employees. For example, when we began donating a percentage of our profits to these causes, I noticed that everyone in the company became very excited about where and how the money was being used. They were much more interested in that information than they had ever been in what our sales were. If you think about your own workplace for a moment, how many people can you really expect to be interested in sales and profits? But when you start to share your profits in ways that the community can see and feel, enormous interest and pride is generated in your workplace. When, for example, the town of Kennebunk asked how we could help with recycling, we came forward with a grant to buy curbside bins, so that the whole community could participate in a curbside recycling program. The effects of that kind of contribution can be seen by every employee, and each one can feel proud to have been a part of it.

What is the correlation between selling all-natural toothpaste and putting your energy into helping the community with curbside recycling? The correlation is simple: we are living out our beliefs in every aspect of the company. The same is true in our approach to personnel. We recently hired a new head of Research and Development, and the search took an unusually long time because we were not interested in the average scientist—one who only knew his or her chemistry. Because we use only natural ingredients, we were interested in an applicant with specific knowledge of plant chemistry—ethnobotany and ethnopharmacology—as well as an understanding of and sympathy with our mission statement.

The final choice was a Nigerian scientist of great knowledge and skill, as well as love of nature. In the final interview, I asked him why he wanted to work for Tom's of Maine. He said, "I think this company is a very bold experiment, and it has everything that I believe in and want to be part of." The values-orientation of the company brought this man out of a very successful, fast-track life to settle with his family in a small town in Maine and work with us.

But living the mission statement and managing the company by humanistic values has not always been easy. In many ways, it is an ongoing process in which we are always learning. The best and simplest way that I can describe our understanding of managing by values is this: it is not about simply writing a check to the right organization; it is not about just coming up with a more aggressive health plan or 401(k) profit-sharing plan. It has to do with a fundamental attitude of respect for the people you work with, for the customers you serve, and for the environments and communities you are part of. We say in our mission statement that we want to be a profitable and successful company while acting in a socially and environmentally responsible manner. We are saying we want it all: we want profits, we want to be responsible, and we want to be environmentally sensitive.

In order to have it all, we must embrace two basic goals simultaneously: one is to make a profit; the other is to demonstrate our respect for the earth and everything on it. These goals must be embraced both intellectually and emotionally, as well as in tandem. The trick is not to be profitable on Monday and respectful on Tuesday; the trick is to be both in every action, every day. It is, in the understanding of the Hindus and the Buddhists, a concept of the middle way, in which you have your mind and eye on both shores. As you come to make a decision—as you're working with your teams, working with your people to solve problems—you are keeping both views in mind. It is a learned and acquired capacity that one might call balance. Some might call it compromise; I would call it integration.

This is difficult to achieve, but I would say that we have achieved it. Our profits are higher than they have ever been, and we've taken a lot of shelf space away from our competitors, the major commodity brands. That is, after all, part of what we're here to do—not just to provide good, natural products but also to take a market share away from Proctor & Gamble, Colgate, and Lever. We are competitors, but of a different kind. We call our approach common good capitalism, because it involves learning how to attend to both the profit side and the concept of goodness in the way we make decisions.

It is impossible to take this approach without making some mistakes, and we have certainly made some. For example, soon after we wrote the mission statement, we formed a mission implementation committee—an interdepartmental group designed to help managers run their departments according to goals articulated in the statement. Not only was this plan not enthusiastically embraced by the managers, but it was met with quite a bit of resistance. I realized that part of it had to do with our new commitment to unhierarchical forms of decision making. The mission statement is intended to empower everyone in the organization, but when the middle manager is suddenly called upon to implement such a statement, he or she may well say, "Wait a minute. I've been working very hard for a number of years to get to a place of power in this organization, and now, due to this new set of ideas, the power just went right by me." Situations like that will arise, and they have to be talked through. The people who feel resentful have to be heard and respected; their concerns must be voiced and addressed.

There are many ways in which a company can show its respect for its members. Some are complex and take a lot of research and planning, such as devising a new profit-sharing and retirement plan, which we did just a few years ago. We felt we had a responsibility to share profits and help people plan for their retirement. But though our employees were pleased with the plan, it is hard to communicate the tangibility of sharing in profits, and many people were not very interested in the specifics of it. But when we decided to put fruit in every common room every day, so that anyone taking a break could have an orange, an apple, or a grapefruit, the employees responded to that. I was astounded, in fact, at what an impact the simple act of making fruit available throughout the day, free, had on our staff. Though simple, this act communicated to our employees that this company cares about and respects them.

The task of bringing soul into business has had a profound effect on my own life. Emotionally, I am more committed to the company than I have ever been. I'm excited about what I do because I'm living out my inner beliefs on a daily basis with my team. When I began as an entrepreneur, I felt this same way; I was very energetic, because my creativity was constantly called upon in the making of new products. Then, when I bought into what our culture defines as "professional" ways of running a business, I bought into a very dry way of doing things. What is the reward for doing it well? Do it again next year. That's your reward. But trying to run a business ethically and with soul brings constant challenges to my abilities and my creativity. It is a much more rewarding way to work.

The process of running a business by ethics is by definition complicated. Business people often fall back on the old motto, "Keep it simple, stupid." I am afraid, however, that this piece of wisdom is no longer useful. You can keep it simple if your only goal is to make a profit. If you want to be ethical, and to run a business that demonstrates in a daily way its respect for human life, that endeavor is, by definition, complex. Our businesses are made of people and created for people; we live, each of us, in communities of people; therefore, we have to respond to the reality that people are complicated. They are made up of many aspects—emotional, intellectual, and spiritual—and each part needs to be honored. Such an endeavor takes a lot of tolerance, patience, and hard work, but it is well worth it.

It is also of crucial importance right now. Ethical and soulful values are not just relevant to our businesses and our workplaces. Currently, our whole culture is in desperate need of attention to such ideas. Every day, the earth communicates to us the effects of all our abuse. Human beings are indicating—in the workplace and on the streets—that they have lost faith in the future, in the possibility of positive change. If we want to restore, maintain, and celebrate the good and meaningful things in life, we have to find the capacity to put them back into every aspect of our lives, including our business planning. That capacity begins in each of our hearts.

Chapter 19

Singing the Soul of a Community

YSAYE M. BARNWELL

Ysaye Marie Barnwell is an unusual blend of artist, academic, and technology specialist. Trained as a violinist as a child (she was named after the Belgian violinist Eugène Ysaÿe), she later earned advanced degrees in speech pathology and public health. Today she juggles the roles of actress, composer, and singer with the internationally known African American women's a cappella quintet Sweet Honey in the Rock, while advising community health projects and informally encouraging progressive grassroots organizations to use on-line databases and computers to enhance their networking and communications capabilities.

She is also known for her workshops on vocal community, offering both brief (two-and-a-half-hours) and extended (five-day) workshops at sites in the United States, England, and Australia. In this context, she introduces participants to African rhythms, calls and chants, Spirituals, Gospels, hymns, and the music of the civil rights movement and other contemporary struggles.

In her essay, Barnwell explains how music and other arts are integral to everyday life in traditional African culture and how they express the soul of the community.

A frican and African American music has spread all over the world. From Spirituals to rap, from traditional rhythms to rock, you can hear our music or feel its influence almost everywhere and anytime you turn on the radio or the television set. Although the sounds continually surround us, most people are not generally aware of their origins, underlying structure, or meaning. A discussion of the worldview from which this music has arisen can set a clearer context for the experience of becoming a vocal-singing community.

When I ask young people in this culture to tell me where they see art, they invariably say "in the museum" or "in galleries." Likewise, in order to hear the music that is defined as art, they have to go to concerts. However, to children in a traditional culture, the concept of art, as we experience it, might be nonexistent; for them, art is such an integral part of everyday life that it does not distinguish itself from other instruments of daily or ritualistic practice.

In traditional contexts, particularly if writing is not the method of choice for recording and transmitting history and culture, the arts—music, dance, masks, totems, poetry, paintings, and so forth—serve to achieve those ends. The arts are the method by which events, knowledge, feelings, and values are recorded, preserved, and transmitted from generation to generation. The arts are a glue that connects elements along two possible continuums of reality: one between the invisible world and the visible world, and the other between the past (ancestors and elders), the present, and the future (the as yet unborn). Through the arts we effect change—within ourselves as individuals, within our communities, and through the things we create.

In his autobiography, *The Dark Child,* Camara Laye recounts the experience of watching his father work as an ironsmith and goldsmith in Guinea, West Africa. To encourage him to respond favorably to a request to begin work on a gold trinket, he is serenaded by a griot, or praise-singer, who chronicles in song the greatness of his genealogy, the lofty deeds and skilled craftsmanship of his ancestors. Through song he is told that he is the descendant of a long line of artisans and that he is about to begin his work.

You can imagine how proud this man feels. As he begins to work he can be seen uttering incantations into the pot as he stirs the gold in order to energize his creation. If the artisan, healer, teacher, farmer, or cook does not energize the thing he or she is creating, the end product may not serve the purpose for which it was intended. If the blacksmith does not sing or pray energy and spirit into the tools he is making, his locks may not keep the enemy out, or the weapon of war he makes may injure or kill its bearer.

When we sing, we actually practice magic. That magic can influence us in many different ways. Each one of us probably has a song that energizes us, or a piece of music that transforms our sadness into happiness. Some of us like music that creates or reinforces the sadness within us. There is also music that moves us to action, moves us to dance, to meditate, to join a movement, to vote, or to investigate an issue further. There is music that can symbolize a lifetime of experience, for example, a national anthem or the song played during your first kiss. In the African worldview, music and the other arts are functional; they do not exist as "art for art's sake," as in many Western cultures. The fact that Western cultures have adopted writing as a way of recording human experience means they do not need to use the arts for that purpose.

This fact also influences the way certain arts are performed. With the advent of writing, music and dance could be transcribed and therefore reproduced repeatedly outside their original contexts. Thus the expectation of consistency began to dominate the performance arena: an expectation that a piece of music or a dance would be performed the same way each time, or that the performer would simply get better and better at performing what was documented on the page. In this view, once the artist has attained a certain level of perfection, he or she is expected to maintain it. Consistency defines the artist's technical proficiency and genius as a performer.

The highest celebration of the European musical art form is going to specific places on specific occasions in order to create an audience that watches the artist display his or her technical virtuosity. However, this concept does not exist in African societies, where art is a part of everything that one does and therefore cannot be separated out and placed on a mantel for safekeeping or exclusive showings. Art loses its significance and its meaning if extracted from its context.

When art is part of everyday life, it can contribute to the strengthening and building of the community. We see this particularly in three major performance aspects of African music: polyrhythms, call and response, and improvisation. Polyrhythm means that there is more than one rhythm occurring at the same time. It is important to understand how this works and why it is significant to the life of a community. In a drum orchestra in Africa, there can be as many as twelve or more musicians, all of whom are playing different instruments and different rhythms. There is usually someone playing a bell, and you can hear it pierce through everything. It is important to have that bell or a similar sound as a focal or reference point to listen to or else the players can get quite confused.

The bell player is doing his or her thing; each drummer is doing his or her thing, which is quite different from anyone else's. It could very easily become a big mess if no one is listening. For this music to work, each instrument's player has to listen carefully. Each player listens first to the bell, then measures where he or she is in relation to that pattern. Then each player measures where he or she is in relation to another prominent rhythm and then to the larger and larger structure. But even this is not all of what each player listens for. The player is listening for the sound that nobody is playing, the sound that you hear when you experience everything coming together perfectly. That is the magic. That is the deepest thing that could possibly happen; it is the sound created only when everything is in correct relationship to everything else.

How, you ask, does the African drum orchestra and the concept of polyrhythm connect with our regular lives here in the Western world? It connects because it illustrates the possibility and power of diversity in community; it is a metaphor for coalition, for organization. People, each of whom has his or her own interest to protect, preserve, and promote, agree to come together. You are doing your thing and I am doing mine, but we are listening very carefully and respectfully to each other and we are listening for the larger melody. We make minor adjustments in our rhythm in order to maintain the integrity of our relationship. We are in cooperation, not in competition. We are working toward the larger good, which no one person or entity could produce alone.

We can learn much about ourselves by performing polyrhythmic music firsthand and then asking the following questions:

What was the larger melody created by all of the parts working perfectly together? Were you able to hear it?

Did you ever sense that your part was in perfect rhythmic or harmonic relationship to another?

If you were sitting next to or encountered a person singing another part:

Did you delight in singing along with someone who was singing something different?

Was it more comfortable and exciting to find somebody who was singing your part?

Did you try to sing louder to influence a person singing differently from you?

Did you allow someone singing differently to sway you into singing his or her part?

Were you lost and in need of rescuing?

Responses to these and similar questions can function as metaphors for how we live in community and in the world.

In traditional societies, much interaction, particularly for teaching, occurs in a pattern of call and response. Singing in this pattern is a way of determining that your message has been received and interpreted accurately and of involving all who are present in the process that is occurring. It is similar to the communications training technique in which one person makes a statement and another listens and responds, "You said . . . " The original speaker knows immediately whether or not he or she has been heard correctly. Next, the original speaker must listen carefully to try to determine if the message has been interpreted correctly. The leader often challenges the listener(s) to repeat more and more difficult messages and to listen for certain messages that indicate that the nature of the communication or interaction will change.

In drumming terminology, such a message is called a break and indicates that everything is ending. The nature of the break indicates if the end is final or that things will begin again, possibly at a much faster pace. The levels of communication and cooperation in this process can be quite amazing both to witness and to participate in.

Another important aspect of music made in community is the phenomenon of improvisation. Often when people think about performing or participating in African or African American music or dance, they have the attitude that "anything goes"; you can do anything you want. I think that this attitude comes from the sense of freedom and accessibility that this music engenders. However, this attitude is uninformed. African and African American music and dance are very structured and disciplined. Improvisation, or creation in performance, happens within a structure that is known and understood by each performer. The boundaries of spontaneous creation in performance are defined by the structure of the piece being performed. Those who do not know the structure usually cannot interpret the situation correctly.

For example, people who visit a black Pentecostal or shouting church may get the mistaken impression that it is all right for them to get up and dance if they feel like it. If they understood the structure, they would know that the dancing they are observing is the "holy dance" of those upon whom the Spirit has descended. Dancing as a social phenomenon may not be permitted in the church or by the church at all. When you go to jazz performances, you often see that a piece begins with the entire group playing and then each person in the group assuming the lead. I once heard Branford Marsalis instruct some youthful jammers. He emphatically stated that "you only take a lead if you have something to contribute to the conversation." You do not take a lead just to show off or to compete; as he put it, "You gotta have something to say." Often what we have to say comes from another, higher source and in that sense is inspired in the same way that "holy dance" is inspired. If Spirit truly descends, the piece will sing itself. This is when dancers seem to fly and when singers seem to sing with the voices of angels and when all present are filled.

Other factors that become clear in some improvisational settings are that there is more than one leader in the group and that leadership revolves. There is an expectation that leadership will move to the next person who has something to say, and that those who have been the leaders will assume a supportive role for the person now leading. Again, it is cooperation and not competition.

A people's music reflects their sense of community. When African people were brought to this country, their music changed significantly because their experiences changed. There were new things to document, new emotions to catalog, new values to sift through. There was a new dialectic that needed to be set in motion because of the phenomenon of slavery.

Though several different kinds of music evolved out of slavery, to me, the most powerful body of song is the Spiritual. Spirituals make up the major body of music written by slaves brought to this country; they are oral history. Through Spirituals, we hear the expression of what life was, what death was, what it felt like to be alienated, to be torn away from everything they had ever known. Spirituals reflect both African spirituality and Christian concepts.

As slaves began to embrace Christianity, many songs emerged that specifically named biblical figures and told their stories. There is a song about Daniel in the lion's den; about Jonah in the belly of the whale; about Joshua, who fought the battle of Jericho; and about Moses, who led his people out of slavery in Egypt. The songs became affirmations because their purpose was to remind the singers and the community that if those biblical men and women could overcome adverse circumstances, then surely there was a way to overcome slavery.

There were Spirituals that negotiated whether a slave should remain enslaved or try to escape. "Staying songs" reflected the belief that slaves should stay and work within the system because where the problem is, there also is the solution. "Balm in Gilead" is such a staying song. There are also the songs that talk about leaving: "Oh Freedom . . .

Before I'll be a slave, I'll be buried in my grave and go home to my Lord and be free," "Swing Low, Sweet Chariot," "Deep River," "Get on Board, Little Children."

"Steal Away" is an excellent leaving song because it is a call. It says, "Steal away, steal away, steal away to Jesus . . . I ain't got long to stay here." There are several theories about these lyrics. One is that "Jesus" refers to freedom. Jesus was also the name of a slave ship—the good ship *Jesus*. If you are going to get back home, one of the ways is to go back the same way you came—by boat. This song is really about escape and has a strategy buried in it. The verse says,

> My Lord he calls me.
> He calls me by the thunder
> The trumpet sounds within my soul.
> I ain't got long to stay here.

Some people think that these words refer directly to escaping during a storm, when there is a lot of natural commotion and people would normally stay inside. If you used the storm as an opportunity to leave, your footprints and scent would be washed away by the rain, and by morning the dogs would not be able to follow you.

There are many other leaving songs. One such song that I especially like is "Follow the Drinking Gourd." The drinking gourd is the Big Dipper headed by the North Star. The song says,

> Follow the drinking gourd.
> For the old man is awaiting for to carry
>   you to freedom.
> Follow the drinking gourd.

Who is the old man waiting to carry you to freedom? Moses. But who is Moses? Harriet Tubman. Harriet managed to lead over three hundred slaves to freedom on her many trips along the Underground Railroad as far north as Canada.

There are distinct differences between Spirituals and Gospel music. Spirituals are that body of music created by African slaves from the 1600s to the 1800s. They are of rural origin, unaccompanied, and anonymous. No one actually wrote them down. In all probability, they were developed by the community, not just one person. We know that because many of the melodies are similar, and the words of one song can often be found in another. If you are working in community, there is shared ownership of your songs: you sing something or you hear something sung a certain way, and it gets repeated in a variety of different settings.

Gospel music, on the other hand, developed as a result of the great migration of blacks from rural to urban areas during the early twentieth century. It is urban in origin, composed by individuals in the twentieth century, and usually is accompanied. We know who composed these songs because they wrote their names on the music, copyrighted it, printed it, and sold it. You can buy these songs today. We know who the great Gospel composers were then, and we know who they are today. The pioneering Gospel composers included Thomas A. Dorsey, Lucy E. Campbell, Charles A. Tindley, and William H. Brewster.

When people came to the cities, they began to hear the blues and other new music that was developing. They began to absorb new instruments into the sacred music of the times. Today it is natural to find all kinds of instrumentation in Gospel music. You can hear strains of blues and jazz because both are urban-based music, and because African Americans tend not to fragment things. Western cultures tend to push us to distinguish between what is sacred and what is not. But for the African American community, the distinctions are not always clear. That is why it is not unusual to hear blues sounds inside a Gospel song. It is also not unusual to hear rap inside of Gospel because again we don't always make hard-line distinctions. When Mahalia Jackson was asked why she was singing religious music that sounded like the devil's music, she replied, "Why should the devil have all the good songs?" If you are trying to attract the people who are influenced by the devil, you have to sing something that they will listen to, or you will never be able to recruit them into your camp.

During the migration from rural to urban areas between 1915 and 1945, African American communities began to develop vocal quartets. Quartet singing does not restrict itself to four people singing. It means you have four solid parts, usually with one voice that sails on top. A whole movement developed around quartets. There were men's quartets as well as women's quartets. A cappella groups began to develop into larger and larger ensembles. Now we sometimes have massive choirs with hundreds of people singing Gospel.

Music during the civil rights movement in the 1960s was important because it was the glue that brought people together in mass meetings. Singing fortifies people and binds them together. By being together and producing this collective sound, we can go forward as an entity larger than each of us as individuals.

Because the civil rights movement was a nonviolent movement, the only weapons that people had were determination, their bodies, and the power of their collective voices. It was the thing that people heard for miles before the marchers arrived. It was what would recruit people standing on the sidelines, those who couldn't make up their minds whether or not they wanted to join in.

The police officers—with their billy clubs, guns, and fire hoses—were confronted by a powerful bubble of sound that couldn't be penetrated. Even when the police beat people and sprayed them with fire hoses, the sound didn't stop. They put them into the paddy wagons, and the sound didn't stop. They put them in jail, and the sound didn't stop. The jailers said, "We will take your damn mattresses if you don't shut up," and the sound didn't stop. It was empowering—not much different from the blacksmith singing to the objects he was creating.

The songs of the civil rights movement also recorded history and reported to the public stories that had not been reported in the newspaper. If you heard or know the song "Birmingham Sunday," then you heard or knew the names of the four little girls who died in the Birmingham church that was bombed. If you heard "In the Mississippi River," you heard that there were many, many bodies of missing black people dragged from that river as a result of the search for one white civil rights worker.

The songs in the civil rights movement came from everywhere. They came from the Spirituals that talked about being free; they came from Gospels that talked about salvation. The songs even came from the radio—rock-and-roll songs like Ray Charles's "Hit the Road, Jack"—and from children's games. One children's song was actually written by an adult, who could see that the dog that belonged to the white kid and the dog that belonged to the black kid were playing together. "So," he asked himself, "how come the kids couldn't play together?" He wrote a song that goes,

> My dog loves your dog. And your dog loves my dog.
> So why can't we sit under the apple tree?

If one were to compile the songs of African American people, the work songs, calls, field hollers, Spirituals, ring shouts, jubilees, blues, rhythm and blues, Gospels, raps, and so on, one would have a firsthand account of the history of our people.

When we sing together, we are celebrating our history. We are practicing culture that is functional and communal. Singing fortifies us and binds us together; it teaches us the value of cooperation, of revolving leadership, and of listening to one another. By producing a collective sound, we can go forward as an entity larger than each of us as individuals. It is my hope that what people experience singing together— hearing and feeling the power and beauty of the sounds that they produce—will make a difference in their lives and in the lives of their communities.

Chapter 20

The Journey of the Adolescent Soul

DAVID OLDFIELD

At a time when young people, particularly in our cities, are more imperiled than ever, David Oldfield's work with adolescents is particularly important. Director of the Center for Creative Imagination at the Foundation for Contemporary Mental Health in Washington, D.C., he focuses on adolescence as the bridge between childhood and adulthood and works to develop appropriate ways to offer guidance for crossing that bridge.

Oldfield is the author of several books, including The Journey: A Creative Approach to the Necessary Crises of Adolescence, *which outlines a modern rite of passage for adolescents and has been used in schools, mental health facilities, churches, and youth centers all over the country and in Europe. Though best known for his contributions to the lives of young people, Oldfield applies his understanding of the importance of myth, ritual, and the imagination to devising programs and rites of passage for groups of all ages.*

Not long ago, I invited a fifteen-year-old boy I was working with to draw an image of how it felt to be where he was on his life path. His picture captured perfectly the predicament of adolescents in our culture. On the right side of the drawing were representations of the childhood he was leaving—a cold, blue-gray landscape of once-beautiful flowers, now limp and dying. On the left was the world of adulthood, vague and misty, dominated by a huge, menacing sun that blinded him so he could not see what he was moving into. He had drawn himself trying to cross a suspension bridge from one side to the other, but the bridge was rotting—wherever he placed his feet, the planks broke through. The bridge had gone untended for too long and was in obvious need of repair, but no one was around to fix it. The boy was left to make his way alone, or die trying. In this drawing, the movement from childhood to adulthood was expressed as a tenuous, threatening, and lonely passage.

This image captures the essence of the experience too many young people have today. From time out of mind we, as a species, have known that the passage of adolescence requires a profound shift in the way we live our lives. That shift has always necessitated two different but balanced movements: outward, toward mastery and self-sufficiency in the world, and inward, to awaken the dormant depth-dimension of the psyche. It is a soul journey and, as such, is tremendously important—not only to the individual being and her family but to the renewal of the life of the community, the nation, and the planet. Yet most of us are not consciously aware of how significant the inward passage of adolescence is to our adult lives. Developmental psychology has made it clear how integral early childhood attachments are to our ongoing mental health and emotional stability. We need to remember that this need for attachment is no less critical in adolescence, when the scope of our attachment increases. If the primary work of being a child is to acquire a sense of self and attachment to family, then the great work of adolescence is to transform that sense of self by bringing it into attachment with the world.

Adolescence is an emergence: we emerge into society—into what it means to be male or female, to be a member of a particular family or ethnic tradition, to be an American, to live on this speeding, shrinking planet. These are overwhelming tasks that cannot be accomplished simply by growing older. They must be stimulated and contained, experienced and expressed in sanctioned, dignified ways that underscore rather than deny their importance. Unfortunately, in our culture we have no such containers for adolescents coming of age. In modern America, there are no formal rites through which young people can express the yearnings of soul that usher them from childhood into adulthood. We do not honor the inward journey of adolescence with vision quests, like the indigenous peoples of North America, or help the young cultivate the wisdom of their dreams, as did the ancient Greeks. If anything, the soul's journey is blocked by the pounding omnipresence of modern materialism. By their actions—be it withdrawal into drugs or the antisocial expression of gangs—young people are attempting to communicate to us the agony of this absence.

Because the soul's yearnings are ontological, an adolescent cannot simply say no to them. The soul in adolescence craves occasions to express itself and its needs however and wherever it can. If mainstream society cannot or will not provide a context for that expression, the young are forced to create one for themselves. We see the results of this struggle in the harsh media footage of adolescent violence, in gangs running amok, in numbing national statistics of downward spirals in literacy and life expectancy, in the growing ranks of adolescents who are disenfranchised and disengaged. We look at these expressions as problems in need of solutions (which most often translates into "get rid of the kid") rather than as symptoms of a much deeper malady. J. Krishnamurti once said, "It is no sign of health to be well adjusted in a profoundly sick society." We would do well to heed this warning, for we may be blaming the young rather than facing the hard truth about ourselves: we are failing to provide the next generation with the occasion and the structure they need to awaken their newfound souls and bring their depth into expression.

Right now, the systems and institutions that we rely on to help us raise the next generation in healthy, soulful ways are disintegrating before our eyes. The old models of both mental health and education are in a state of profound transformation; the old paradigms are dying.

Mental health, as a system serving adolescents, has been relegated to providing symptom relief—most often in the form of prescribed drugs that "stabilize" the mood—to the dangerously distressed; "deviance" continues to be redefined downward, admitting more and more hostile and antisocial activity into the "normal" range because we simply don't know what else to do with it. Education—from the ancient Greek word *educare,* which means "to lead out"—has become an arena for cramming in data that will lead to high scores on standardized tests. Our immediate task is to create a new paradigm, a new lens for looking at adolescence that brings focus to the unique soul yearnings of this life stage. One way to begin is to reexamine the essential movements in the passage of the adolescent soul.

In the twenty-two years that I have been working with adolescents, I have become aware of two basic truths about this transitional time of life. The first is that the soul journey of adolescence is primarily heroic. In adolescence, we are called to move out from the safe center of life as we have known it into a quest for what is larger, deeper, more worthy of being served than our individual egos. By definition, adolescents stand on a threshold; the movement they represent is through a doorway that leads away from a life that is simply not big enough or deep enough for them anymore. Whether the doorway leads out into the world or down into a deeper region of the self, adolescents stand in a place of anticipation and preparation. They are no longer children, not yet adults. The Hindus call this place *neti, neti,* meaning "not this, not that."

The passage from here to there is made difficult by the fact that, as a society, we fear transitions and change. Without knowing it, groups develop myriad ways to ignore, demean, and denounce profound transitions like that of adolescence, not because we don't want young people to grow up, but because in the act of their growing up, they remind us of our growing old. Simply by their presence, adolescents remind us of the threshold experiences still awaiting us, and bring us face to face with our own fears. We think that if we clamp down hard on the kids—if we trap them with rules and structures and extraneous responsibilities to deflect their attention from the profundity of their transition—we will, in some way, keep our own fears at bay.

This, of course, is a fruitless endeavor and just the opposite of what adolescents need. Periods of transition require freedom to move, to discover the new, to stretch. There is much to explore, and the anxiety that so often surrounds our encounters with the unknown can consume the quest if it is not contained and cared for in dignified ways.

Sadly, this is rarely the case. One of the most widespread complaints about adolescents is that they act out too much. We fail to see through this style of behavior into what is being said. Acting out behavior is only a manifestation of their essential energy. Everything in adolescence is bursting forth, blooming, expanding in its adult capacity. The physical body is bursting its skin; hormones drive emotions to new heights and depths; the social world expands in intrigue and complexity. Our soul at this time yearns for engagement with life's grandest mysteries: Who am I? What matters? Knowing I will die, how shall I live?

These are the movements that drive the adolescent. Rather than acknowledging the natural shape of their needs and their quest and providing appropriate and meaningful avenues of expression, we sit young people at desks for six or seven hours a day and require them to deal with everything but themselves and their natural concerns, reprimanding them for any displays of emotion that haven't been civilized or made genteel. We are perhaps rightly concerned about the nation's declining rates of literacy and numeracy. But what of *emotional* literacy—the ability to know one's moods, particularly one's relationship with anger? What of *social* literacy—the ability to experience the Other (other gender, other ethnic group, other age group) as a gift rather than a threat? What of *imaginal* literacy—the ability to dream dreams worth dreaming and to know what to do when hope is lost?

Because adolescence is a transitional space, it is impossible to be accountable for all one thinks and does during those years. Ancient and indigenous people knew that much of the life-wisdom gained in adolescence came from trial-and-error explorations, and thus they removed young people from the scrutiny of family and tribe while the painful, awkward process of "finding yourself" took place. Passage experiences most often took place in the wilderness or in solitude. Today, young people feel as if they are under a microscope.

For example, my eleven-year-old son is friends with a girl his age who is losing her hair from stress. She has internalized a message (from family? school? the culture at large?) that her entire future depends on how well she does in school *right now*. Right now, her grades must be good enough to get her into the honors track next year, where she must excel enough to get her into accelerated classes in ninth grade, so she will be eligible for advanced placement classes her junior year, so she can get early admission to the college of her choice, so she can get into the "right" graduate school, so she can get a good job, *so she won't have to worry!* All this on the head of an eleven-year-old, struggling to concentrate on her homework while an ocean of anxiety washes over her. She has already decided she is a failure, and it would seem that her body is in psychosomatic revolt. But the adolescent soul has a different agenda. To the soul, such outward and visible benchmarks of success are just so much cultural trickery. What matters to the soul is authenticity: is this me, my path, my life, or am I acting out someone else's fantasy of me?

The second essential truth governing the soul journey of adolescence is that it needs to be guided by those who have already made the passage. In most traditional and indigenous cultures, it is the sacred function of elders to initiate, to guide a formal process in which adolescents can be introduced to their souls—to the mysterious depths of themselves—and so discover their individual journeys. Left untended, the energies of adolescent soul become chaotic and can be perverted to destructive ends. The unique energy of adolescence is frequently likened to that of a fire: it has tremendous energy and potential, but requires care so that it doesn't rage out of control. Simply put, initiation banks the natural fire of adolescence, shaping its size and intensity for the benefit of the individual and his or her community. We cannot bank the fires of adolescence by suffocating the flame. We bank the flames with awareness, compassion, and a sense of being connected to an entity greater than our own small selves. Establishing these vital connections between one's own inner fire and the community was the responsibility of the elders.

Unfortunately, elders in the true sense of the word are hard to come by these days. The role of elder has been divested of its natural power and spread thinly over a variety of disciplines. We divide the functions of initiation into various specialties: we are educated in the classroom by professional teachers; healed in a clinic by professional doctors; consoled in a church, mosque, or synagogue by professional clergy; and taught values in the home by parents who read books by experts telling them how to do it. But in reality, values are taught everywhere; learning occurs every moment of the day; the potential for healing is present everywhere people touch each other's lives. Those without professional degrees have been co-opted into thinking that they have little to offer young people, but nothing could be further from the truth. The soul, particularly at adolescence, is nourished by being in the presence of those living soulfully. We are, each of us, much more important in the lives of our neighborhood children than we can possibly imagine.

In Hawaii, there is a wonderful tradition of people called aunties. Aunties are women in a community who feel called to "adopt" a neighborhood child. Typically, sometime in the child's first year, a woman will drop by to announce to the parents that she is the auntie of their child—a boon few parents would dream of refusing. From that time forward, the auntie and the child are connected: they visit, they converse, they teach, they play. If problems arise at home—if the child has an argument with a parent or sibling and needs a place to retreat—he or she goes to the auntie's house to stay for a while. This is a marvelous example of the way indigenous people create opportunities for young people to attach themselves to the community in the same way that they attach themselves to their families.

People have been eldering since the beginning of time, and there are wonderful "maps" available to us that can be revived to help us understand and guide the movement of the adolescent soul. Mythology, particularly heroic mythology, provides just such a map. Mythology is the psychology of antiquity. Embedded in the language and structure of myth are ancient understandings of the realm of our own souls.

The genre of the heroic myth captures most clearly the movement of the adolescent soul. Every culture has heroic myths that can help young people with the events of their lives. Heroic myths suggest the need to be called into an adventure in life. They give context to pain and suffering.

They provide role models that allow young people to see through the folly of the world and to learn to think for themselves. They provide a backdrop of meaning for an adolescent's natural drives, often sanctioning what parents and society will not.

For example, many of the myths of adolescence are about edges: coming to the edge of what is civilized and safe, and then going on. From Icarus to Alice in Wonderland, heroes and heroines are drawn to the edges of experience and either step or fall over; they are called to move from one realm to another. "Character," that mysterious entity that begins to flower in our youth, is evoked by how we respond to the experience of our edges in adolescence. Heroic myths give us clues as to what we can expect from life should we make this choice or that. Jung characterized therapy as the process of discovering a new story-container for our lives, to give a new context to our ever-expanding experiences. The soul of an adolescent needs just such a container to understand itself.

The other "map" available to us comes in the form of formal rites of passage. Until recently, such a notion sounded too primitive, too pagan, for modern ears. We assume that maturity comes with age, and that one simply grows into manhood or womanhood. But rites of passage suggest that coming of age is an event to be consciously engaged, not only by the young person, but by the community as a whole. In indigenous cultures, rites of passage were a proving ground to establish one's worthiness for life's next stage. Ordeals of body and soul, of wit and will, were created by the community to give birth to the new adult.

Both myths and rites of passage are containers; they give shape and structure to the otherwise chaotic and volatile energy of youth. They direct the movement of the soul toward expression in the world. Though the details of such a journey vary from person to person, there are essentially five phases to the passage from childhood to adulthood.

The first phase I have already mentioned: the soul awakens to itself. Children, by and large, are happy living essentially through their five senses. There is enough wonder and magic in the sensual world to captivate them. In adolescence, a deeper dimension opens up. We realize there is space—a whole universe, really—inside us that has power and direction. What can be difficult and even shocking at this time of life is that the power and direction of the emerging soul often run in contradiction to the individual's persona. For example, the adolescent's persona may want to be socially adept and popular, while the soul yearns for solitude. Holden Caulfield in J. D. Salinger's *Catcher in the Rye* is a classic example of the ongoing friction between the social persona and the soul of an adolescent.

The second phase occurs when the soul begins to seek its own path. Once it becomes aware of itself, the soul craves expression. This can be troubling for the adults in a young person's life, for the forms of expression the soul experiments with are often radically different from the child's previous expression, and once again, friction exists between the inner and outer life.

I saw an example of this played out in the life of a fourteen-year-old girl in a class I taught. She was extremely introverted and would try to become invisible in social situations. When I asked the group to draw images of themselves, she drew herself, not as she looked to all of us, but as a very colorful character she called Niambi the Exotic, who was trapped in a bottle. In sharing, she revealed that while she always appeared plain and shy on the outside, she felt something new growing on the inside—a bold, self-directed young woman she named Niambi. But like a genie, Niambi was stuck in a bottle, and the girl wanted Niambi to come out so the rest of the world could see her beauty. How might Niambi free herself?

So the group began to talk about ways Niambi might get out of the bottle: break it (but Niambi might get hurt); rub it like a magic lamp (no, no one else could release her). Then someone remembered an old television commercial in which Ella Fitzgerald sings an impossibly high note, shattering a wine glass, and suggested, "Maybe Niambi needs to find her own voice and sing so loud she can shatter the bottle with her song."

The girl immediately took to this suggestion, and it became her therapeutic task to give Niambi a voice. One Friday as she left a meeting, she said, "When I come back on Monday, you're in for a surprise." Monday morning, this shy, reticent little girl came to school with bright green hair spiked in all directions, wearing wild, mismatched clothing, her ears jangling earrings from multiple new pierced holes. Even her walk was different. She came bopping into the room, looked us in the eyes with tremendous satisfaction, and said, "I'm out."

Her parents, as you might imagine, were right behind her, saying, "We'd like to see David Oldfield. We hear that this has something to do with some 'journey' she's on." Their mood was less than happy, and who could blame them? They wanted their quiet, shy little girl back, and they knew that their daughter would never be that little girl again. But neither would she stay this wild and loose for long. Often the first expressions of soul in adolescents are extreme because the soul needs momentum to burst through the crust that has held it in for so long. This girl—the young woman—in time evened out her appearance and found an equilibrium in her style that lay somewhere in between the closed-in little girl and the eccentric Niambi. We need to remember what ancient peoples knew: that this time is full of surprises and is often quite messy.

The third phase of the journey is what is referred to, in heroic mythology, as the road of trials and obstacles. There is a profound and driving need, in adolescence, for the soul to be tested. As children we live more or less comfortably within the bounds of other people's rules and reality descriptions. In adolescence, the soul declares itself through its own descriptions of what is real, what is valuable, what matters; now the soul craves dialogue with the world. That dialogue occurs in its encounters with obstacles, with ordeals that make it stretch, with dangers that make the soul tingle with its own vitality. Ancient rites of passage seem always to have led the young into situations of danger, where they were forced to confront fear, self-doubt, and self-limiting mental models. In this way, they proved their worth and fitness to the adult community.

There is valuable learning for us here. For all the rigors associated with schooling, present culture offers few formal, sanctioned opportunities for adolescents to test their worth. The need for such tests is so great that if the culture fails to provide suitable challenges, the adolescent soul will seek its own. It is no accident that teenage gangs are often begun by the most disenfranchised, by young people whose needs—for identity, for a sense of personal power, for membership in an entity larger than their own egos—go unmet. The sacredness of the suffering involved in ancient rites is perverted into two boys standing toe-to-toe, hitting each other in the chest repeatedly just to see who flinches first. They intuit their need for testing; they just don't know how to go about it. Rather than condemn their activity, we need to distill for adolescents the questions that will help them identify the right ordeals for their soul journeys, questions such as, What do you seek? What quest is worthy of your energy? What sacrifices are you willing to make in pursuit of your goal? What will you serve?

The trials and obstacles in this phase prepare the youth for the central ordeal: the confrontation with death. Death—both literally as a signal of our mortality and symbolically as a metaphor of transformation—speaks directly to the adolescent soul. In times of profound change, death imagery is much more likely to erupt in the mind, telling us the story of what it feels like to be changing, as a part of us does indeed die in order to allow another to be born. As a child, my son Jeremy had a dream that reflected this process. He was a week shy of his fifth birthday, an enormously important experience in a child's life: at five, you leave home—you go to kindergarten. It is a year of learning to swim, to ride a bike, to eat meals away from home—incipient independence everywhere you turn! A week before this event, he told me he had dreamed that he and I were on a boat together. He was diving off the side of the boat, then swimming back, then diving off again, while I watched. Then he dove in and didn't come back. I began to get worried and dove in after him, swimming to the bottom of the ocean looking for my son. All I could see were crabs and sea snakes. I swam back up to the boat to tell the captain that Jeremy had died. When I got to the wheelhouse, Jeremy was there, steering the boat. He had become the captain. When he saw me, he smiled, then turned the boat around, heading for home. All this from a preschool child, who somehow knew that being five required that he first "die" to four.

After the ordeals and encounters with death comes the fourth stage of the adolescent journey: rebirth and return. This is the time for honest self-reflection and integration, typically involving a great deal of solitude in which the soul can sort out what it has learned and what it now has to offer the world. On this point, the wisdom of heroic myths and rites of passage is clear: the treasures won on the soul's journey are not possessions to keep, but gifts to offer. Try to hoard it, and the soul's treasure will torment you or turn to dust in your hands. Before young men and women reenter the community, time and care must be taken to help them understand the nature of their unique gifts, match them with the needs of the community, and discover in what form their gifts might best be offered.

The fifth and final phase of the soul's journey in adolescence is ceremony, or formal acknowledgment. Ritual and ceremony are necessary activities in human existence; they contain us and our anxiety as we face experiences too vast for our individual psyches to handle alone. Ritual removes us from time's normal flow and places us in proximity with the eternal. In baptisms, weddings, and burials, ritual whispers, "You stand now at a threshold where countless generations before you have stood, where myriad more will stand after you. As you experience this threshold, you do so for all of us, and all before and after you are present with you now."

We need to create similarly affirming ceremonies honoring adolescents' passage into adulthood. In the groups of young people I work with, we design ceremonies of passage together. Ceremony must be authentic, a true reflection of the people gathered and of the way their personal experience is woven into the fabric of the world. Our access to the rituals of other cultures has led many to sample from this tradition or that, as though the world opens itself to us as a spiritual supermarket. But we err if we attempt to take on the trappings of another culture's ceremonial traditions—sweat lodges or Sufi dancing—because to do so is to minimize the importance of our own experience and our own soul's creative propensities. Caucasians of European descent are most prone to making this mistake, because many of us come from traditions bereft of powerful ceremony. But the very vacuum we feel is nourishment to the soul; with patience and humility, the soul will fill that vacuum with an authentic expression of itself.

The young people I work with begin thinking about ceremony by getting in touch with what matters most. This usually leads us directly to a discussion of food: What will we eat at this ceremony? One group asked their parents to bring their favorite food from childhood—our buffet table was filled with macaroni and cheese, Twinkies, and canned spaghetti. Another group baked a cake for their parents because they wanted to say, "No longer are we only in need of feeding by you; now we can also feed you." They wrote words on the cake in icing that represented traits they felt they would need as adults, such as courage, wisdom, and patience. As they passed the pieces of cake around, anyone could take a bite from any piece, as long as they were willing to tell the group why they wished for this trait in their lives. Both the young people and their parents were willing to speak movingly of what they needed along life's journey.

It is crucial for parents to witness this ceremony of passage and to sanction the change. The passage must be acknowledged by members of the older generation, for it is they who must accept the new status of the young person in their midst. This is a process of incorporation, of bonding the soul's youthful energy to the needs of the community. In the process of a rite of passage, a common ground of experience reveals itself, linking what once seemed two distant generations. This is an occasion for storytelling, for sharing experiences. Young people are not always fond of advice, but they relish hearing about the exploits of their parents' teenage years: the mistakes made in the way their parents rebelled against authority, the insights that got them through the tough times.

The key for those who wish to engage adolescents deeply and effectively is to remember those times. There is a great deal to the modern adolescent's soul journey that is unique to this generation: AIDS, the information explosion, the oversaturation of our senses by external media, and violence directed at one another and our planet, to name just a few examples. But much more is timeless, experienced by each generation. Compassion—the willingness to be present and to suffer with others—is an astonishingly potent healing force, and compassion springs from shared stories. The bridge between childhood and adulthood may have fallen into disrepair, but the soul still calls. The passage must be made. It remains for us to rebuild that bridge, so that the soul of the young can renew us all.

Chapter 21

From Aging to Sage-ing:
Restoring the Soul of Eldering

ZALMAN SCHACHTER-SHALOMI

In a culture that worships youth and treats aging as if it were a disease, the voice of Zalman Schachter-Shalomi provides a much-needed perspective. An ordained rabbi, Schachter-Shalomi is dedicated to exploring and recovering ways in which we can expand our spiritual awareness to match our life span. In 1989 he founded the Spiritual Eldering Institute, a Philadelphia-based organization that offers workshops and seminars all over the country in which people explore the challenges and opportunities of mid to late life. Schachter-Shalomi is the author of many books, including From Aging to Sage-ing: A Profound New Vision of Growing Old *(1995), which he coauthored with Ron Miller.*

Schachter-Shalomi is also interested in exploring the links between various religious disciplines. While at the forefront of the Jewish Spiritual Renewal movement, he has also entered into dialogue with Sufi masters, Native American elders, Catholic monks, and Buddhist teachers, as well as transpersonal psychologists. Drawing on the wisdom of these diverse disciplines, he has constructed a vision of aging that can benefit all generations by restoring dignity and passion to the aging process and allowing young people the benefit of good mentoring.

Many people talk about the benefits of an extended life span, about how lucky we are, at this time in history, to have the blessing of living longer than any of our ancestors. But to have an extended life span without an extended awareness of what it means to live a life isn't really a blessing at all. Who wants to hang around in a body that is constantly being diminished? For someone my age, every day brings with it a little decrease in my physical powers, a little bit less that I can do. So I might ask myself, am I really experiencing an extended life span, or am I just prolonging my dying?

In order to experience an extended life span full of awareness, consciousness, and blessing, we need to have models for getting older. Right now, we have models for many of the earlier parts of our lives but not for our elder years. If you think of a full year, with all its seasons, as a metaphor for a lifetime, you can see that we have models for those parts of our lives that correspond to the end of winter, the spring, and the summer, but very few for how to get through the fall and back to winter again.

If we say that every seven years is equivalent to one month, by the time we are seven years old, we have finished January; our second teeth start coming in, and we're ready for the next phase. February takes us through the beginning of puberty, up to the time of bar mitzvah or bat mitzvah. March, the beginning of spring, is equivalent to the years from fifteen to twenty-one; you're moving into adulthood during those years. Between April and May, you're beginning to find your role as an adult, to define it a bit more for yourself. By the time you get to June, you are expected to have a sense of yourself as an adult in the world so that in July, August, and September—which takes you from forty-two to sixty-three—you can participate in the summertime of life, when you do the work that you have prepared yourself to do.

In this culture, we have role models for every phase up to this, but when we reach October, November, and December we don't have any models. That leaves us with a predicament—how do I groom myself, whom do I emulate, when the fall and winter arrive? All the pictures of aging I am presented with in this culture are pictures of decrepitude or ineptitude—pictures of people who can't do what they used to do. On the one hand, I'm expected to be wise; on the other, as I look around, the only models I see are of breakdown. This is why it is so important to create another model.

Models are necessary for a number of reasons, but one of the most important is to help us with our fears. When I talk to women who have participated in home birth—those who rejected the "let the doctor handle it and knock me out so I shouldn't feel anything about the labor" approach—many of them tell me that it was crucial to have someone there who had already been through the process, who could tell them what they might expect and what they should do about it. If we have that, then we can prevent our fears from turning into panic. If someone can tell us what we are likely to encounter and how we might handle it, then what seems like a terrifying process becomes accessible and replicable; we can do it again, and we can show somebody else how to do it as well.

My work is to show people what they can expect about growing older. I talk about what is expectable and normal in those fall and winter months. I also talk about how the physical diminishment that accompanies aging doesn't mean the rest is going bad—we have other parts to our organism, and when we jettison the physical, we still have more life available to us in other realms. If we learn to transfer our attention from the physical realm to the inner spiritual realm, then when the physical drops away, we have another plane to work on. That is attending to the soul of eldering.

It seems to me that there are two main tasks to approaching eldering from a soulful perspective. One is to leave something good behind for the next generation; the other is to make a finale that is right for us. We have the opportunity now to create a template for growth into the elder years that includes both these tasks, an opportunity that was never available before this period in history.

One thing we might want to do in order to leave something good for the generations after us is to take care of the karmic pollution we've caused in our lifetime. If anyone tells me they've never caused any karmic pollution, I don't believe it. There are so many choices in a given lifetime that no matter how careful you are, at some point you've done something wrong.

And that in itself is fine. We are here to learn, and the way most of us learn is by making mistakes. One problem with our school system is that it is built to educate us through the transfer of information, which is not how we learn best. We don't give kids enough of a chance to make controlled mistakes and to learn from them. This carries over into how we view our own mistakes as adults. Often, we have a hard time seeing them as learning situations, as opportunities to clean up our karma so that when it comes time for us to leave this life we can be satisfied with what we leave behind.

If you believe in reincarnation, then you believe that whatever you leave behind this time, you will still have to face the next time you come around. If you don't believe in reincarnation, you might look at this as a sense of tradition. Tradition is not something put on my shoulder that I have to drag for a lifetime. Tradition is what was left behind by the last generation so that the next generation doesn't have to start from scratch, reinventing everything for itself.

For example, imagine that a man has made a lot of money, and it is his time to die. He goes to Switzerland, opens a numbered bank account, and tells the bank officer, "I want you to invest this money very carefully, very conservatively. Several years from now, someone will come to you with a certain code. When he does, give him the money, don't ask questions."

So the money is invested very carefully and conservatively, and finally the time comes when the person with the right code comes to Switzerland to get the money. If you believe in reincarnation, then it is still the same person who made the money to start with; if you don't, you can look at that person as the next generation, the inheritors. In any case, this person asks for his money and gives the correct code. When the bank officer hands it over, he asks, "What are you going to do with it?" The man says, "I'm going to invest it in very risky ventures."

This is the business of tradition and renewal in every generation. One generation will do something very conservative in order to protect and even increase their resources. Then there will always be mavericks who come along, like Matthew Fox, the former Dominican priest, to whom many people say, "Hey, what are you doing to tradition?" And he responds, "I'm going to take all kinds of risks. This is the time to invest in new ventures."

When we can accept that life is a cycle and that this is a learning place, we can let go of many of the negative assumptions, the pollution, that we leave behind for our children. Civilization is the deposit of what we have learned in the past. It is what we leave behind so that the next generation doesn't have to start from scratch. Unfortunately, we are better with this concept in some areas than in others. One area in which we fail is sexual education; there, each generation seems to have to figure out everything for itself. In everything else, my papa was able to show me how to be a man; in that area, we couldn't even talk to each other. It's a pity that we haven't yet learned how to spiritualize our sexuality in order to be able to transmit to the next generation a way of loving that is sacred, that honors the earth and our lives and one another.

That is one of the big jobs of eldering—to leave something behind that is positive for the next generation. The other is to make a finale that is right for us. Part of that has to do with watching the processes that we go through and not expecting ourselves to think or feel in the same ways that we did when we were younger. For example, as I started to look at myself as an aging person, I learned that something had changed. When I was younger—and especially as a teenager—I was always troubled if I had to be at home on Saturday night. It seemed to me that alone meant lonely. But now, when I come home and I don't see any blinking lights on the telephone answering machine, and I have no place to go and nothing to do, it feels good. Now alone means solitude, and there is a big difference between loneliness and solitude.

One of the rewards of eldering can be solitude: having time to talk to yourself. When we're younger, so much of our concern has to do with what is going on outside of us. Think, for example, of what it means to be a mother, how there is always someone tugging at you. Often, in a very active life, when you're exerting yourself too much, living too much on the outside, your only chance to rest is when you get sick. You get a headache or a cold—the body saying, "Could I have a little solitude? Could I have a little time to be with myself? Could I have a chance to figure out where I am on the journey of my life?" It often takes being lifted out of the traffic of life to be able to have some time for reflection. Again, as we grow older, our bodies lead us to this. Often the natural tendency of elders is to be silent and watch.

One of the important ways that we go about making a finale is to bear witness to the next generation's activities. That is how a traditional council of elders works. You don't have to do anything else but to hold the field—to keep your intentions clear and to bear witness. Because we live in a youth-oriented culture, often that kind of still watching isn't valued—it doesn't yet have a niche, and again, we have no models for it. The models we admire now tend to be the ones who do the opposite— who "die in the saddle." People admire, for example, Malcolm Forbes, the millionaire who rode his motorcycle until the day he dropped dead. We want our elders to continue to work too hard, to have sexual conquests, to demonstrate that they're still virile people instead of allowing them to be wise people. So we need to create a social template that will encourage and allow for wisdom.

Unfortunately, we value information, but not wisdom. Information is something we can measure, but wisdom—Where does it come from? How do you get it? If we say that wisdom comes from good judgment, that still leaves us with the question of where good judgment comes from. It seems to me that good judgment comes from experience, which comes from bad judgment. In other words, wisdom comes from all the mistakes that we have made. Part of being able to make a good finale in your life is to accept that your mistakes have given you the wisdom you have now. Wisdom comes from garnering, reconstructing, and reconfiguring what we have done in order to use the information we have gotten from the mistakes we have made. This is how we harvest a lifetime.

Many people, when they look back over their lifetime, only see the mistakes and not the wisdom gained from them. They see failures in business, in marriage, in relationships with their children. Then they just want to stop looking. If the past were a filing cabinet, for most people, it would be divided like this: good memories, maybe two drawers; bad memories, a whole wall full.

We don't want to look at these bad memories. We are repelled by the anxiety of opening up those drawers. Imagine, though, that in those files, there are actually stocks and bonds that have matured. While we've kept them in the failure box, they have matured. We don't even know how rich we are, because we don't dare open up those files, pull out those old, bad memories, and look at what we learned from them, how they contributed to our being who we are.

Part of the eldering work is to be able to open up those files. Another has to do with dealing with the present, which can be very hard. In the present I might have trouble with my prostate, my digestion, my blood pressure, or my sight. When I stay conscious of all these losses, the burden might feel too great. So I shut down consciousness to the present, which leads to time disorientation.

As elders, we need to recontextualize the past and hold with the present in such a way that what we see are opportunities, not limitations and failures. In this way, we can embrace the future, too. There can be a wonderful liberation that comes at this point in life—a friend of mine said to me recently, "I'm now seventy years old and I don't owe anyone anything anymore. The rest of my life I can just owe to myself." Often, elders can take the opportunity to read or study something they never had a chance to. I know many people who grew up during the Depression and didn't get a chance at the education they wanted; now, in their elder years, they can pursue the things they always wanted to learn. How wonderful that is!

Sometimes, when we look back at the things we didn't get a chance to do, we feel the pain of unlived life so deeply that it's too heavy to bear. But if you allow yourself to look at those things you didn't get a chance to do, you might decide to take some chances and have some fun. For example, a couple of years ago, when I was in Rio de Janeiro, I saw that there were hang gliders jumping off beautiful, very tall mountains right by the ocean. I've always envied Clark Kent, always wanted to be able to fly myself. So I took a hang glider run. I didn't fly it myself; there was a pilot, someone who was running the thing. But the time I spent in that wonderful contraption—with no floor and nothing around me but the wind—was amazing. It felt so good to be able to say, "What have I got to lose?" In this business of giving ear to the unlived life, there waits such deep satisfaction because the hungers have been so great. When a person gets to fulfill that which has been delayed so long—how wonderful that is.

We need to remember that an elder is still in pursuit of happiness, joy, and pleasure. A man told me about his elderly mother, who got married, after a very short engagement, and didn't want to tell her children about her plans because she was afraid of their reaction. So often, the attitude is, "Come on, Mom, you shouldn't be doing this," as if after a certain point, people shouldn't want to have pleasure, to act spontaneously anymore. But it is so important to open up a place where the unlived life can be lived. I've often thought that this would be a good use for the computer technology known as virtual reality. Can you imagine a home for the aged where everybody can have his or her unlived life through virtual reality?

If we start to reexamine elderhood, one of the first things that will have to be reformed is our approach to homes for the elderly. An elder is a person. That seems an elementary statement, but when we take a look at how we care for the elderly in this country, I see very little respect for the individual person; so often, what we have is a form of warehousing, a kind of custodial work. We in the United States have managed very well—better than any other place I know in the world, at this point—to give our elders comfortable physical environments with modern medical technology available, but we have robbed them of their personhood. They have now become objects so that the people who work with them can handle them more easily.

For example, let's say a couple moves into an elder-care facility; as the life expectancy of the woman is usually greater than that of the man, he dies first. She is physically in pretty good shape, and she'd love to cook in the kitchen, which would bring her pleasure, but they don't let her. It would be inconvenient; it doesn't suit the way the institution is run. In the institutionalization, she has become an un-person. Sometimes there seems to be hardly any difference between jail and an old-age home. We need to insist that an elder is a person.

We need to remember that an elder is still growing. The notion is that because there is physical diminishment going on, there is no growth at all. But elders are still learners. Think, for example, of the last reconciliation that Elisabeth Kübler-Ross talks about in her work on death—that final "yea-saying" or acceptance of the end. That's still part of growth; we learn how to do that. It has to do with our potential, our power for learning, which is present up until the very last moment.

One way that we can help our elders experience that power for learning is to find ways to talk with them about the processes they are going through. For example, there came a time when I wanted to talk to my dad about his plans for his own death and funeral. Every time I started that conversation, I got into trouble. The message I got from him was, "Back off, I don't want to talk about that. What's the matter, you can't wait for me to die?" It was as if he felt that, by talking about it, we might hurry the process up.

One day I said to him, "You know, I have made some plans for my own death. What do you think about them?" I invited him to enter into the conversation about where my own remains might go, that sort of thing, and then it was so much easier for him to tell me about his own plans. It is so important for us to be able to talk, generation to generation, about these things. If we can't help one another to walk into that unknown place, into death, then we cut people off from their elderhood. We have to be able to look at the end of December, to face that phase with consciousness and enthusiasm for the lessons still to be learned.

The work of spiritual eldering cannot be done by people who are fleeing their mortality. The most important part of the work that we have to do in order to create a new model for eldering is to come to terms with our mortality. Every once in a while I read an article about a new scientific development designed to keep people from ever having to die. I don't want to quarrel with such efforts—let them try whatever it is they want to try. But there are other kinds of immortality that seem to me to be much more worthwhile. All of the molecules that make up my body are going to get recycled. Maybe someday they will actually be a part of another human being; certainly, they will be at some point a part of a plant. That's not so bad.

And there are other ways that we can pass something along that will live after us. A young friend of mine was telling me that when he goes to visit his mother now, he brings a tape recorder; he is using it to record an oral history of her life and the family's life. He was not sure, at first, how she would take this, but it has brought her great joy and delight. Now she often says, could you bring the tape recorder again? Knowing that someone is listening with a tape recorder means that it doesn't go into one ear and out the other; it means that what is being said has value, that it won't be lost.

The moment that an elder can look in the mirror comfortably—without any desire for a face-lift, any turning back of the clock—is a precious moment. The work to create new models of eldering is all about being able to create that moment in every elder person's life. We need to celebrate that time when what has been ripening in us throughout our lives can be embraced and loved. We need to make a space for the soul of eldering to flourish.

Chapter 22

The Journey Home

ELAINE PREVALLET

Elaine Prevallet, a Catholic Sister of Loretto, directs Knobs Haven Retreat Center in Nerinx, Kentucky. She has a Ph.D. in religious studies and has taught at the college level as well as on the staff of Pendle Hill, a Quaker educational center in Wallingford, Pennsylvania.

In her essay, she discusses the metaphors of journey and home in relation to living a spiritual life. She explores their gender associations, the need to pair the two for balance, and the paradox that sometimes the journey is home.

Much in our world today suggests that home is being threatened. More and more people are becoming, if not physically then culturally, homeless. Three years ago there were 17 million refugees around the world. These numbers are increasing as national boundaries continue to shift and create cultural instability across the globe.

In our own society, traditional institutions—the family, educational and medical systems, government, and church—are breaking down. These cultural "containers" that once protected us are becoming increasingly inadequate to the task. We are at sea in the technologies of bioethics and the machinery of war. We do not have national consensus on what's right and wrong in the critical areas of life and death. The larger collective that once grounded us in shared beliefs and values no longer does so.

Additionally, just when we collectively recognized that earth is our home, we also realized that the planet is no longer a safe place to live. There isn't anyplace on earth safe from nuclear radiation, acid rain, or pollution. There are no shelters or sanctuaries where a person can escape environmental problems. Thus, we lack a sense of safety and security that ideally home would provide.

It isn't surprising, therefore, that a longing for the safety of home is emerging. In fact, precisely because of societal and global breakdown, the archetype that we identify as "home" calls to us more strongly, urging us to deepen our interior grounding, to find our *inner* home. When safety, security, and groundedness disappear from our outer world, we need more desperately to find it within.

The word *home* conveys a sense of safety and freedom; of love and comfort; of familiarity, security, and peace. *Home* speaks to the deep desires of our hearts to belong, to be at rest. Home, as we imagine it, is where it is safe to be who we are, without any need to pretend. At home, we can be unselfconsciously ourselves and know we are accepted. We don't have to dress up; we can let our hair down.

We need to recognize, however, that there is often a discrepancy between our idealized notion and the reality of home. Homes are often not safe places; many are less than idyllic. We need to recognize that "home" operates as an ideal or archetype.

In the Christian tradition, for example, home can represent an image of hope, a longing for paradise. A deep and seemingly universal sense that something is wrong with the world, or with us in our human condition, impels us to seek our place of true belonging, our home. A familiar hymn sings of a home beyond this earthly one of ours, where all wrongs will be made right: "Jerusalem our happy home, when shall we come to thee? When shall our sorrows come to an end? Thy joys, when shall we see?"

A passage from *A Course in Miracles* also reflects this view: "We speak for everyone who walks this world, for he is not at home. He goes uncertainly about in an endless search, seeking in darkness what he cannot find, not recognizing what it is he seeks. A thousand homes he makes, yet none contents his restless mind. He does not understand. He builds in vain. The home he seeks cannot be built by him." In contrast, then, to the wrongness, lostness, or restlessness that humans often experience, the image of home gives us a glimpse of what our hearts long for: a place of acceptance, contentment, and peace. A. A. Milne depicts this longing in an episode in *The House at Pooh Corner.** Pooh, Piglet, and Rabbit have gotten lost in the forest. Rabbit, who is playing a nasty trick, gets caught in his own devices:

"The fact is," said Rabbit, "we've missed our way somehow."

They were having a rest in a small sand-pit on the top of the Forest. Pooh was getting rather tired of that sand-pit, and suspected it of following them about, because whichever direction they started in, they always ended up at it. . . .

"Well," said Rabbit, after a long silence in which nobody thanked him for the nice walk they were having, "we'd better get on, I suppose. Which way shall we try?"

"How would it be," said Pooh slowly, "if, as soon as we're out of sight of this Pit, we try to find it again."

"What's the good of that?" said Rabbit.

"Well," said Pooh, "we keep looking for home and not finding it, so I thought if we looked for this pit, we'd be sure not to
find it, which would be a Good Thing, because then we might
find something we weren't looking for, which might be just
what we were looking for, really."

"I don't see much sense in that," said Rabbit.

"No," said Pooh humbly. "There was going to be when I
began it. It's just that something happened to it on the way."

"If I walked away from this Pit, and then walked back to it,
of course I should find it."

"Well, I thought perhaps you wouldn't," said Pooh. "I just
thought."

"Try," said Piglet suddenly. "We'll wait here for you."

Rabbit gave a laugh to show how silly Piglet was, and
walked into the mist. After he had gone a hundred yards, he
turned and walked back again . . . and after Pooh and Piglet
had waited 20 minutes for him, Pooh got up.

"I just thought." said Pooh. "Now then, Piglet, let's go
home."

"But, Pooh," cried Piglet, all excited, "do you know the
way?"

"No." said Pooh. "But there are 12 pots of honey in my cup-
board, and they've been calling to me for hours. I couldn't hear
them properly before because Rabbit would talk, but if nobody
says anything except those 12 pots, I think, Piglet, I shall know
where they're calling from. Come on."

Each of us has the equivalent of Pooh's twelve pots of honey that is
our heart's desire; if we are quiet, we can hear it calling us home. In this
sense, home is a metaphor for love in located form, love embodied in place,
love incarnate. We are made for love, and it's love that's calling us home.

But we can't discuss the metaphor of home apart from its companion metaphor, that of journey. In a 1989 article in *Soundings*, Sharon
Parks describes the metaphors of journey and home as "two great
yearnings": for autonomy and agency, and for belonging and commu-

nion. She suggests that these metaphors correspond to what has been identified psychologically as masculine and feminine: the masculine need for separation and differentiation, and the feminine tendency toward attachment and relationship. She believes that they were once used together but in the last two hundred years were separated by the masculinization of our culture. Women, and the wisdom of their experience, have been relegated to the private sphere of home, while the public sphere has been the domain of the male. Journey, connoting as it does movement, going out, relating to an external and unfamiliar world, connects with the masculine. Home connects with the personal, the familiar, with abiding and belonging, which we typically (correctly or not) associate with the feminine.

Perhaps because of our pioneer heritage, movement seems to be our American cultural preference; for example, we commonly use the metaphor of spiritual journey. Of the two metaphors, journey and home, journey is clearly the one that captures the popular imagination. Indeed, the metaphor of journey is essential to spiritual *development*, speaking as it does to the adventure, risk, dynamism, and movement, the letting-go and moving-on that characterize the life of the Spirit.

But adventure and risk, like everything else, can be ambiguous in terms of their spiritual value; we need to critique the sense of adventure if it is to be integrated into spiritual life. For instance, some of the men who fought in the Persian Gulf spoke of that experience as an adventure that was the high point of their lives. War provides a heroic feeling, a rush of adrenaline, that men have valued through the centuries. In a 1984 *Esquire* article, William Broyles wrote, "War may be the only way in which most men touch the mythic dimensions of their soul. It is, for men, at some terrible level, the closest thing to what childbirth is for women—the initiation into the power of life and death." We need to question, however, whether the experience of war serves life and is of value to the Spirit.

Pregnancy, to follow Broyles's analogy, does carry with it a sense of risk. Women face loss and subsequent grief when pregnancies are miscarried or aborted, when a child is stillborn or deformed. Sometimes pregnancy even threatens the life of the mother. But the risk is clearly in the service of life.

As a culture, we are out of touch with the feminine in our experience, which, according to Sharon Parks, corresponds to the metaphor of
home. We have forgotten that our first experience of home was the
womb. In 1991, as background for her dissertation at Southern Baptist
Theological Seminary, Leslie Smith Kendrick asked a group of women
to reflect on their experiences of pregnancy, breastfeeding, and men-
struation in order to discover how these experiences yielded feminine
intimations of God's presence in their lives. One woman characterized
womb space as safe space, an environment in which we are fed without
any effort on our part. Another described pregnancy as "the sacred
space within which the mystery unfolds." These are astonishingly apt
descriptions of the ideal sense of home.

Biblical tradition, too, has neglected feminine imagery. In the
Hebrew Bible, one of the verbs used for God's love *(rachem)* is, in its
cognate form, the word for "uterus" or "womb" *(rechem)*. The word is
often used to refer to God's compassion for the people, and it evokes the
visceral passion of a mother for her child: womb love. But the feminine
sense of the word has disappeared. God is seen as male, and God's compassion is a father's compassion.

Yet our experience of God's love can be likened to womb love, a
space in which we are fed in ways we're not conscious of. Such a
metaphor can also help connect us to our embodiedness in our earth
home: God's love, in which we live, move, and have our being, can be
compared to the air we breathe while being totally unaware of the complex biological processes by which it sustains us. God's love is like the
ground we stand on, reminding us that we depend on the millions of mi-
croorganisms reproducing and decomposing in the soil, or like the
water of the planet that is in our bodies as well as in the rivers and
oceans. Womb love makes us conscious of the natural environment as
"the sacred space within which the mystery unfolds."

In the Christian tradition, the Gospel of John carries the theme of
home to a profound spiritual level. Using the Greek verb *menein* (to
abide, dwell, be at home), John writes that God dwells in Jesus and
Jesus in God in deep, mutual love. Jesus promises that he and God will
come and make a home in us. That in-dwelling or at-homeness is the

deepest truth of our being. God's love, finding a home in us, frees us to be our truest selves.

However, if God is to make a home in us, we must provide for God a place where God can be God, where God's own being will not be violated. In the same way that home is sometimes unsafe for children because parents try to make the children into their own image, want the children to turn out a certain way without respecting who they actually are, so our home space can be "unsafe" for God if we try to make God into our own image and refuse to let God be God in our lives. Meditation on John's Gospel suggests that only when God is free to be God in us are we truly who we are. That is an extraordinary idea: that God wants to find a home in us and that we are truly who we are only when God is truly being God in us.

Love's calling within us to come home is a call to dedicate ourselves to the process of becoming true. But the love that is the truth of our being also connects us with others. We know, not only from theological images such as the body of Christ but also from physics, that everything is connected to everything else. Thus, we find our truth only in unity with all that is. Far from being an isolated, private, and comfortably individual affair, then, *home* will not let us rest content as long as there are persons suffering from homelessness in the outer world. As long as there is suffering, evil, or oppression, love will push us to compassionate action. And so home and journey operate in a dialectic of rest and motion.

Both metaphors, journey and home, have strengths and weaknesses. The value of the metaphor of journey lies in its capacity to keep us aware of movement, development, and change. These are essential to life, including spiritual life. But journey can feed the illusion that someone somewhere else, some teacher or some holy ground, will open up the holy ground within. People journey great distances—to Tibet, India, Machu Picchu—to gain access to their own holy inner ground. Sometimes a new place in the outer world does in fact open up a new inner space or awareness; outer landscapes can put us in touch with our soulscapes. Outer journey can deepen and even radicalize the inner journey. But it can also be an escape or diversion. The metaphor of journey risks exacerbating the tendency of our extroverted culture to always look to the outer world for solutions or diversions, which only alienate us more from our inner lives. Journeying by moving in the external sense can increase our already epidemic sense of rootlessness and our loss of a sense of place.

Further, if we connect the notion of journey with excitement, adventure, action, and thrills, then the metaphor may mislead us. The inner journey is often not exciting, and, in fact, we can get discouraged if we expect it always to be so. If we connect "journey" with making progress, arriving somewhere, and reaching a goal, again we will find it disappointing. The disciplines we practice as part of our spiritual path are a good case in point. We begin doing them with a good deal of enthusiasm, hopeful that they will be means for us to progress to our goal.

I remember that, as novices, we were given a way to chart our journey of improvement. We each had "conscience beads"—a string of beads worn under our capes where no one could see them. Each of us picked a virtue that we were going to develop or a vice that we were going to weed out. Twice each day, we checked whether we had performed the virtue or avoided the vice. If successful, we pulled a little bead down and recorded it in a notebook. We were measuring our inner progress.

Disciplines such as these can indeed help us begin to put ourselves at the disposal of God's will. To use Jung's terms, they can help the ego learn how to serve the Self. In this regard, progress seems measurable early on. But after a while, it becomes clear that spiritual growth is less under our control than we had imagined. We have to let go of the desire to get somewhere, because the truth is that we no longer know where we want to go. "Really, we are all travelers, only we don't know where we're going," says one of the characters in the film *Into the West*. That is true for the spiritual path. We may not have a sense of getting closer to God, because the closer we get, the more the mystery deepens. We continue the disciplines not because we have ecstatic experiences, and not even because we see that the disciplines are making us better and better. We do them because we have a deep sense that they are integral to our lives. We don't grade ourselves; we simply do them, without trying to measure our progress. We rely on an inner compass to keep us on track, even though the destination becomes increasingly difficult to articulate.

While the metaphor of journey is vulnerable to the expectation that there should always be excitement and progress in both inner and outer life, the metaphor of home has its weakness as well. Home sounds suspiciously like stagnation, like a refusal to grow; it sounds private, comfortable, turned in on itself, quiescent.

Again, all metaphors have limitations. When two metaphors that are intended to be complementary are separated, the negative dimensions of each manifest themselves. If metaphors are to be life-giving, if they are to be useful and to yield their truth in our lives, we need to be attentive to how they change as our lives change. For example, the metaphor of journey may be more useful in early life when development is a conscious goal, when progress enlists our energies and efforts. Home may be more useful in later life, when our own progress is less visible to us, less a matter of conscious effort to improve. At all points, however, the metaphors need to be held together. Most of our lives we move between metaphors. But when we are living most deeply, the journey *is* home.

For example, midlife can be a painful time when one undergoes major changes and has to leave behind skills and values that served one well earlier on. But midlife integration, when it happens, often feels like coming home to oneself. At home, we know who we are, and we know our foibles and idiosyncrasies. We don't have to prove ourselves, even to ourselves. We have lived long enough to accept ourselves and be comfortable with our strengths and our limitations. Midlife, at its best, becomes a time when we know ourselves and we're at home with ourselves in a comfortable kind of inner space.

In his essay "The Integration of Personality," Jung writes, "Personality is the supreme realization of the idiosyncrasy of a living being. It is . . . the absolute affirmation of all that constitutes the individual, the most successful adaptation of the universal conditions of existence coupled with the greatest possible freedom for self-determination." Innate idiosyncrasy means true individuality. It is not in any way like the experimentation of a rebelling teenager who tries on various faces in order to find her or his own style. Rather, idiosyncrasy is unselfconscious freedom and simple being, flowing from within. Unselfconsciousness is a great freedom—the freedom of comfortably belonging in our bodies, and of being at home in the love that is the deepest dimension of our lives.

Idiosyncrasy means individuality, but it does not mean independence. The sense of home, or belonging, means that we know we exist in interdependence with everything that is. The more we are one with ourselves, the more we are one with everything else. Love is the truth of our being: it is less like the passion of falling in love and more like a steadiness of will or a deep intentionality that moves us each along our own individual path, drawing us irresistibly into unity as we go.

Home does not in any sense imply inactivity. As natural as fruit is to the vine, so too are sensitivity and compassionate action in response to injustice, oppression, and deception. As organic as the instinct to grow, so too is the instinct to move toward truth, to shed pretense, to share one's energies, to utilize one's gifts, to serve others' needs. Love keeps us in ever-renewing awareness of how united we are with all that is. As precious, uneventful, and indescribable as the being-with that we enjoy with someone we love, so too is the God-life within us. Home and journey are united; we journey without ever leaving home.

Home is the ground of our being where God's love encompasses and envelops us; little by little, it opens us to recognize our unity with all that is. We belong in unity. We are made for truth and love; truth and love mean oneness with each other and with God. Home is an inner magnet; it is God, drawing us deeper into a life of love.

Chapter 23

Restoring the Soul of Politics

JIM WALLIS

For Jim Wallis, religious commitment and political activism go hand in hand. He is the founder of Sojourners, an ecumenical Christian community based in Washington, D.C., as well as the editor of Sojourners magazine, in which political, social, and economic issues are examined from a spiritual and theological perspective. A preacher and activist, Wallis was the first chairperson of the Witness for Peace Advisory Committee, which traveled to Nicaragua to observe, document, and work to change injustices there, and was an originator of the Nuclear Weapons Freeze Campaign.

Wallis writes as he preaches—with urgency, commitment, and conviction. In addition to his regular column for Sojourners, *he is the author of several books, including* The Soul of Politics *(1994). The material in his essay originally appeared, in a slightly different form, in that book.*

The world isn't working. Things are unraveling, and most of us know it.

Bonds of family and community are fraying. Our most basic virtues of civility, responsibility, justice, and integrity seem to be collapsing. We appear to be losing the ethics derived from personal commitment, social purpose, and spiritual meaning. The triumph of materialism is hardly questioned now in any part of our society. Both domestically and globally, we are divided along the lines of race, ethnicity, class, gender, religion, culture, and tribe, and environmental degradation and resource scarcity threaten to explode our divisions into a world of perpetual conflict.

Our intuition tells us that the depth of the crisis we face demands more than politics as usual. An illness of the spirit has spread across the land, and our greatest need is for what our religious traditions call "the healing of the nations." The fundamental character of the social, economic, and cultural renewal we urgently need will require a change of both our hearts and our minds. But that change will demand a new kind of politics—a politics with spiritual values.

Several decades ago, Mohandas K. Gandhi warned against what he called the seven social sins. He named them as politics without principle, wealth without work, commerce without morality, pleasure without conscience, education without character, science without humanity, and worship without sacrifice. These social sins today provide an apt description of our leading institutions and cultural patterns; they are the accepted practices of the life of the nation.

Several thousand years ago, the writer of the Proverbs warned, "Where there is no vision, the people perish." That ancient warning also applies to our contemporary situation. Without a vision, we are indeed perishing. From the violent carnage of our inner cities to the empty consumerism of our shopping malls, from our shantytowns to our stock exchanges, from the muffled cries of our children in poverty to our twenty-second media sound bites, from our toxic wastes to our time wasted watching television, from our religion of entertainment to our entertainments of religion, from all the substances we abuse to the economic and political institutions that abuse us—we are a society that has lost its way.

During the American election year of 1992, public television's Bill Moyers commented that none of the candidates had adequately spoken a "language that evokes the common bond of a diverse people." Moyers believes the American people have a desire to transcend the old paradigms of politics, "a deep yearning to go beyond Left and Right, to go beyond the nostrums of both the conservative and the liberal movements as they have been manifest in our time." The old political categories we have known are almost completely dysfunctional now. Ideologies and policies of liberal and conservative, Left and Right, have run their course and come to a dead end.

Liberalism is unable to articulate or demonstrate the kind of moral values that must undergird any serious movement of social transformation. The critical link between personal responsibility and societal change is missing on the Left. Conservatism still denies the reality of structural injustice and social oppression. To call for individual self-improvement and a return to family values while ignoring the pernicious effects of poverty, racism, and sexism is to continue blaming the victim.

We can find common ground only by moving to higher ground. Constituency-based politics, with its factional interests, will not lead us to this higher ground. Politics has been reduced to the struggle for power among competing interests and groups, instead of a process of searching for the common good.

The U.S. Census Bureau tells us that more people are now in poverty than at any time in the last three decades, and that 40 percent of the poor are children. Close to half of black and Hispanic children live in poverty, while in the wider society 10 percent of U.S. households own almost 70 percent of the nation's wealth. These are profound realities if we are to take our religious traditions seriously. But the poor are not a political issue when both conservative and liberal politicians merely compete for the votes of middle-class suburban dwellers.

A vision of politics must be articulated that clarifies the essential moral issues at stake in any political discussion. Spiritual values must enter the public square. We are not calling here for the invasion of sectarian religion or theocratic grabs for power but rather for the contribution of neglected values to the political process. Most of us believe that institutional religion and the state must remain separate. But without values or moral conscience, our political life quickly degenerates into public corruption, cultural confusion, and social injustice.

Only a prophetic political morality has the capacity to transcend old ideological categories and forge new relationships and connections between people and issues. Out of these new configurations of moral concern will come the creative political initiatives we so desperately need.

Deep in the American soul exists the conviction that politics and morality are integrally related. But why do our efforts to connect them always feel like mixing oil and water? Today, many doubt that politics can be soulful. But others are already intuiting the need for a new kind of politics based on a renewed moral perspective.

We need a politics that offers us something we haven't had in a long time: a vision of transformation. Cornel West, an African American Christian intellectual, calls it the "politics of conversion." Jewish editor Michael Lerner describes a new "politics of meaning." Dare we aim for the conversion of politics itself? Dare we seek the soul of politics?

But the politics of power will never yield to the politics of values without fundamental change. The moral issues at the heart of the public debate are often unrecognized and ignored or, worse yet, manipulated and twisted for politically self-serving and ideological purposes.

We witness the spectacle each election year. Genuine moral discourse and discernment seem out of place in the media's political coverage and the endless polling of voters. When moral issues do come up, they tend to be narrowly defined and often become the basis for excluding others rather than opening doors to compassion and justice.

Political discussions around local or national elections reduce many citizens to a choice of the lesser of two evils or the temptation to withdraw altogether in support of hopeless nontraditional candidates. More often, the result is noninvolvement. Only half of us bother to vote anymore, and the level of real citizen participation, especially between elections, is alarmingly low for the health of political democracy. Instead of letting our values remove us from politics, perhaps it is time for us to trust those values and allow them to become a bridge, both to the majority of disaffected citizens and to the still-unmarked path to a morally sound political vision. We must broaden and deepen our definition of politics beyond "Republicans and Democrats." Many Americans today often find themselves with an unrepresented point of view on many issues, a political ethic not being articulated by the views of the opposing camps.

We long for political leaders who would be community builders, not polarizers; public servants who practice the art of bringing diverse peoples together for projects of common good, instead of power brokers who represent only those who have the most clout. Building consensus, creating common ground, and finding workable solutions to intractable problems are far more difficult tasks than endless ideological posturing and partisan attack.

It is possible to evoke in people a genuine desire to transcend selfish interests and respond to a larger vision that provides a sense of purpose, direction, meaning, and community. Real political leadership provides that very thing; it offers to lead people to where, in their best selves, they want to go.

Politics is the discourse of our public life. There are real limits to what politics can provide to better the human condition. But politics can make a great difference, for good and for evil, in the ways that we live together. Political leaders can appeal to people's best instincts (as when Martin Luther King Jr. proclaimed, "I have a dream") or manipulate their worst impulses (as when George Bush exploited the case of Willie Horton). Which values or fears are awakened or appealed to is, perhaps, the best moral test of politics and politicians.

But we must also expand our definition of political leaders to include more than elected officials. Those who could and should help shape a new political direction include teachers, farmers, poets, scientists, workers, entrepreneurs, union organizers, religious leaders, human rights activists, children's advocates, and representatives of grassroots movements and communities.

Daniel "Nane" Alejandrez, a barrio veteran, directs the Coalition to End Barrio Warfare, an organization active in over fifty cities across this country. At forty-four, Nane is the third oldest male remaining in an extended family of 250 people. He and his compañeros at Barrios Unidos are beginning a series of community-based economic development projects to provide alternatives to the drug traffic and to help strengthen local neighborhoods.

After a new wave of drive-by shootings against Latino families in Los Angeles, Fred Williams, an African American community leader, brought black young people along with him to stay overnight in the homes of Hispanic families. A clear message was sent, and the violence subsided.

Dr. Janelle Goetcheus and her family left their comfortable white middle-class existence to establish medical facilities in Washington, D.C., for homeless street people, undocumented immigrants from Latin America, and children. Her persistent advocacy for those with no health care has made her a thorn in the side of the medical establishment and has won her the distinction of being named Family Physician of the Year by the American Academy of Family Doctors.

Don Mosely and other members of Jubilee Partners have provided hospitality and assistance for almost two thousand war refugees making the transition to new lives. Traumatized Vietnamese boat people, Central Americans fleeing tyranny, and Bosnian Muslims escaping "ethnic cleansing" have all found an open hand and a welcoming community just outside the little southern Georgia town of Comer. An offshoot of Koinonia Farm's early experiment in racial reconciliation, Jubilee seeks to practice the ancient spiritual discipline of welcoming the stranger.

Eugene and Jackie Rivers, along with a corps of young black men and women from Harvard University, Massachusetts Institute of Technology, and other schools in Boston, have moved into drug-infested, violence-torn Dorchester to establish the Azusa Community—an African American congregation dedicated to reclaiming the street youths who have been abandoned by virtually everybody else.

Lucy Poulin and an intrepid group of Mainers have created a whole network of economic cooperatives, housing construction projects, and cottage industries in one of their state's poorest counties. In the tradition of Dorothy Day's Catholic Worker Movement, Home Coop has created a land trust, homeless shelters, organic gardens, a service center, and a welcoming community for the rural poor.

At our own Sojourners Neighborhood Center, twenty blocks from the White House, Nathan Jernigan, a Howard Divinity School graduate from the projects of Chicago, and Barbara Tamialis, from the suburbs of Detroit, codirect a program in which sixty African American young people are doing more than improving their reading, math, and other educational skills. They are becoming "freedom fighters," who are learning to remember their past, claim their present, and choose their future.

These men and women have learned that political morality grows from experience, from concrete human situations that need attention—homeless people, lack of health care, hungry children, a toxic environment, family breakdown, violence on our streets, domestic abuse, abandoned economies, violence against women, young people at risk, jobless parents, death from AIDS, international disregard for human rights, hate crimes, or the casualties of war—rather than from theoretical and ideological concerns.

They demonstrate that social change will be based upon reclaiming the values of personal responsibility, social compassion, and economic justice. New visions of community spirit, democratic participation, and political empowerment can transcend both liberal and conservative categories. Transforming individual character, social policy, and our physical environment is the key to change.

We should not place our trust exclusively in government programs or in appeals to personal self-improvement; neither can we rely merely on private volunteerism or public spending. Rather, we must generate a new moral and political will to change our lives and our communities. Both private and public support will be needed for the kind of community-based initiatives that empower individuals and families to change their own circumstances and their neighbors' well-being.

We begin not by searching for new macroeconomic systems to replace the ideological dinosaurs that have failed us. Instead, we start by subjecting all projects, initiatives, decisions, and policies to new

criteria: whether they make justice more possible for all of us and especially for those on the bottom; whether they allow us to live in har-
mony with the earth; and whether they increase the participation of
all people in decision making. In other words, we must learn to judge
our social and economic choices by whether they empower the power-
less, protect the earth, and foster true democracy.

All these criteria are derived from our best moral, religious, and political traditions and serve as examples of how our spirituality could
help shape a new social direction. Gandhi said that when you begin a
new project, "Recall the face of the poorest and most helpless [people]
whom you may have seen and ask yourself if the step you contemplate
will be of any use to [them]. Will [they] be able to gain anything by it?
Will it restore [them] to control over [their] own life and destiny?"

Regardless of our political backgrounds, we could agree that the political status quo is simply not acceptable. Too many people are not
making it and are being left behind. Neither the injustice built into our
social systems nor the irresponsibility they generate are tolerable any
longer. Controlling or abandoning the poor are not the only alternatives. Most of our religious traditions teach that justice is best understood as the establishment of right relationship among peoples,
communities, and the earth itself.

Additionally, the false choice between economy and environment is
suicidal, as is the failure to respect and value our racial and ethnic diversity. Encouraging a consistent ethic of life for both the unborn and
the already born might bring us together without criminalizing desperate choices and backing women into vulnerable and dangerous corners.
Changing the way we think about gender is the best way to make violence and discrimination against women unthinkable. We should know
by now that if we ignore the demands for human rights, peace, and a
healthy environment in other parts of our community, nation, or world,
we will ultimately jeopardize those same things for ourselves, because
our world is interconnected.

I believe that a prophetic politics rooted in moral principles could
again spark people's imagination and involvement. We need a personal
ethic of responsibility, a social vision based on bringing people together,

a commitment to justice with the capacity for reconciliation, an economic approach governed by the ethics of community and sustainability, a restored sense of our covenant with the abandoned poor and the damaged earth, a reminder of shared values that calls forth the very best in us, and a renewal of citizen politics to fashion a new political future. But to shape a new future we must first find the moral foundations and resources for a new social vision.

During the civil rights movement it was said that your perspective comes from what you see when you get out of bed in the morning. The things we see, hear, taste, smell, and touch each day determine our view of the world. More than things we've read or the ideas we've heard, it is our vantage point that most affects our social and political perspective.

For me, that perspective comes from waking up in one of the poorest and most violent neighborhoods of Washington, D.C. A popular slogan today is that you can't understand America and the world from "inside the beltway." That's only partly true. Indeed, the reality of this country cannot be understood from inside the offices of the Washington lobbyists, media pundits, and politicians who inhabit the corridors of power. What they wake up to in the morning are the busy schedules, sheltered lives, and privileged positions of those who fill the upper echelons of American decision making.

But just a few blocks away are neighborhoods like mine, where the realities of life provide a stark and revealing paradox to the wealth and power of official Washington. Here people wake up to a profoundly different reality. The contradiction between their view and the view from government halls provides the most revealing insights into the truth about this country and, indeed, the rest of the global economy. It is with this paradox in mind that we must work to build a soulful vision of politics.

Chapter 24

Making the Earth Whole Again

ROSEMARY RADFORD RUETHER

Rosemary Radford Ruether is one of the most respected and widely read feminist theologians in the Christian tradition or, indeed, in any tradition. When many other women have chosen to leave the Catholic Church, Ruether works instead to change it from within. Her analysis of sexist ideologies in Christianity and her prescriptions for change have had a profound influence on the work of countless other theologians and scholars.

Ruether teaches at Garrett Evangelical Seminary at Northwestern University in Evanston, Illinois. She is the author or editor of twenty-five books on theology and social justice, including New Woman, New Earth: Sexist Ideologies and Human Liberation *(1975), and* Gaia and God: An Ecofeminist Theology of Earth Healing *(1992).*

Ecofeminism brings together ecology and feminism. It explores, in a full, deep form, the way in which male domination of women is linked to our domination of nature. To understand ecofeminism, one must see that this connection between the domination of women and the domination of nature is not simply symbolic or metaphorical—as when we talk about virgin territory, for example—but deeply present in our social structures. This is not to say that the metaphors our culture uses for women and for nature have no impact, but that these metaphors point to a society structured so that the subordination of both women and land is considered appropriate.

Because of the profound effect that theology has had on the way we view women and the natural world, it has become very popular, in some ecofeminist literature, to name the Bible as the main source of the problem—to say, for example, that the Bible is the primary tool through which we legitimize systems of patriarchy and domination. There is some truth to that assessment, but it is too simplistic an analysis. There are, in fact, several stages to the development of the way in which Western society constructed our relationship with nature and with women and other subjugated people.

The roots of this construction are based in a social and economic system, developed between 3000 and 4000 B.C., that we can call patriarchy. What I mean here by patriarchy is not simply the subjugation of women—in fact, the subjugation of women came somewhat late in that development—but a system constructed by a priestly military and an aristocratic elite who owned all of the land and subjugated the rest of the people to serfdom or slavery. The development of a serf-and-slave-labor system ensured a monopoly on land and power for an elite group that became increasingly male as they disenfranchised women of their own class. This was done primarily through the male monopoly on tools of war and coercive violence, derived from the earlier male monopoly on weapons for hunting. It is not surprising that some of the earliest myths of creation describe the relationship of gods to humans as one of masters to slaves. Only gradually does the master-slave metaphor become clearly applied to relationships of male over female.

In the process of developing that pattern, various mythic, cultural, and religious structures had to develop in order to validate it. These structures supported the idea that both subjugated people and land are body rather than mind, objects rather than subjects, and that the male mind and sovereign power are separate from and better than the realm of earth and the feminine. One example of this is the Babylonian creation story, the *Enuma Elish*, which was reworked from earlier creation stories to celebrate and support the social order of the city of Babylonia. In this tale, the young warrior god Marduk slays Tiamat, an ancient mother goddess, who was thought to carry the forces of both creativity and chaos. Marduk meets her in hand-to-hand combat, kills her, cuts her in half, and orders the cosmos out of her dead body. That in itself is interesting: the model of creation is military killing, and what is created is made from matter that has been already rendered dead.

Then Marduk kills Tiamat's consort, Kingu, and fashions humans out of Kingu's blood mixed with clay. Marduk imposes servitude on the mortals he has created, in order to leave the gods free for leisure. The hierarchical pattern of thought reflected here developed gradually from the ancient Near East into Hebrew and Greek thought, and then was synthesized in Christianity.

However, within the Jewish and Christian traditions, there remains a residue of the sense of nature as, if not divine, at least sacramental— of being something that we don't have a right to exploit. Thus, rather than blaming biblical myths for the current destruction of the earth and oppression of women, we must look at the modern world, and at the ways in which our faith in science and technology contribute to a patriarchal, split view of the world.

Our contemporary myth, similar to that Babylonian creation story, is that the universe is a machine: dead matter in motion. In fact, our basic contemporary model of a relationship—with nature, with other people, and with our own bodies—is of a relationship with a machine. Every time I go to the doctor, I am reminded that our whole medical system is constructed along these lines: it is based on addressing what is wrong with a specific part of the body without any sense of the human being as a whole, living organism. The machine metaphor has taken over contemporary consciousness.

This consciousness has led us to the ecological crises we face today. The earth, which to our ancestors—and, until very recently, to most of us—seemed like a vast, infinite source of power, has suddenly taken on another face. We recognize the fragility of the earth; we see it as delicate and susceptible to destruction. The next step is to form an accurate and adequate analysis of what this crisis is all about—to probe its cultural roots, its social roots, its technological roots, its spiritual roots—and then to find a pattern of healing that can replace this destructive system and can sustain and support humans, trees, and a rich diversity of creatures for our children and our children's children. We can begin by noting seven converging trajectories of crisis that have developed as a result of both the ancient and the contemporary worldviews I mentioned above. These seven trajectories of interacting crisis are population, food, energy, pollution, extinction of species, poverty, and militarism.

The first trajectory is the exponential growth of the human population. In the middle of the nineteenth century, there were one billion human beings on the earth. A mere eighty years later, in 1930, the number had doubled to 2 billion; forty-five years later, in 1975, it had tripled to six billion. By 1975, only thirty years later, it was 6 billion. At this rate, we are facing a population on this planet of 12 billion in the early twenty-first century.

Of course, there have been efforts at birth control, and they have had some effect. Sadly, one of the major sources of population control now is the death rate of the poor, particularly of poor children. But the trajectory of population growth continues to rise nonetheless. If we want to avoid living in a world where the primary tools of population limitation are war, starvation, and disease, what we need is a mobilization of birth control education and availability that aims at the empowerment of women. Most important, we need to recognize that the social, economic, and cultural equality of women is the most important aspect of enabling women to be decision makers about their own reproduction. This, of course, is the last thing that most government agencies are prepared to do, although the 1994 United Nations Conference on Population and Development, held in Cairo, affirmed gender equality as the key factor in limiting population and promoting sustainable development. The expanding human population interacts with problems of food sources and production. We can foresee an upcoming crisis in the actual capacity to produce enough food for an expanding population. At this moment, however, the primary food crisis is one of distribution rather than production. The problem has two dimensions. One is poverty: large numbers of people, including many people who are the actual primary food producers, don't have the money to buy enough food to eat. Many Guatemalans, for example, produce luxury foods for export to other countries but don't have enough money to buy enough to eat themselves.

Poverty is also connected to the other dimension of the crisis, which is a pattern of food production that emphasizes, at least for the affluent classes, eating off the top of the food chain. According to this pattern, we feed basic grains to pigs and cows in poor countries to produce hamburgers and steaks; then we fly those steaks to the elite who are far away from the place where the animals were raised. Cows fed in Guatemala become hamburgers at a McDonald's in the United States. One of the problems with this is that the ratio of pounds of grain protein fed to these animals for pounds of animal protein produced is roughly ten to one. So the cheaper sources of food protein are not available to human beings, but rather are fed to animals to make much more expensive sources of nourishment. Then, because this kind of food is flown into wealthier countries from poor countries all over the world at a very high transportation cost, the people who actually produce this food— who tend the cows and so on—are paid the lowest possible wage, often far too low for them to afford a healthy diet.

The third trajectory of interlocking environmental crises is that of the burning of fossil fuels, on which our whole modern energy system is based. Fossil fuels are the residue of ancient buried forests; from those forests, we derive coal, natural gas, and petroleum. These resources are in fundamentally limited supply. If we continue at our present level of petroleum use, for example, available supplies will be more or less gone in roughly forty years. A finite source of fuel is being used as though it were infinite. In addition, the accelerated burning of fossil fuels affects the level of air pollution, causing the greenhouse effect and acid rain, which are having a destructive effect on the climate and on trees. Then there is the potential for wars over who controls the petroleum. We have already had our first petroleum war; in fact, our whole Middle East policy from the beginning of this century has been largely predicated on the goal of Western control of oil. What we have is a chain of interacting crises resulting from our present energy system.

The fourth trajectory is that of pollution. Our systems of production avoid what we might call the third part of the life cycle, which is death and disintegration. A healthy forest without any human presence produces no trash because natural systems, when undistorted by humans, complete the life cycle. In other words, whether we're talking about trees or animals, everything that dies disintegrates and is reabsorbed through recyclers such as insects and vultures. The natural system is one in which death is recycled into new life.

What humans have done—and there is a cultural dimension to this—is avoid the disintegration side of the life cycle. We avoid it by throwing away our wastes. In demonizing waste as pollution, we have, ironically, created pollution. If we don't reintegrate our garbage peels, our paper, our human and animal excrement, they become toxic. Prime matter for fertilizers becomes toxic waste because it is tossed into streams.

There are also new kinds of pollutants, such as nuclear waste, that nature simply cannot handle, and that remain toxic and dangerous for millions of years. Our denial of the natural cycles of life has expanded to include creating materials that cannot fit into the cycle at all. Until we are able to rethink our approach to waste, we will continue to have profound problems of toxicity of land, soil, air, and water.

The fifth trajectory is that of extinction of species. We are living through the gravest period in evolution: that of the rapid demise of the diversity of plant and animal species. There are many reasons for that, including toxic wastes. But the basic problem is that human beings are destroying many natural habitats. The problem of extinction of species will not be solved by saving certain particularly cute creatures in the zoo. We must stop destroying the natural habitats by which the great diversity of species are sustained.

The last two areas of crisis in this web are poverty and militarism. These two problems are so complex that an essay of this length cannot do more than touch on some of their more obvious aspects. As for poverty, it is easy to see that our present pattern of development is pushing people lower and lower on the economic scale. Fewer and fewer people participate in the affluent strata—currently, roughly 10 percent of the world. In the United States, obviously, the percentage is a little higher, but not so high as we might think. An increasing proportion of human beings are falling off the other end of the scale, with larger and larger numbers of people barely surviving. This is combined with economic policies that dictate that the bulk of productive wealth goes not to develop alternative systems, but to the support of military power. Military expenditures worldwide have expanded continually for the last twenty years, with funds going largely to enormously expensive, unused nuclear weapons that have to be continually refurbished in order to keep the threat of possible use alive. Military expenditures have drained countries all over the world of funds that might have been used to solve the problems of hunger, illiteracy, and lack of housing.

Given that we now recognize these seven interconnected areas of crisis, how can we get at the sources of healing? I would suggest that we need three dimensions. One dimension is culture consciousness, which includes a transformation of our spirituality. Recently, I met with a group of scholars at Harvard Medical School who are working to relate therapy and consciousness to a variety of social issues. We started by asking ourselves, "What kind of deadening of consciousness allows us to know that nuclear war is a danger and not respond to that danger?" It's a question of ecological numbing—we know there is a crisis, but we can't overcome our inertia and respond to it. This particular group is trying to get at the psychological and spiritual roots of that inertia, and to develop practices of meditation and even liturgy by which people can reclaim an affective sense of relationship to the natural community.

The second dimension of healing is to change our technology. To deal with the problems of fossil fuel—in terms of both its limited supply and its effects on air, water, and soil—we have to discover and shift over to a technology based on renewable energy sources. The earth has one final energy source, the sun. One way to solve some of our problems might be to return to the sun, the most renewable energy source we have. That would entail a far-reaching technological transformation, not just in terms of the machines we've developed that run on fossil fuels—it is not clear, for example, whether you can run jet engines on other than petroleum products—but also in terms of the ownership of sources of energy. Solar energy lends itself to many small, self-owned systems rather than the monopoly of a few big companies, which would obviously be healthier for everyone.

Finally, we need to develop an economic system of sustainable production and consumption—one that can appropriately feed and sustain all of the creatures on the earth rather than providing a huge share of resources for a certain shrinking elite while more human beings drop out of the bottom and increasing numbers of species are destroyed. This may be the most complex dimension of all, but it has to be addressed if we want to survive on this earth.

All three of these dimensions of healing need to take place together. Unfortunately, there is a tendency among some people concerned about spirituality and psychology to want to work with only the first dimension—that of changing consciousness. There is also a tendency among certain people who work with technology to be concerned only with the second dimension—developing ways of using alternative energy sources. Very few people, it seems to me, want to address fully the interconnections of all three. I think that one way to work toward all three aspects of the healing process is to work within community groups.

In these groups—extended households or networks of households—we would take on, consciously and seriously, the task of living an ecologically healthful life. On the one hand, we would examine the internal wounds that support the deadening of our consciousness, the roots of our disregard for our own bodies and for nature. We would work at healing our sense of relationship to ourselves and the earth.

Simultaneously, we would analyze the structure of our daily lives in terms of what we consume and what we waste. Because we have more autonomy in our home base than outside of it, we can begin there to analyze things like our own food production and consumption, our methods of transportation, our recycling. We can think of this as a "pilot project," a way to find out not only how ecologically we are living but how our individual patterns connect to larger systems—city waste-disposal, for example, and public transportation.

This would lead us to use our local communities as bases of political organization and action. For example, if we build a network of groups to create a recycling system and then have our recycled materials picked up, we can't rest there; we have to find out where the material is being taken and how effectively it's being recycled. This might lead to developing some local industries that will actually use the recycled material; to pressuring local businesses to reexamine their own ecological responsibilities; or to running candidates for local, regional, or ultimately, national offices.

If this sounds like a daunting task, we might look to what women have been able to accomplish in our churches in the last thirty years or so. The Christian churches have been powerfully changed by the movement of women into ministry. There was a time when women ministers were unthinkable; now, mainstream Protestants, Episcopalians, and Lutherans all have women in the ministry, and the issue is at least on the table, if not accepted, in Catholicism. This can create a profound transformation in our spiritual consciousness.

Part of that simply has to do with the symbolic power of having a woman at the altar. Even if a particular woman minister is not involved with explicitly feminist things—she may be an Episcopal priest constrained by the *Book of Common Prayer* to refer to God in exclusively male terms—her very presence as a female in those vestments has a seismic effect. It transforms our images of what divinity and sacred power can be and, in fact, acts to heal that splitting of the male mind from the feminine and the earth that I referred to earlier.

Think, for example, of what it might mean to have a pregnant woman leading a service. Those who oppose women being in the ministry often give this possibility as an example of what we have to fear: they see a pregnant woman on the altar as an affront. What they fear, it seems to me, is how such an event would bring together so many things that our culture has split apart—sacredness and the body, divinity and feminine fertility. A pregnant woman on the altar would manifest, in a whole, healing image, precisely the connection between the natural and the divine, and between the feminine and the divine, that our culture has consciously repressed or forgotten.

In order to heal our connection to the earth and to the feminine, we need to find such images. We need to remember that the earth is not something beneath us, but all around us, and that we are essentially dependent children living in the midst of a vast circle of life. I see an image of this in many Asian paintings, in which nature is usually quite vast— large mountains, trees, and rivers—and the people, by comparison, quite small. We need to find healthy, healing images like these and to act on them if we are to prevent major ecological disasters. Time is short: the Worldwatch Institute estimates that we have roughly forty years to effect changes that will avert the collapse of life-sustaining systems. We need to work, with committed love, to make life whole again.

Afterword:
What Is Common Boundary?

Common Boundary is a private, nonprofit 501(c)(3) organization founded in 1980 to foster communication among and support for mental health professionals and others in the helping and healing professions who are interested in exploring the relationship of psychology, spirituality, and creativity.

In order to do this, Common Boundary publishes a bimonthly magazine, holds a conference each November in Washington, D.C., and organizes seminars and invitational think tanks on important issues in the field. Annual awards of $1,000 each are made to the author of the outstanding master's thesis or doctoral dissertation on a psychospiritual topic and to an individual whose project communicates the interdependence of ecology, psychology, and spirituality. Common Boundary also publishes a Graduate Education Guide, which lists training opportunities and educational resources for those interested in personal growth or professional development in psychospiritual and holistic areas.

For more information contact Common Boundary, Inc., 5272 River Road, Suite 650, Bethesda, MD 20816. Telephone (301) 652-9495.